THE IDEA
OF AFRICA

African Systems of Thought

General Editors

Charles S. Bird

Ivan Karp

Contributing Editors

James W. Fernandez

Luc de Heusch

John Middleton

Roy Willis

THE IDEA
OF AFRICA

V. Y. MUDIMBE

INDIANA UNIVERSITY PRESS
Bloomington and Indianapolis

JAMES CURREY
London

Published in North America by Indiana University Press,
601 North Morton Street, Bloomington, Indiana 47404
and in Britain by James Currey Publishers,
54B Thornhill Square, Islington, London N1 1BE.

The paper used in this publication meets the minimum requirements of American
National Standard for Information Sciences—Permanence of Paper for Printed
Library Materials, ANSI Z39.48-1984.

 ™

Manufactured in the United States of America

Library of Congress Cataloging-in-Publication Data

Mudimbe, V. Y., date
The idea of Africa / V. Y. Mudimbe.
p.   cm. — (African systems of thought)
Includes bibliographical references and index.
ISBN 0-253-33898-0 (alk. paper). — ISBN 0-253-20872-6 (paper: alk. paper)
I. Title. II. Series.
B5310.M83 1994
96—dc20   94-1183

1 2 3 4 5   00   99 98 97 96 95 94

British Library Cataloguing in Publication Data

Mudimbe, V. Y.
Idea of Africa. – (African Systems of Thought Series)
I. Title II. Series
199.6
ISBN 0-85255-234-3 (paper)

For Daniel and Claude

Anthropologie ist jene Deutung des Menschen, die im Grunde schon weiß, was der Mensch ist und daher nie fragen kann, wer er sei. Denn mit dieser Frage müßte sie sich als selbst erschüttert und überwunden bekennen.

Anthropology is that interpretation of man which fundamentally already knows what man is and, therefore, can never ask who he is. For with this question it would have to acknowledge that it is shattered and overcome.

—Martin Heidegger, "Die Zeit des Weltbildes." In *Holzwege* (Frankfurt am Main: Vittorio Klostermann, 1950), 69–104, p. 103, "Addendum 10."

PREFACE

This book is about an idea, the idea of "Africa." What is it and how is it related to contemporary literature? In returning to this question, I forced myself to face a simple issue: what kinds of stories should I tell my two "Americanized" children about Africa?

It would have been easy, too easy, to exploit the exotic representations and categories of Africa as illustrated, say, in English or French literature, and to marginalize Africa in the field of what Bernard Mouralis has called "Contrelitteratures." There is, as we know, a tradition which, for centuries, has conveyed this exotic idea of Africa. Instead of grounding this project from within this controversial and controverted literary tradition, I prefer to understand the concept and history of this literature in such a way that I can transcend the continuity and pervasiveness of an exoticist imagination and, at the same time, account for its conception. Consequently, my references and analyses may surprise. They juxtapose, in effect, very different sources and conventions. They constitute a mosaic which, although bearing witness to an idea of Africa as expounded within the Western tradition, including, indeed, Africans' reactions to the idea, does not elaborate on ancient descriptive designations of the continent, but rather invites questions about their credibility, about the authenticity of the African identities, geography, and mythology presented in the literature.

Let us note that the very name of the continent is itself a major problem. The Greeks named it Libya and used to call any black person an *Aithiops*. The confusion begins with the Romans. They had a province in their empire known as Africa, and their intellectuals used the same word for the "tertia orbis terrarum pars" (e.g., Sallustius, *Iug.* 17, 3), that is, the continent as we know it, being the third, after Europe and Asia. With the European "discovery" of the continent in the fifteenth century, the confusion becomes complete.

A sequel to *The Invention of Africa* (1988), this book presents journeys into the multifaceted "idea" of Africa. As approached and circumscribed here, this idea is a product of the West and was conceived and conveyed through conflicting systems of knowledge. From Herodotus onward, the West's self-representations have always included images of peoples situated outside of its cultural and imaginary frontiers. The paradox is that if, indeed, these outsiders were understood as localized and far away geographically, they were nonetheless imagined and rejected as the intimate and other side of the European-thinking subject, on the analogical model of the tension between the being In-Itself and the being For-Itself. In any case, since the fifteenth century, the idea of Africa has mingled together new scientific and ideological interpretations with the semantic fields of concepts such as "primitivism" and "savagery." The geographic expansion of Europe and its civilization was then a holy saga of mythic proportions. The only problem, and it is a big one, is that as this civilization developed, it submitted the world to its memory; but, at the same time, it seemed itself to be sanctioned by and to produce the most unimaginable evils a madperson could have imagined. To focus only on the last five centuries, let us note three remarkable monstrosities which seem intrinsically part of Western history: the slave trade and its politics since the fifteenth century, colonialism and imperialism at the end of the eighteenth century and throughout the nineteenth, and fascism and nazism in the twentieth.

In this work, I proceed from a French translation by Blaise de Vigenère (1614) of the Greek Philostratus's *Icones* and from the Englishman Robert Burton's treatise on melancholy (1621) to a synthetic survey of the Greek contacts with the continent, to issues of relativism, to the Greek paradigm and its power, and finally to the politics of memory. I also consider the present-day reactivation of Greek texts by black scholars and discussions of "ethnological reason," primitivism, and colonial "domestication." Finally, I face a contemporary predicament: which idea of Africa does today's social science offer? To put it simply, these five chapters are stories written for my "Americanized" children born in Africa.

The intellectual space covered outlines Africa as a paradigm of difference. For the Greeks, such a peculiarity did not seem to mean more than what the words Africa, Ethiopia, Libya signified, as Alain Bourgeois has demonstrated (1971). Asians and Northern Europeans were "barbarians" too, and functioned in the Greek imagination as a uniform order of alterity. It was, I think, fifteenth- and sixteenth-century Europe that invented the savage as a representation of its own negated double. Exploiting travelers' and explorers' writings, at the end of the nineteenth century a "colonial library" begins to take shape. It represents a body of knowledge constructed with the explicit purpose of faithfully translating and deciphering the African object. Indeed, it fulfilled a political project in which, supposedly, the object unveils its being, its secrets, and its potential to a master who could, finally, domesticate it. Certainly, the depth as well as the ambition of the colonial library disseminates the concept of deviation as the best symbol of the idea of Africa. I do refer to this colonial library, which beyond its adjustments and arrangements offers traces or reflections of a longer tradition. In fact, I have tried to circumvent its epistemological violence by including its nightmares as well as the fragile presuppositions of its ponderous knowledge.

It might be useful to note that *The Idea of Africa,* like *The Invention of Africa,* is not about the history of Africa's landscapes or her civilizations. Since the 1920s, African scholars, and most notably anthropologists and historians, have been interrogating these landscapes and civilizations and reconstructing, in a new fashion, piece by piece, fragile genealogies that bear witness to historical vitalities that, until then, seemed invisible to students of African affairs. Further, *The Invention of Africa* was not a presentation of the history of African anthropology, nor even that of the colonial conversion of the continent. And *The Idea of Africa* is certainly not concerned with such a perspective. At any rate, it does not analyze what one could call African achievements.

The Invention of Africa stemmed from a very simple hypothesis. In all societies, to refer imprudently to Paul Ricoeur's *The Conflict of Interpretations* (1974), one always finds, in principle, a sort of zero degree discourse: a primary, popular interpretation of founding events of the culture and its historical becoming. That this discourse should be qualified as conveying a body of legends and myths is of no importance since its ordinary function is to witness, naively for sure, to a historical dynamism. Silent but permanent, this discreet and, at the same time, systematic reference to a genesis marks the everyday practices of a community. Families reenact this discourse in their ordinary lives; mothers consciously transmit its rules to their children (teaching the origins of a culture as they force upon the child an internalization of a civilization, its spiritual and cultural rules, and its values), and the community as a whole—through its procedures of initiation, schooling, and socialization—will make sure it produces a citizen who has the "feel" of a tradition and who thus, as an adult, will act and react normally and correctly in everyday life. The thought that determines the behavior is consistent and silently refers back to a master charter even if the movement is not conscious when it actualizes itself in the practice of daily life. The Torah is such a charter in the Jewish tradition. The New Testament served a similar mission in the Christian West.

There is, also in principle, very explicitly in certain societies and less in others, a second level of discourses. These deploy themselves critically and actualize themselves as intellectual disciplines—history, sociology, economics—of the culture, that is, as disciplinary knowledge transcending the first-level discourse and, by their critical power, domesticating the domain of popular knowledge and inscribing it in a rational field. It is at this level that the identity of a culture and its dynamics manifest themselves as project and invention, as a construct claiming to hold in a regulated frame the essentials of a past and its characteristics, or, if one wishes, the "spirit of culture," in the specific sense illustrated, for example, by the romantic concept of *Volkgeist*.

The rupture from the level of founding events is neat. In fact, what this discontinuity renders is a question mark opening up other discursive practices, if one accepts Pierre Bourdieu's grids of classification: on the one hand, phenomenology as a critical and autocritical reading beginning within a determined subject and rigorously apprehending the perceived and rendering it as both discourse and knowledge; and, on the other hand, the dangerous ethnophilosophical enterprise, so well illustrated in African Studies by Placide Tempels and his disciples. Negating its subjective foundation, ethnophilosophy claimed to be a perfect "scientific" translation of a "philosophical" implicit system which is out there in the quotidian experience, and it qualified itself as an objectivist discourse, proposing thus that the primary *chose du texte* animating the practice of everyday life can be trapped faithfully within a

discourse and forever. Such an ambition seems excessive. Even the most objectivist discourses of the second level—e.g., history or sociology in the social
sciences, physics or chemistry in the sciences—do not negate that their propositions do, indeed, transform and regularly change in a radical manner preceding voices, translations, and apprehensions of what supposedly is out there.

Finally, there is a third-level discourse, one which, in principle, should be
critical of the other discourses (interrogating their modalities, significance, and
objectives) and, at the same time, by vocation, one which should be autocritical. It must be clear that the deviation between the second and third level is
in practice a spurious one, as witnessed to, say, by Hegel's philosophy, which
subsumes magnificently all the a prioris of the second-level discourse in the
European experience and history. In any case, at least theoretically, nothing
prevents us from conceiving this third level as one on which a meta-discourse
could bring about a history of histories of a given culture, or, as Lucien Braun
has demonstrated in his book, the possibility of a "history of the history of
philosophy"—and, in our case, the usefulness of a history of histories of
African anthropology and history. And that will be just a first step in an
indefinite critical and autocritical enterprise. From this perspective, it is obvious that to approach the questions "What is Africa?" or "How do we define
African cultures?" one cannot neglect a body of knowledge in which Africa
has been subsumed by Western disciplines such as anthropology, history, theology, or whatever other scientific discourse, as I have tried to demonstrate
very concretely in *The Invention of Africa* and in *Fables and Parables* (1991).
This is the level on which to situate this new project.

As I read some critics of my books, my first reaction was to remain silent.
To use a metaphor, why should I be forced to play chess with people who do
not seem to know the rules of the game? In effect, beyond positivism, I have
been trying to understand the powerful yet invisible epistemological order
that seems to make possible, at a given period, a given type of discourse about
Africa—or, for that matter, about any social group in Africa, Asia, or Europe.
As Michel Foucault put it: on the one hand, the history of science traces the
progress of discovery, the formulation of problems, and the clash of contro-
versy; it also analyzes theories in their internal economy; in short, it describes
the processes and products of scientific consciousness. But, on the other hand,
it tries to restore what eluded that consciousness: the influences that affected
it, the implicit philosophies that were subjacent to it, the unformulated the-
matics, the unseen obstacles; it describes the unconscious of science. This
unconscious is always the negative side of science—that which resists it, de-
flects it, or disturbs it.

I do not doubt that there is in the primary discourses of African cultures a
reading that could possibly relate to *la chose du texte,* to its fundamental local
authorities. Yet, the fact is there: African discourses have been silenced radically or, in most cases, converted by conquering Western discourses. The
popular local knowledges have been subsumed critically by "scientific" disciplines. This process meant not only a transcending of the original locality, but

also, through translation (which is, in reality, a transmutation), what I call the "invention" of Africa took place. In *The Invention of Africa* and in *Fables and Parables* I observe and analyze this fact and try to distinguish levels of interpretation and orders of historicity. As noted in *The Invention of Africa,* Western interpreters, as well as African analysts, have been using categories and conceptual systems that depend on a Western epistemological order. Even in the most explicitly "Afrocentric" descriptions, models of analysis explicitly or implicitly, knowingly or unknowingly, refer to the same order. What does this mean for the field of African studies?

In this *Idea of Africa,* I explore the concept of Africa by bringing together all the levels of interpretation, and I examine their roots in and reference to the Western tradition, focusing on some of their past and present constellations and involving myself as reader. The variety of texts chosen reflects my aesthetic and ethical codes. Does my apprehension and analysis of this confusing and confused "idea of Africa" (confused by both its history and its interpretation, confusing by the different levels of its perception) relate validly and authentically to my subjectivity and experience as an African teaching cultural anthropology and the history of ideas? To put it differently: is it or is it not valid? If it is not valid, it is without interest and should be discarded; if it is valid, it demonstrates the obvious, and thus should be discarded too. Therefore, the correct or incorrect realignment of the "idea" of Africa on well-known histories of exoticism or on celebrations of alterity is just a story and it can be challenged.

In many ways, *The Idea of Africa* is both the product and the continuation of *The Invention of Africa* insofar as it asserts that there are natural features, cultural characteristics, and, probably, values that contribute to the reality of Africa as a continent and its civilizations as constituting a totality different from those of, say, Asia and Europe. On the other hand, any analysis would sort out the fact that Africa (as well as Asia and Europe) is represented in Western scholarship by "fantasies" and "constructs" made up by scholars and writers since Greek times. That such constructions have simplified cultural complexities and made complex *the being* of these continents as objects should be obvious. In the case of Africa, the constructions have been obeying an external order and formulating paradigms that today we might tend to link with the prehistory and the history of Africanist narratives. In the name of a difference, the constructions have always invoked a right to a particular visibility. The history of this right, in itself, witnesses paradoxically to a will to truth on the part of the Western order that has been "inventing" Africa for centuries. The recent history of cultural anthropology may provide the best example.

From evolutionism to post-structuralism—through diffusionism (illustrated by Schmidt's school of Vienna), Malinowski's functionalism (and its derivations in England and America), French ethnophilosophy, initiated in the early 1940s by Marcel Griaule and thematized by the Belgian missionary Placide Tempels, author of the well-known *Bantu Philosophy* (who found himself caught in the uncomfortable position of being rejected simultaneously by both professional anthropologists and philosophers), to the magisterial works of Claude Lévi-Strauss and Luc de Heusch—the history of cultural anthropology indicates very clearly that the discipline does not comment on its own great mutations but on rules for advancing correctly disciplinary propositions. As Michel Foucault said, "what is supposed at the point of departure is not some meaning which must be rediscovered, nor an identity to be reiterated; it is that which is required for the construction of new statements. For a discipline to exist, there must be the possibility of formulating—and of doing so ad infinitum—fresh propositions" (Foucault 1982). The negative contemporary reactions to functionalism or to structuralism vividly act out a distorted perception coming from the so-called post-modernist critique, in the domain of humanities and social sciences. Evolutionism in anthropology is not the childhood of functionalism; and diffusionism does not necessarily announce structuralism. And in any case, as Ivan Karp reminds me in a personal note, we should not reject them out of hand, but see them as phases in the development of a discourse—with both positive and negative aspects.

The positivist myth of a causal history—a simplified and, alas, lazy nineteenth-century transplantation of natural science models—has been obscuring the fact that from the evolutionist period at the end of the eighteenth century the very objective of anthropology was to account for difference. The causalist trap so magnificently rendered by Edward Burnett Tylor and Thomas Frazer, in its naiveté, does not indicate, for example, the necessity of structuralism, in exactly the same manner that Diodorus Siculus or Philostratus is not silently present in Herodotus's histories written five centuries before. Genealogies, causalities, etc. are just tools that one can use to organize hypothetical grids for understanding transformations of paradigms, the peculiarity of narratives, their cultural and political negotiation power. Thus, insofar as African anthropology is concerned, the most pertinent question might not be about the unity and the signification of the field; still less about the creativity, originality, and progressive sophistication of contributions brought about by successive savants from, say, Tylor to Claude Lévi-Strauss and Luc de Heusch. Instead, by considering as events currents such as evolutionism, diffusionism, functionalism, structuralism, and by facing the issues of what were and are their conditions of possibility, we may ask a major question: to what intellectual configurations do they witness? From this perspective, it becomes interesting to remark that no one in the history of the discipline should be seen as "aberrant"; and, for a student of the history of ideas, the vexing interrogation would then be, for instance, why is not Sir Evans-Pritchard or Meyer Fortes thinkable in the seventeenth century and how do we understand Herskovits, Lévi-Strauss, or Mveng as twentieth-century products? In sum, the real problem seems to be about epistemological configurations and the types of discursive practices they make possible.

*   *   *

I wish to acknowledge the contributions of a number of colleagues and friends. Katya Azoulay, Arnd Bohm, Elisabeth Boyi, Stanley Blair, Gaurav Desai, Marjolijn de Jager, Denise McCoskey, and Rigobert Obongui helped, advised, and supported me. I am immensely grateful to Bogumil Jewsiewicki, Ivan Karp, and Allen Roberts for their criticism and suggestions. My gratitude goes also to Rita Henshaw, who typed the first version of this book, and to my direct collaborators in the Duke Graduate Program in Literature, Priscilla Lane and Dan Pillay, for their skilled and patient assistance. I owe also sincere thanks to Janet Rabinowitch of Indiana University Press, and to my editor, Nan Miller, whose copyediting went far beyond what I could expect.

Some parts of the book appeared elsewhere in journals or in collective projects. I am grateful to the editors for permission to rewrite them and include them in the book, and particularly to Henry Finder *(Transition)* and to Susan Vogel of the New York Center for African Arts. An excerpt of this book, "Amazons, Barbarians, and Monsters," was published in an issue of *South Atlantic Quarterly* edited by Frederic Jameson on ongoing research by Duke University faculty.

The bibliography includes books I consulted and had in hand. They are not necessarily original versions. Their dates specify the edition and its publisher. By preference, I chose to use and refer to English versions even when I knew well the original in a foreign language. Thus, when, in the bibliography, I refer to a non-English original, the translation from it in my text is my own.

I dedicate this book to my two children Daniel and Claude, and, in a sort of echo, to Monsieur Willy Bal, who, thirty years ago, at Lovanium and at Louvain, taught me the essentials of techniques I am still using in decoding cultures and histories. As a matter of fact, the project of this book comes from a reaction I had when I read his June 1990 report to the monthly meeting of the Belgian Academy of Literature on what it means to be a "Wallon 'wallonnant' et 'tiers mondialiste,'" what it means to read oneself as a margin in narratives conceived and written by those who have discursive power.

THE IDEA
OF AFRICA

Hoc Opus Eruditissimo et
Dilectissimo Magistro WILLY BAL
discipulus gratus dedicat.

I.

SYMBOLS AND THE INTERPRETATION OF THE AFRICAN PAST

From the French Fate of Hercules to Robert Burton's Exotic Spaces

> Credenda sunt omnia, nihil enim est
> incredibile.
> Facilia Deo omnia sunt, nihil est impossible.
>
> —FICIN, *Theol. Plat.*, 301

The French Fate of Hercules in Philostratus's *Icones*

In the *Icones*, Flavius Philostratus, a Greek from Lemnos born A.D. 170, tells the story of Hercules among the Pygmies of Libya and moralizes about the misery of human existence. (Keep in mind that Libya in ancient Greek geography designates the African continent.) After his victory over Anteus, "the pest," the Greek hero is exhausted and decides to rest. Hercules is attacked in his sleep by Pygmies, who are depicted as an "army" of black ants. They are pictured as "children of the earth," that is, like Anteus, "children of the flesh." By trying to avenge the death of Anteus and destroy Hercules, they confirm the tension between earthly and spiritual realms, strong and weak individuals, and affirm the prevalence of the latter. Indeed, at the end of the story Hercules gets up, crushes his assailants, puts them all in his bag, and takes them to Euristee.

No doubt Blaise de Vigenère's 1614 French translation, *Les Images*, magnifies the scene and its message by linking to its argument the economy of a full-page plate illustrating Philostratus's moralization.

> Le pauvre Hercule ayant sué sang et eau à nettoyer le pays de cette peste d'Antée, ce loup-garou, brigand et bourreau infame; tout las et travaillé du combat encore [. . .] le voilà [. . .] agacé, assailli par une petite racaille [. . .]; lesquels bouillonant de la terre à guise d'une fourmilière, sans mesurer leurs forces à la sienne, sans peser ni considérer l'événement de la chose, ayant plus

le coeur de nuire à autrui, que de se conserver eux-mêmes [. . .] (Vigenère 1614: 482)

> After sweating blood and water in cleaning up the country of Anteus, the pest, that werewolf, bandit, and infamous tyrant, poor Hercules, still tired and exhausted by the combat, is provoked, attacked by a little rabble coming out from the earth, bubbling in the form of an anthill. These attackers do not estimate their strength compared to that of Hercules; they do not judge the situation correctly, since their will to harm seems to them more important than their will to survive.

The plate (Vigenère 1614: 480) visualizes and echoes these contradictions and the lesson. Anteus was a son of the earth and a bandit. His powerful body has been vanquished. It lies now abandoned on the site of the struggle, but in perspective, at the top of the plate, as if it belonged to a faraway past. Hercules is depicted in a profound sleep, his muscles relaxed, yet his being still illustrates an emphatic force and dominates the center of the plate. At the bottom, all around the hero, coming from the ground, militarized "ant-pygmies" attempt to fight Hercules. It seems hardly necessary to elaborate on the message: wisdom consists in knowing oneself and not minding others' business, particularly when one is objectively weak.

Hercules, the model! He has here all the prestige of physical strength, intellectual awareness, and spiritual wisdom. His role as a model depends not only upon his own virtues and capacities but also on the fact that these qualities are carefully arranged by a space and a tradition whose structures serve as the creation and affirmation of his being. His healthy self-awareness and body speak of a paradigm: power is historical, cultural, and, in this case, visibly descends from the divine. The plate, the story, and the commentaries regulate this paradigm or normality to the extent that Hercules' opponents cannot transgress the fatality of their role: that of being aberrant, morally sick little "things," springing from the soil like ants.

Let us specify that in Philostratus's text (1931), as well as in de Vigenère's French translation, the Libyan Pygmies function visibly as a mythical memory and as a historical antiparadigm. Strictly speaking, they constitute a privileged example by converging, in what they represent, the measures of these two different imaginations; the mythical superimposes itself on a supposedly historical and objective knowledge. Indeed, the notation added to Philostratus's story quotes classical sources by Homer, Pliny, Ammianus Marcellinus, and others, to which we shall refer in a coming section. Yet, strangely, it is introduced by what seems to be an ethnographic approach:

> Of these pygmies [*pygmées*] not only Poets but also historians and naturalists have spoken with certainty as of something true and real. That dwarfs [*nains*] exist is a common and well-known fact that cannot be doubted. I remember being in Rome in 1566 at a banquet of the late Cardinal de Vitelli where we were served by some thirty-four dwarfs, very small and most of them misshapen and deformed. (Vigenère 1614: 483, my translation)

Hercules among the Pygmies. A reproduction from the Bodleian edition of the *Icones* of Philostratus translated by Blaise de Vigenère, 1614. *Les Images ou Tableaux de Platte Peinture.* Paris: Chez la Veuve Abel L'Angellier.

The polarization between antagonists becomes unbearable. There is no doubt that the representation of the whole story illumines something else. Yet it would not make sense at this stage of analysis to confront Philostratus and de Vigenère about the veracity of their texts. Did they really believe in the parenthood of Anteus and the Libyan Pygmies, in the reality of an antlike culture, and in the likelihood of the whole event that pits Hercules against the Pygmies? These are idle questions, insofar as we face discourses that seem to transcend the present-day opposition between true and false (see, e.g., Veyne 1988). Our authors claim to be capable of distinguishing, for example, an "Indian" from an "Ethiopian," several types of "Negroes," and many more strange creatures. In any case, they pay attention to travelers' accounts about faraway continents and countries and their inhabitants (e.g., Vigenère 1614: 870–72).

The texts themselves in the exploitation of the mythical story provide what is a fairly clear meaning of their project. First, by confusing the signifiers "Pygmy" and "dwarf," they establish a nonexistent entity that they can signify in the fable as exemplary of stupidity: "Dum vitant stulti vitia, in contraria currunt" (in attempting to avoid mistakes, stupid people end up making them); and, as a consequence, "decidit in Scyllam, cupiens vitare Charybdim" (in trying to avoid the rock of Charybdis, the fool finds himself against the rock of Scylla). Second, they make explicit the exceptional cultural tension existing between Hercules and the Pygmies, who are qualified as "children of the earth," that is, those who live according to the passions of the body, completely subservient to its pleasures and violences. Thus the commentator can, in the annotations, move from the first qualification to a second one: "the Holy Scriptures call them children of men." An authoritative quotation from Albertus Magnus allows a transfer from this distinction to a classification of beings, situating the Pygmy at the bottom of the human scale just before the apes: "Albert au troisième chapitre du premier livre des Animaux, appelle les Pygmées hommes sauvages, participant de vrai aucunement de notre nature, en tant que touche quelque premier motif de la délibération" (Albert, in chapter three of his book on Animals, calls Pygmies savages because they do not share our nature insofar as reflection is concerned) (Vigenère 1614: 484–85). Thus the story imposes itself as a parable. In what it expounds, in the paradoxical richness of its conflicting sources, models, and hypotheses, it aims at uniting at least three things: a legacy of knowledge that goes back to the Greeks and Latins, a new understanding about the place of human beings (their similarities and differences) in nature, and issues about philosophical anthropology. In the meantime, what one learns in this confusion seems simple: the texts are, strictly speaking, second-level *legenda*, a mixture of facts, stories, symbols, presuppositions, and the like arranged according to a contemporary grid.

This confusion attests to a search for both a readaptation of an old order of knowledge and its reformulation as a radically new perspective (see, e.g., Groethuysen 1953). What Michel Foucault says of Aldrovandi's studies could, therefore, be expanded to include not only our authors but most students of human varieties (see, e.g., Hodgen 1971) in the sixteenth century and the early seventeenth.

> There is no description here, only legend. And, indeed, for Aldrovandi and his contemporaries, it was all *legenda*—things to be read. But the reason for this was not that they preferred the authority of men to the precision of an unprejudiced eye, but that nature in itself is an unbroken tissue of words and signs, of accounts and characters, of discourse and forms. When one is faced with the task of writing an animal's *history*, it is useless and impossible to choose between the profession of naturalist and that of compiler: one has to collect together into one and the same form of knowledge all that has been *seen* and *heard*, all that has been *recounted*, either by nature or by men, by the language of the world, by tradition, or by the poets. (Foucault 1973: 39–40)

I would like now to invoke another text, a more concrete illustration, specifically the general economy of Robert Burton's *Anatomy of Melancholy* (1621) and its guidelines for a mythic anthropology, in order to rearticulate the fable of Hercules among the Pygmies according to the whole and complex system of resemblances, sympathies, and antipathies referred to by Foucault and in which the Pygmy, as a sign, would exemplify another abstraction, that of the savage. The latter, as Michel de Certeau suggested (1982), would have been, as a cultural figure, the step preceding the "economic subject."

Robert Burton's Exotic Spaces

> Insanus vobis videor, non deprecor ipse quo minus insanus.
>
> —PETRONIUS, AM, DTR: 120

It was Michel de Certeau who observed that "In history, which leads from the subject of mysticism in the sixteenth century to the subject of economics, primitive man lies between the two. As a cultural (or even epistemological) figure, he prepares the second by inverting the first, and, by the end of the seventeenth century, he is erased, replaced by the native, the colonized, or by the mentally deficient" (see de Certeau 1982: 227). At first sight, *The Anatomy of Melancholy* does not pertain directly to this kind of cultural figure. Burton's text, voluminous both in size and in scholarship, has another design: to cover "scientifically" the territory of melancholy, to analyze its forms, causes, and symptoms, and, finally, to shed light on the most adequate techniques for its cure. Nevertheless, the text hails from a particular period, from the era that encouraged "collections of curiosities" (Hodgen 1971: 162–201) and, in a general manner, collections of customs and traditions. One might cite, for example, the stories of J. Boemus, *Omnium gentium mores, leges, ritus, ex multis clarissimis rerum scriptoribus* (1520), the work of F. Deserpz, *Recueil de la diversité des habits qui sont de présent en usage tant ès pays d'Europe,*

Asie, Affrique et Illes sauvages, le tout fait après le naturel (1576), or the treatise by A. de Bruyn, *Omnium pene Europae, Asiae, Aphricae atque Americae gentium habitus* (1581). It is a period remarkable for authorizing and liberating this new form of knowledge, a period that, coming out of the fifteenth century, interprets the world, its virtues, and its evocations according to the expansion of European space, as the planisphere, published by Mercator in 1569, represents.

On that ground, the figures of the "savage" compel recognition: in the scientific and philosophical discourse, they express the negative, they are superimposed as a question, as irony, or as a provocation to orthodox texts, and they simultaneously put the order of knowledge and that of tradition to the test. Thus they are multiple, as de Certeau states. For example, they might indicate "a 'popular' wisdom as compared to the networks of 'civility' and to the professionalization of scholarship; an 'extraordinary' case as compared to a normalization of behaviors and methods; an off-course wandering through the space distributed by the established Churches or by the States issued forth from earlier Christianity; etc." (1982: 278). But also, and in a characteristic way, these figures stretch across the full dimension of geographic expansion. The European histories of the conquests of the navigators and the explorers overseas will coincide with the rigor of knowledge and in the fidelity of the colonizing spirit to culturally integrated or rejected images.

Disagreement then appears as a powerful criterion. It arranges the gap which distance and difference have created in light of these colonizing practices, which on the whole, will remain constant from the sixteenth to the twentieth century: the scenarios of reducing other landscapes, other peoples, and other values (see Mouralis 1975: 66–105) to a normative paradigm.

If, by its intention, *The Anatomy of Melancholy* diverges from the path of the explicitly exotic "corpus" of the early seventeenth century, it still bears witness to it: first, because it is solidly in keeping with a prevailing conception of the period (Hodgen 1971: 184); second, because the figures of the primitive offered in this work are those which emerge at the borders of the normative values in the geographic European circle. They are also those which, within or outside of this context, appear as monstrosities or as exuberant and excessive bodies. Indeed, this second reason sows confusion into the exotic space of *The Anatomy of Melancholy*. The "savage," integrated or rejected, is faceless, colorless, and obviously voiceless. He is a pretext. If he (she) appears, he (she) is simply a result or, more generally, a metaphor that has emerged in a straight line from the dreams and the readings of Robert Burton, who wrote a voluminous treatise on melancholia in order to avoid succumbing to melancholia himself (AM, DTR: 20).*

---

*The edition I am using is Holbrook Jackson's, the complete title of which is *The Anatomy of Melancholy: What it is, with all the kinds, causes, symptomes, prognostickes and severall cures of it* (New York: Random House, 1932; paperback edition, 1977). I have compared the quoted passages to the 1638 version, the fifth edition, corrected by Burton. In my text, AM is the abbreviation used. DTR, the abbreviation for *Democritus to the Reader,* stands for the foreword

Robert Burton was an Englishman and a man of the Church. He was born in 1577 in Lindlye (Leicestershire), and he studied at Brasenose College and at Christ Church. In 1616 he became vicar at St. Thomas (Oxford) and, from 1630 until his death in 1640, he was pastor at Seagrave. One might expect that England, the West in general, and Christianity in particular, would hold keys that would render it possible to interpret the exotic space that comes out of his work. But what we have is only this: of England he states sarcastically that she "is a paradise for women and a hell for horses, while Italy is a paradise for horses and a hell for women" (AM III: 265). If Burton celebrates the "beauty" of God, the preparation of the Revelation, and its tradition in the West (AM III: 313–18) as a pessimistic skeptic, he also takes a firm position, and more lengthily so, on the extent of idolatry, of unbelief, and of the extravagancies of evil in the world. "There where God possesses a temple," he writes, "Evil will have a chapel; there where God receives sacrifices, Evil will receive offerings; there where God is celebrated in ceremonies, Evil will have its traditions" (AM III: 321). It is, one might say, a cynic who remarks: *"Divisum imperium cum Jove Daemon habet"* (AM III: 322): the empire has been divided between God and Satan.

A cynic? In the foreword, while explaining the symbolism of his pseudonym, Democritus Junior, he humbles himself according to the requirements of the period: *"parvus sum, nullus sum, altum nec spiro, nec spero"* (AM, DTR: 17): I am a little one, nil, and do not aspire to much. But it is only the better to pose as a ghost, to haunt his readers. He thinks that he descends from a race of voluntary outsiders, in the image of that little Democritus who, according to Hippocrates and Diogenes Laertius, was melancholic by nature and "avoided the company of men and, in the solitude of his garden in Abdera, devoted himself solely to his studies" (AM, DTR: 16). It is under this symbol that Burton interprets both the roots of his existence and the organizing signs of his research and his philosophy. "I have led," he says, "a life of silence, sedentary, solitary, discreet, *mihi et musis,* entirely filled with study, almost as long as that of Xenocrates in Athens till his old age, *ad senectam fere;* like his, a life entirely devoted to the apprenticeship of wisdom" (AM, DTR: 17). He clarifies:

> I am not poor, neither am I rich, *nihil est, nihil deest;* I have little, but I need nothing: all my wealth lies in the tower of Minerva. . . . In imitation of Democritus in his garden, I lead a monastic life, *ipse mihi theatrum,* far removed from the tumult and the noise of the world, *et tanquam in specula positus,* but, so to speak, above all of you in the manner of a Stoic, *Stoicus sapiens, omnia saecula, praeterita praesentiaque videns, uno velut intuitu.* (AM, DTR: 18)

---

which opens the volume. The books which contain the actual treatise on melancholy are referred to by their corresponding Roman numerals. Thus, for example, II refers to the second book of the treatise. The translation of Latin extracts and the modern adaptation of the English are my own. As a rule, however, I have kept the author's Latin quotations as they stood.

The world is a show for him. But although the idea he has of life certainly depends on this, he is not at all constrained by it. Burton sees himself as a stoic, but also as a visionary, and assumes a rather radical project: with the help of his senses, he plans to demolish and thwart meanings in the name of his right to reason. "I am only a spectator," he confesses,

> one who watches the fortunes and adventures of others, listening in on the news and rumors: wars, epidemics, fires, massacres, assassinations, celestial movements of the meteors, miracles, apparitions, etc.: I am an attentive reader of all that is published and an observer of what happens: paradoxes, schisms, heresies, philosophical or religious controversies, etc.

In short, his is an intelligence, and at the same time an eye and an ear, that is simultaneously near and far, contemplating the confusion and the disorder of the world from above. Like the models he invokes, Diogenes and Democritus, he too has gone into the world and into the fray, *non tam sagax observator, ac simplex recitator* (AM, DTR: 19), more as an observer than a recitator. Of course he did laugh at the rampant folly, and did sympathize with the misery which he could not lessen. It is, nevertheless, with a vivid sense of helplessness that Burton would return to his solitude, but at the same time with the thought of contributing his understanding of polarity to the knowledge of the madness of the world. All there is left to do then, he thinks, is to reinvest the nostalgia for antiquity and, via the contemporary transgressions and aberrations, find again the primary meaning of the plan of Democritus the Elder. One of his lost works dealt with the seat and the significance of the *atra bilis,* that is to say of melancholia. But, adds Burton, he is living this application of an ancient dream in the manner of Vectius in Macrobius, in order to bring to his reader, the human species, pleasure and knowledge: *simul et jucunda et idonea dicere vitae/Lectorem delectando simul atque monendo* (AM, DTR: 21).

This is the posture, one might say, of the philosopher or the skeptic of the early seventeenth century. Yet, that which this posture denies the life that it analyzes from on high, it questions in its desire to suggest meaning to that same life. It does not directly defuse madness or folly in detailing throughout the treatise the states and the impulses of melancholia, but rather it dangerously subverts them into other forms of desire: the sacred royalty of antiquity and the power of the prophet.

In short, we find an image that quite closely approximates the "savage man" of whom de Certeau speaks: "a brilliant invention of the fourteenth and fifteenth centuries which preceded (and undoubtedly shaped) the Western discovery of the 'savages' of the New World in the sixteenth century," an image that "introduces into the symbolic that which the city exorcises, at the time that the carnivals, excluded from holy days as being too costly, turn into nocturnal sabbaths of sorcerers and witches" (1982: 272). De Certeau finds the image of the vanquished, but of a vanquished one who "speaks of what cannot be forgotten." In other words, one could say that Burton, by default, opens the door to what is still possible. He is neither a Huss nor a Luther, nor even one of those mystics of the early seventeenth century who contribute to the reorganization of religious and social topography (de Certeau 1975). He is, rather, an aesthete who works on the real or potential resources of countries, beings, and virtues: by turns theologian, philosopher, philologist, geographer, prophet, he meditates on the precariousness of the world, the body of distant continents, and the raptures of the universe that he would like to create. These kingdoms are, in reality, only mirrors: they find their source in the powers, the obsessions of the author himself, in the memory of his geographic space, and in his cultural tradition.

Take, for example, his notes on Africa, America, and Asia. Africa is a place of laughable interests. Her inhabitants are as wretched as the Indians of America and, according to Leo the African, *"natura viliores sunt, nec apud suos duces majore in pretio quam si canes assent"* (AM I: 351). Their life is simply the utmost in misery: *"miseram, laboriosam, calamitosam vitam agunt, et inopem, infelicem, rudiores asinis, ut e brutis plane natos dicas"* (AM I: 351). What Burton presents is far from a geographic description. It is not even an ethnologic body of work in the style of Michel de Montaigne's commentaries. It is a construction of vague recourses to knowledge gained from books and travelogues. From these references the theme and the insistent image of the African continent as a "refused place" arise: a hot piece of land on which pathetic beings live on roots, herbs, and camel's milk (AM I: 230); a monstrous place and, therefore, as Bodin indicated (Brown 1939), above all a place where madness and melancholia reign supreme (AM I: 237–38). Indeed, were this not so, how can it be explained that Africa produces and sustains the life of so many venomous beasts, while these do not live in Ireland, for example? (AM II: 43). Therefore, Africa is a "refused continent" and a place of negative extremes, even in her achievements, which, in other places, would constitute the promise of balance and salvation: just think of the confrontation of Priest John's Christianity in East Africa, and the horrors of polygamy, circumcision, harsh fasts, an aberrant cult with regard to St. Thomas, etc. And yet, paradoxically, this "refused space" could one day be converted into another body; it could find meaning, as America and the Terra Australis did, in the arrival of colonies of immigrants (AM III: 246).

America falls in the same abject category as Africa: she is barbaric (AM I: 97), out of proportion (AM II: 36 and 41), has strange fauna (AM II: 43). Her inhabitants are superstitious and idolatrous pagans (AM III: 322). Nevertheless, a sign has been planted in history for her benefit and her awakening: it is by divine order that Christopher Columbus discovered this continent (AM II: 60) and, from that moment on, the Spanish of Mexico, for example, began to reestablish the dignity of humankind by suppressing monstrous sacrifices, such as the daily offering of the hearts and contents of still living human bodies, *viva hominum corda e viventium corporibus extracta* (AM III: 360).

Asia does not appear to exist as a geographical body. The mysterious kingdom of Priest John might be found there, a hypothesis that Burton duly noted (AM II: 36). But in the work itself, Asia is only a qualifier. She displays Arabia and China, the former as an immense desert, a scorching, harsh, dry land (AM II: 47), the latter as an enigma, a land at the far end of the world, a civilized country, peaceable, governed in an exemplary way, free of all madness, a place where Aristotle's *commune bonum* seems to rule. For Burton, China is the realization of the victory of the mind over madness, just as Italy was under Augustus (AM I: 79 and 102). But Asia unfolds other symbols, signs that are ambiguous in their flamboyance, such as Babylon and its hanging gardens (AM II: 75), Cairo with its hundreds of thousands of courtesans and its triumphant vices (AM III: 247). The Middle East, one of Asia's gateways, is, at the same time, the entry to the West. Polygamy, the beauties of the night, the handsome young men of Cairo are canceled out by the dark temptation known in Fez, Rome, Naples, Florence, Venice, and any number of other large cities of Europe. This temptation indicates a trajectory (AM III: 247). It is from these very regions, too, that dangers, both fascinating and frightful, have risen: the history of ancient Egypt and its superstitions, the Syrian and Persian enterprises, as well as bands of Christian heretics, etc.

Actually, the exotic circles and the imaginary savagery so much a part of the reports of sixteenth- and seventeenth-century ethnologists (Hodgen 1971; Hammond and Jablow 1977) do not contain Burton's essential intention. If, when he deals with "civilized" or "barbaric" nations, the civility of the one appears positive compared to the supposed perversions of the other, it is not motivated by fascination, nor even by the fact that it is the topic of study. Burton looks for proof and counterproof, in order to make a case. The value of "kingdoms" as beings, whether they be in Europe or elsewhere, arises from a singular connection: the one Burton establishes between the scheme of his discourse and the naked, the absolute truth, to which, he writes somewhere, Luther would be a "heroic witness" (AM III: 334).

Africa and America are, obviously, exotic bodies, but without mystery. That is because they are transparent and unveil themselves as spaces upon which the versatility of disorder, the reign of evil, and the all-powerful force of false gods play themselves out (AM III: 365–66). These bodies, like that of Asia, can be defined through a cutting away, or separation, or even rejection, through that which expresses a gap, as from the norm. Thus, marginality is, all at the same time, (historic) accident, (religious) malediction, and fortunately also (eschatological) promise of a possible reconciliation with the center-norm.

From there on, Burton's thesis, if one can speak of it as a thesis, seems to signify a negation of any and all diversity and a reduction of every marginal space. It is, in fact, dangerous to speak of a thesis. What brings the author of *The Anatomy of Melancholy* back to reality is the spirit of an era that thinks and rethinks a "redistribution of space" according to a "Same" which is "an historic form, a practice of dichotomy, and not a homogeneous content" (de Certeau 1982: 30–31). Concretely, the spatial marginalism of the non-Western space would be dissolved in the expansion of European geography and history, to the extent that these consider themselves sufficiently powerful to reestablish the uniformity of Genesis by deleting the accidental monstrosities that resulted from the diverse marches of history (see Hodgen 1971: 254-349). In any case, this is the theme Burton sets forth in the dichotomy between the Christian and the pagan universe. The latter would superpose a corrupted spiritual geography upon the physical world.

On the other hand, if the first domain implies the real existence of a Christian space, it does not mean this exclusively: there is no homology between the Christian universe and this concrete space which is "Christian Europe." The Christian universe would rather declare a manner of privilege that is historically exceptional; or, more precisely, it would be a place where sense (and thus good sense) is practiced exactly, and where sense and *desire* are colonized by truth. Indeed, Burton says, look at the pagans: "they depict God and, in a thousand ways, mutilate the understanding one might have; our heretics, schismatics, and certain scholars are not very different in their ways of acting" (AM II: 59). Thus, in opposition to the Christian universe, the pagan kingdom or field of disorder is also a cultural area: according to the strict geographic style of Edward Brerewood (1565–1613), if the regions of the known world were divided into thirty equal parts, the Christian part would be represented by five units, the Moslem part by six, and the idolatrous part by nineteen (Hodgen 1971: 218–19). But Burton understands the kingdom of evil as a spiritually undefined stretch of space. The geography of the exotic spaces—those of Africa as well as those of America—is then nothing more than the unfolding of desire for an intractability equally present in Europe. It offers a sketch of the immense detrimental work done by Evil and its agents: heretics, imposters, politicians, false prophets, and preachers (AM III: 328).

The resumption, that is to say the founding, of a new space of civility and of meaning—a commonwealth that would embody the negation of savagery and madness (AM, DTR: 97)—becomes, in a concrete way, a prophetic celebration for the reversal of all that Burton despises and the sincerity of which he questions, notably, the ancient and modern mythologies, the papacy and Catholicism, messianisms, superstitions, and the politics of nations in general (AM III: 325–72). It is an immense world that he denies in favor of a utopia, the new Atlantis, in which, he writes, "I will freely reign, will build cities, establish laws, and issue decrees as I see fit" (AM I: 97). Dictatorship or theocracy? He answers: "*pictoribus atque poetis,* etc.—you know the liberty that poets have always taken and, furthermore, my predecessor, Democritus, was a politician [. . .], a man of law as some people say; why then, could I not follow in his footsteps?" (AM I: 97–98).

Burton's kingdom is, symbolically, outside of the known world. It might be situated equally as well in the *Terra Australis Incognita,* on some barely accessible island in the Pacific Ocean, as in the heart of the American continent or on the northern shores of Asia (AM I: 98). In any event, he would put it "in a temperate place, or perhaps below the equator, that worldly paradise, *ubi semper virens laurus*" (AM I: 98). It is obvious that the new Atlantis is a sign for something else. Nevertheless, one should remark that the mythic character of its location does not issue only from the multiplicity of possible places and their imprecision, but also, and perhaps more so, from the fact that the vague references to these places apply to classically exotic spaces. And the sought-for effect asserts itself: Burton was dreaming of a meaningful place that would reconcile a disorder lived and an ideal present since the beginning of time.

Burton arranges this utopia rigorously with the help of three normative principles: control over physical and human space, control over the spirit of the city, and control over the founding rules of the order of human life.

Control over physical and human space is, properly speaking, a tool for the establishment of a "rationally" organized kingdom. The new Atlantis will be divided into a specific number of provinces: twelve or thirteen. Each province will have a metropolitan center which will be its geographic heart. All the cities will obey precise canons as to their site and their construction: they will be situated along a waterway, they will demonstrate a harmonious shape (square, rectangular, or circular), and they will have uniform houses, and useful institutions and buildings (churches, hospices, hospitals, schools, prisons, marketplaces, sports fields, possibly a citadel), all constructed with state money *ex publico aerario* (AM, DTR: 99). These plans, including the details Burton suggests regarding waterlines in the cities, the distribution of land, or the organization of collective food reserves, are configurations of a utopian project. But within the unobstructed vision of that dream, they offer a critique of the existing society and, at the same time, propose new social and economic formulas.

His desire to control the spirit of the city and the norms which govern people's lives is, in this respect, most revealing of the design of the society that Burton has in mind. He rejects the egalitarian society as being utopian and judges Campanella's *City of the Sun* as well as Bacon's *New Atlantis* to be purely fables, simple fancies. To go even further: the platonic community is, he says, in many ways "impious, absurd, and ridiculous" (AM, DTR: 101). What Burton proposes is proportional equality, reflecting a hierarchy that is both fixed and flexible in its structure (from the three kinds of noble titles—by birth, by election, by bestowal), functioning in a monarchy. For—and here he invokes a monarchist adage—liberty functions well under the administration of a good monarch: *"numquam libertas gratior extat, quam sub rege pio"* (AM I: 101).

A monarchy, surely, but one which would be a model community for Burton (AM I: 102–03). He perceives it as a providential State (the blind, the feeble, the needy, the aged, will all be taken care of by the common good); a pacifist State (no one may carry weapons in the city and there will never be an offensive war); a legalistic and paternalistic State (*Nisi aliter dispensatum fuerit,* no marriages for men before the age of twenty-five, for women before twenty; in the case of widowhood, no remarriage until six months have passed after the death of the spouse; a housekeeping code that would teach couples how to live, etc.); and, in a most outstanding way, a moral State. Thus, in this kingdom there would be priests who would truly follow Christ's example, men of law who cherish their neighbors, modest and gentle physicians, an honest aristocracy, and philosophers who would know themselves. Harsh punishments would be meted out to those who chose vice and sinfulness: sacrilege would be punished by cutting off the hands, and perjury by cutting off the tongue; the thief would be sent to the galleys or the mines, the murderer and the adulterer condemned to death.

In short, Robert Burton is remaking the world. And the myth of the new Atlantis that he designs with extreme norms is established within a totalitarian purity. This follows from his starting point: a rejection of a corrupted society. The invocation of exotic spaces as founding sites for the virtuous monarchy has already shown us that the prophetic utopia would be erected as a symbol of something else. The return to Democritus the Elder, the father figure, gives Burton the right to power: both to rewrite lost knowledge into the memory of the time, and also to pronounce his expertise and judgment on the manner in which the Christian spirit functions. The double heritage gets confused in ambiguity. The signs of melancholia and madness appear, from that point on, as the roots of an obvious and general ill: "the entire world is melancholic, mad, rotten, and so is everything that lives in it" (AM, DTR: 120).

Everything and everyone are affected. An encyclopaedic mass of information multiplies the games and the functions of madness, recites by fits and starts an off-centered universe, burned down in the lightning flashes of abasement and meaninglessness. On the one side there are human beings. They are all unbalanced, alarming, lost. Look, he points out, philosophers, writers, scholars, these dictators of knowledge, *priscae sapientiae dictatores* (AM, DTR: 110), all more or less uttering beautiful stupidities, *ineptiarum delicias* (AM, DTR: 113); lovers, naive in their faith in reconciling love and knowledge, *amare et sapere,* are, all of them, mad; youth is stupid, *stulti adolescentuli* (AM, DTR: 114); man, every man, by his virtues, his knowledge, his faults, bears witness to only one thing—madness; epicureans, atheists, schismatics, heretics, alchemists, those who are irascible, envious, ambitious, lascivious, courageous, wise, the princes of the world—those of yesterday as well as those of today—they are all mad. In fact, he says, echoing Ulrich Hutten, nobody is really sane: really, no one knows anything, no one is without vice, no one is pure, no one seems happy with his or her condition, no one really loves anyone, no one is good, sage, happy: *"nam, Nemo omnibus horis sapit, Nemo nascitur sine vitiis, Crimine Nemo caret, Nemo sorte sua vivit contentus, Nemo in amore sapit, Nemo bonus, Nemo sapiens, Nemo est ex omni parti beatus"* (AM, DTR: 117). As for objects, they bring or inflict the same kind of vertigo. It would be a Herculean task, Burton writes, to record all the madness of constructions, works, and luxury, *"insanos substructiones, insanos labores, insanum luxum"* (AM, DTR: 116). And everything is mentioned: books, architecture, exploits, actions, movements, until, in a word, nothing works, nothing is healthy; reason and equilibrium are beautiful lies. The boat, he says—quoting Fabatus—is mad:

> it never stays calm and the sailors are mad to expose themselves in this way to certain danger; for the waters consist of a crazy rage in constant motion; and the winds, like everything else, have lost direction, they neither know from whence they came nor where they might be going; and the men who embark and in this way go out to sea are the most insane of all. . . . (AM, DTR: 116)

Madness as the apocalypse of the world is a metaphor into which Burton locks himself as well: "*Nos numerus sumus,* we are a multitude, I confess: I am as foolish and as mad as anyone else [. . . .] And my only wish, for myself and for everyone, is to find a good doctor and to have a better spirit at last" (AM, DTR: 119–20). The apparent fanatic thus embodies neither purity nor excellence of reasoning, only a secret desire to work against the world's instability, to decipher the trivial, to reduce the role of evil and its subversion: "the principal demons subvert the Christian world; Jews, Gentiles, and Muslims are out there, *extra callem;* their resistance being relatively nonexistent, *eos enim pulsare negligit, quos quieto jure possidere se sentit*" (AM III: 364). The text thus brings the morality of a culture to its zenith. If the accusing finger is then turned around, it is to point at the ultimate vocation of an elected space. The meaning becomes "ethnocentric." The exotic horizons and their nuances are dissipated. What remains are pictures of illnesses to be cured and, a little behind that, the stubborn figure of a philosophic prophet who pontificates the path to salvation of the bodies and souls of his people: "do not live in isolation, do not be idle. *Sperate miseri, cavete felices,*" have faith you poor people, be careful you who are happy (AM III: 432).

What to Believe?

Burton proposes a utopia in which myths and mythmaking interact and are interdependent. It is clear that he distinguishes between them in his mind, yet it is in their connection that a thesis elaborates itself: "savages" are everywhere, and it is imperative to go back to the Greek model in order to save the fabric of civilization. Geography separates and determines *a priori* universes of madness and savagery, as opposed to those which should stand for and incarnate sense, wisdom, civilization. Thus, despite the adjacency actualized by Burton's treatise between savages from within—who are such because they are morally and spiritually corrupt—and those from without, their drawing together does not displace the geographic deviation and what it signifies culturally and historically. And to this argument can be linked the fable of Hercules among the Pygmies.

Like Burton's treatise on melancholy, Philostratus's *Icones,* with its commentaries from Blaise de Vigenère, also belongs to a moralizing genre. In both cases, mythic paradigms take over from one another in successive relays, and in the most idealizing manner each paradigm justifies a culture as an incomplete project, its best and fundamental values and its fate inscribed in the signs that made it possible. The discourse is autocentered. It explicitly promotes the unequivocal cultural vocation it wants to convey, counterbalances the identity of its spatial and historical experience to that or those occupying the margins of its concrete as well as its symbolic space. The "savage" *(Silvaticus)* is the one living in the bush, in the forest, indeed away from the *polis,* the *urbs;* and, by extension, "savage" can designate any marginal being, foreigner, the unknown, whoever is different and who as such becomes the unthinkable, whose symbolic or real presence in the *polis* or the *urbs* appears in itself as a cultural event: *"comment peut-on être Persan?"* This question stipulates more than a simple problem of representation as in the fable of Hercules. The question defines, in fact, an egocentric foundation of an experience, its contents and values. It suggests also, in the same movement, that the Other cannot be but the other side, the negative proposition of oneself that should be mastered in its very contradiction and absolutely converted to the ideals of one's truth. If necessary, history—a memory codified as a lesson about what happened in the past—would function as both justification and a right for such possible violence. Yet, as Paul Veyne puts it, we do know that

> Historical reflection is a criticism that diminishes the pretensions of knowledge and is limited to speaking truly about truths without presuming that a true Politics or science exists.
>
> Is this criticism contradictory, and can one say that it is true that there are not truths? Yes, and by this we are not playing the game, taken from the Greeks, of the liar who is lying when he says, 'I lie'—which therefore is the truth. One is a liar not in general, but in particular when one says this or that. An individual who would say, 'I have always made up stories,' would not be making up a tale in saying that if he specified, 'My storytelling consisted in believing that my successive imaginations were truths inscribed on the nature of things.' (Veyne 1988: 126)

Do Philostratus, Blaise de Vigenère, or Robert Burton present truths? A negative or a positive response does not seem important, since their texts unveil themselves as results and reflection in an intellectual chain and its determinations. To check the fidelity of their references and the authenticity of their sources might make sense. To question their autocentric representations of the I and the Other seems useless. To adapt a statement of Origen to my point, I would affirm that historic events, as well as mythic interpretations, cannot be subject to logical proof even when they are or seem authentic.

> [Origen adds:] "To be fair, without letting oneself be fooled nonetheless, it is necessary when reading history books to discriminate between authentic events, to which we adhere; those in which we must discern a secret allegorical meaning and which are figurative; and, lastly, events unworthy of belief which were

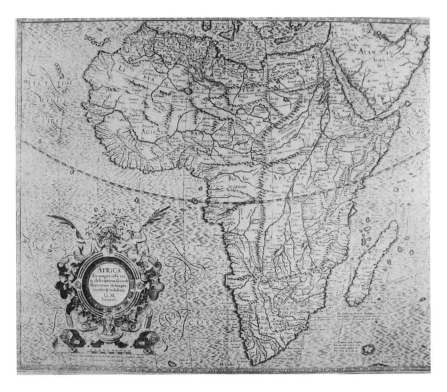

Map of Africa from the world atlas of Gerard Mercator, 1595. Source: Oscar
I. Norwich, with bibliographical descriptions by Pam Kolbe, *Maps of Africa:
An Illustrated and Annotated Carto-Bibliography*. Johannesburg: Ad. Donker,
1983.

written to procure some pleasure" (the text here is questionable; others read:
"which have been written to flatter certain people"). (in Veyne 1988: 143)

When Was Africa Discovered?

> For it is only in the case of the well-known
> and reputable regions that the migrations,
> the divisions of the country, the changes in
> the names, and everything else of that kind,
> are well known. Indeed, our ears are filled
> with these things by many, and particularly
> by the Greeks, who have come to be the
> most talkative of all men.
>
> —STRABO, *Geography*, 3, 4, 19.

Africa was discovered in the fifteenth century. That, at least, is what most
history books say. Professors teach it, students accept it as truth. In any case,

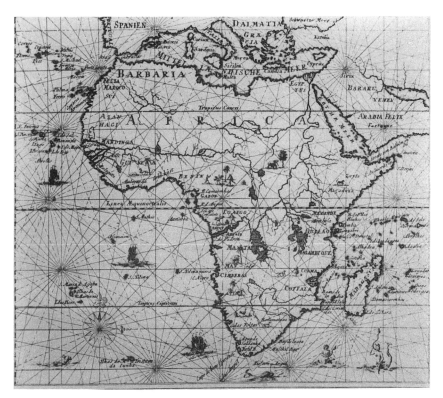

Map of Africa from J. W. Heydt, *Alterneuste Geographisch und Topographische Schau-Platz van Africa und Oost-Indien,* 1744. Source: Oscar I. Norwich, *Maps of Africa,* 1983.

why doubt? The media propagate the veracity of the fact in the sagas of European explorers. Taken at its first meaning, this discovery (that is, this unveiling, this observation) meant and still means the primary violence signified by the word. The slave trade narrated itself accordingly, and the same movement of reduction progressively guaranteed the gradual invasion of the continent.

Thus, doubtless, it was a discovery in this limited sense. Yet, one might very seriously wonder, is it really historically true that the continent was discovered in the fifteenth century? We do know what is inscribed in this discovery, the new cultural orders it allowed, and, in terms of knowledge, the texts that its discourses built and whose achievement is to be found in what I term the "colonial library." Looking again, however, it becomes apparent that indeed the fifteenth-century discovery was not the first contact of the continent with foreigners. Hence that discovery spells out only one viewpoint, the European. Let us consider some evidence.

Necos's *periplus* took place long before, in the sixth century B.C. Herodotus details the enterprise of the Phoenician crew working for the Egyptian Pharaoh, specifies the first known exploration of the continent, "which is encompassed by the sea save only where it borders on Asia" (IV, 42), and, finally, unknowingly, gives proof of the circumnavigation: "it was in the third year that the crew rounded the Pillars of Heracles [the Cape of Good Hope] and came to Egypt. There they said—what some may believe, though I do not—that in sailing round Libya they had the sun on their right hand" (Herodotus IV, 42). Indeed, the sun in the Southern Hemisphere could not be but on the right of the crew sailing the Cape. What seemed unbelievable to Herodotus is, paradoxically, the key proof that the circumnavigation was real. One notes also that, for Herodotus, the name of the whole continent is Libya.

Sataspes, an Achaemenid prince (the son of one of Darius's sisters), tried to repeat—very probably between 485 and 465 B.C.—the achievement of Necos's expedition, but this time by circumnavigating the continent from west to east. The mission failed, because, according to Herodotus, Sataspes "feared the length and the loneliness of the voyage and so returned back without accomplishing the task laid upon him by his mother" (IV, 43). Unlike Necos's Phoenicians, who did not bother to meet local peoples, Sataspes' team did. That is the story he told Xerxes, when he came back after his failed mission: "Thence coming to Xerxes, he told in his story how when he was farthest distant he sailed by a country of little men who wore palm-leaf raiment; these, whenever he and his men put in to land with their ship, would ever leave their towns and flee to the hills" (Herodotus IV, 43). If they ever existed on the west coast of Africa, the "little men" seem to have disappeared a very long time ago.

Another expedition, assuredly more exciting but full of mysteries and incoherences, was organized from the continent itself by the Carthaginians (Hannon 1855). Its date is unknown, probably at the end of the sixth century B.C. Its objective was twofold: to organize colonies on the coasts (and, according to documents, sixty ships and thirty thousand immigrants—men and women—took part in the expedition), and to explore the continent. Hannon's expedition apparently reached Mount Cameroon (see also Mveng 1972: 45–46).

Finally, I would like to mention a little-known text, the *Periplus of the Erythraean Sea* (our present Red Sea), by an unknown author, probably written at Alexandria, and dated between 130 and 95 B.C. (see Huntingford 1980). It is without doubt a firsthand description and, as noted by G. W. B. Huntingford, "a text moreover which shows every sign of being the work of a man who had himself been to most of the places he mentions" (1980: 5). Its account of the eastern coastland goes from Muos Hormos (very probably the present Abu sharm al-qibli on the Red Sea, about 300 miles south of Suez) to Rhapta on the coast of Azania (the Tanzania of today). As suggested by G. Mathew, Rhapta possibly "lies lost in the Rufiji delta" (in Huntingford 1980: 100). The *Periplus* details the goods exported from the coast and indicates their specific origin. These include cinnamon, fragrant gums in general, incense, ivory, rhinoceros horn, and tortoiseshell.

African women, from Odoardo Lopez and Filipo Pigafetta, *Relatione*, 1591.
From left to right: a slave, a common woman, and an aristocrat.

If the history of the area—called Troglodutike by Ptolemy (*Geogr.* IV, 7, 27)—is quasi-inexistent, the ethnology does sound vague but intriguing and should be compared to other ancient descriptions such as those by Agatharchides and Strabo. Some interesting features were noted: circumcision, as still practiced, by the Nandi and Masai; burying the dead by covering the body with stones, as is the custom among the Galla (Ethiopia), the Masai (Kenya), and the Zande (Congo-Sudan); and, more remarkable still, as Huntingford puts it, "the custom of laughing at a funeral. The Nandi used to bury a very old person with no show of sorrow and with laughter and talking, for, they said, 'He has now arrived where he expected to arrive a long while ago'" (1980: 145). The practice of laughing at funerals has always been widespread in eastern and central parts of the continent.

To these *peripla* one could add, among many others (see Mveng 1972), the brief report of Skylax of Caryanda exploration of the west coast (Müller 1882, I: 152–53), that of Polybus, synthesized by Pliny (V, 1), and that of Eudoxos (Pliny II, 67).

Reactivating Ancient Texts

The *peripla* constitute only an expression and, on the whole, a highly limited collection of the Greek and Latin gazes on the continent. There are other gazes, other texts, commentaries, and reproductions through artistic representations of what has been seen, said, or learned about the continent called Libya. Alain Bourgeois, a French scholar and for a certain time a resident in Senegal, in *La Grèce antique devant la négritude* (1971), summarizes the essentials, distinguishing three main themes: Greece and Africa; Negroes as perceived by Greeks as to their anatomy, alimentation, habitation, wars, luxury, political systems, society, mores, religion, wisdom, languages, etc.; and Negroes in Greece. At the end of his research, amazed, he notes:

> Que conclure, enfin, sinon que les rapports de la Grèce et de la Négritude, qu'on eût pu croire *a priori* négligeables ou presque nuls, se sont révélés d'une insoupçonnable richesse? Il n'était pas nécessaire que les écrivains fissent grand étalage de leurs connaissances sur l'Afrique, au demeurant bornées et fragmentaires, nécessairement. Mais en fait ils ont su beaucoup plus qu'on ne s'y serait attendu et de ce qu'ils ont su, ils ont tiré un parti extraordinaire. (1971: 124)

> Finally, what to conclude except that the relationships between Greece and Negritude, which one might a priori have thought to be negligible or almost nil, appear to be of unsuspected richness? It was necessary for [Greek] writers to show off their knowledge of Africa, which was, and necessarily so, limited and fragmented. In fact, they knew much more than one would have expected, and, from what they knew, they made the best of it.

> Il est réconfortant de voir que, au rebours de tant de peuples qui se sont tournés vers l'Afrique que par convoitise, pour sa richesse en or, en ivoire, en main-d'oeuvre, les Grecs d'il y a plus de deux millénaires ont regardé avec admiration les Nègres en tant qu'hommes, fraternellement. (1971: 125)

> It is comforting to see that, contrary to many nations concerned with Africa only for her wealth in gold, ivory, and manpower, two millennia ago the Greeks looked at Negroes as human beings, with admiration and in brotherly fashion.

Bourgeois's research has an ancestor that it recognizes and integrates: A. Berthelot's *L'Afrique saharienne et soudanaise, ce qu'en ont connu les Anciens* (1927). Yet, it can be seen as representative of a post-1940s current that intersects the romanticization of the *Négritude* movement's quest for an African identity. *Négritude*'s objective, since its launching in Paris in the 1930s by Aimé Césaire, Alioune Diop, Léon-Gontran Damas, and Léopold Sédar Senghor, is to celebrate the values of blacks' historical and cultural experiences. The concept of *Négritude* is in the title of Bourgeois's book and runs also throughout the text, which, by the way, is introduced by Léopold Sédar Senghor. From this intellectual and ideological background, Bourgeois discloses and reactivates traces and designations of Africans in Greek texts. These ancient texts are investigated on the basis of their explicit references to Africans, the cohesion of their positive evaluations, and the visibility of concrete representations, as in the case of paintings and sculptures. In return, the message they unveil, which has been ignored, blurred, or muted by centuries of Western scholarship, is represcribed silently to a twentieth-century project: black is beautiful. The adjustment between the two poles obeys, at any rate, the new politics of philological readings or, more exactly, original contemporary textual politics (see, e.g., Mveng 1972: 205–14).

As one begins reflecting upon the image emerging from Bourgeois's excellent book, two main issues present themselves. First, the Greek texts cited are handled as a sort of synchronic totality. Yet they cover several centuries and are not only influenced by markedly different cultural sensitivities but also depend upon these extremely diverse and often contradictory norms. Bourgeois, the philologist, knows that as well as he knows how to separate the credibility and conventions of mythological sources from those of literary and artistic productions. Contrary to the Renaissance handling of knowledge, the genres are distinguished here, and their irreducible difference is recognized as well as the status of their content. Yet, since the project is to evaluate a Greek representation of black peoples, none of the genres is excluded. All receive the same attention and are called upon as a means of forming an "ikon." Thus, for example, Homer's flattering invocations (*Il.* 1, 423; XXIII, 206) of faithful and pious Negroes appear to belong to the same descriptive order as, say, Herodotus's description of Egyptians and black peoples (e.g., II, 104; IV, 55; VII, 70), as does Pindar's celebration of the Ethiopian garden of Zeus (*Pyth.* IX, 53) and the materiality of an object such as the negroid profiles on the Theban vase of Kabirion picturing Circe offering a beverage to Ulysses.

Second, this integration of genres has a strange effect, that of incorporating the maximum information in a canvas. Instead of a rudimentary and realistic picture—after all, compared to Aristotle, Homer knew little about Africans—we get a full-fledged beautiful monster: a religious concept celebrated in the sixth century B.C., a body represented in the fourth century, and a psychology coming straight from third-century descriptions. Indeed, a text such as that of Bourgeois does not indulge itself in the naïveté of the writing of resemblances and differences of, to refer back to my beginning fable, Hercules among the Libyan Pygmies. Nevertheless, despite its magnificent achievements, Bourgeois's text involuntarily employs reflective metaphors rather than the spontaneous, limited, always incomplete figures which we can draw apropos of ancient representations. One should also recognize that the comprehensiveness of the picture does not exclude signs of contradiction brought about by the very demands of the method. For example, in the study of the anatomy of the black, one reads Herodotus, who, in the midst of many sensible observations, writes quite seriously that the sperm of a black man is black (III, 97), and then one still has to be dazed by Aristotle's hypotheses on the nature of black peoples' hair and teeth (e.g., III, 9).

What results from an enterprise such as that of Bourgeois is both a project of knowledge and, specifically, a new manner of relating Greek passages on Africa and Africans to today's discourse and perception of history. In sum, the African right to dignity enunciates itself in reactivating ancient texts and by interrogating the objectivity of history.

This event can be dated. The reality of an African history, particularly for the sub-Saharan part of the continent, does not seem to exist, at least academically, before the 1940s. In effect, African history was supposed to have begun with the European discovery of the continent in the fifteenth century, and

African societies became historical at the moment of their colonization. The forces at work from the 1920s to the 1940s, influenced progressively by the concepts of subjectivity, regional autonomy of cultures, and relativism of values, questioned the universality of the Western experience and its will to truth in a critical reappraisal. The concept of history metamorphosed itself (see, e.g., Braudel 1980) and it became possible to restore the past of non-Occidental cultures independent of a Western presence. Jan Vansina's *De la Tradition orale: essai de méthode historique* (1961) was certainly surprising, but those practicing the "art" of history knew very well the sacred importance of written documents for the examination, interpretation, and constitution of a past. From this viewpoint, Bourgeois apparently plays it very safe: he uses only written evidence. Yet, he is as subversive as Vansina, perhaps even more so. First, he regroups the references to what may seem a simple curiosity: Africans present in the smooth, neutralized, and perfectly sanitized world of Greek civilization, a universe solidly occupied by centuries of Western scholarship commenting upon its own cultural roots. Then, using these bearers of nothing but a vague color, some doubtful names (Libyan, Ethiopian, etc.), and their most obvious manifestations—in rare texts and on vases, for instance—Bourgeois surreptitiously demands a reinterpretation.

> Il est clair que les Grecs, tant de l'époque homérique que de l'époque classique, voire de l'époque alexandrine, poètes, historiens, moralistes, ont, de près ou de loin, connu et apprécié les Nègres, non avec une curiosité de dilettantes, sans le moindre préjugé racial, mais bien au contraire avec les sentiments les plus favorables et dans les termes les plus flatteurs. (Bourgeois 1971: 125)

> It is clear that the Greeks, not only during the Homeric and Classical periods, but also during the Alexandrine period—poets, historians, moralists—knew Negroes far and near, appreciated them without a dilettante's curiosity, without any racial prejudice, on the contrary with the most favorable sentiments and in the most flattering terms.

Léopold Senghor understood the message. It affirms well his own convictions. Protecting himself by referring to the authority of one of his former professors, Paul Rivet, he writes, in the Preface to Bourgeois's book:

> Quand les Indo-Européens, quand les Grecs—grands, les cheveux blonds et les yeux bleus—débouchèrent sur les flots de la Méditerranée, ivres de soleil et de fureur, ils y trouvèrent un peuple *brun,* doux et poli, paisible et raffiné; un peuple métis, composé de Négroïdes et de Sémito-Chamites. (Bourgeois 1971: 8)

> When, drunken by the sun and fierce, the Indo-Europeans, when the Greeks—tall, blonde, blue-eyed—arrived on the Mediterranean beaches, they found there a brown race, mild and polite, peaceful and refined; a mixed race composed of Negroids and Semito-Chamites.

Thus we encounter a revision of traditional history. What might seem to be an idiosyncrasy of Bourgeois and Senghor is actually the most prudent

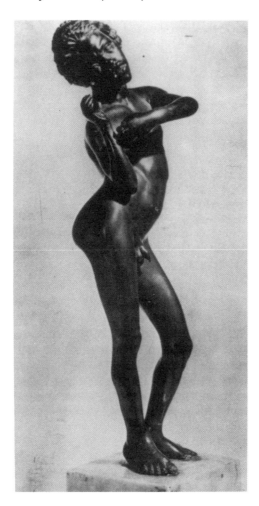

The Young Barberini Musician. c.200 B.C.
Bronze. Bibliothéque Nationale, Cabinet des
Médailles, Paris.

undertaking in the 1940–1950 reevaluations of the history of the continent.
Eugène Guernier, a professor at the Institute of Political Sciences of the University of Paris, had already articulated, in his *L'apport de l'Afrique à la pensée
humaine* (1952), a whole system indicting traditional history. He emphasized
the African origin of humanity and human consciousness, the African roots
of the *homo artifex,* the originality of Egyptian civilization, and the large
contribution of the northern part of the continent, which he calles *Berbérie,*
to the constitution of European rationality and knowledge. The Senegalese
scholar Cheikh Anta Diop, an Egyptologist and a physicist, furthered the
theses in two books, *Nations nègres et culture* (1955) and *Antériorité des*

civilisations nègres (1967), in which he linked Black Africa to Egypt. The new orthodoxy found its most elegant expression in Joseph Ki-Zerbo's *Histoire de l'Afrique* (1972). This perspective was rigorously reworked in two monumental undertakings: the Cambridge and UNESCO histories of Africa. More recently, Martin Bernal's *Black Athena* (1987 and 1991) strongly accented Cheikh Anta Diop's hypothesis by diffusing the Senegalese scholar's "black factor" into "Afroasiatic roots" of classical Greco-Roman civilization.

In actuality, what information the Greek corpus offers about the African continent is relatively limited compared to that available for Asia, for example. R. Lonis (1981) has suggested that the Greek description of Africa could be reduced to three main approaches: a mythic representation, from the time of Homer to sixth-century art; an anthropological reflection, from the mid fifth century in inconographic data and from the Hellenistic period in literary texts; finally, the representation of the African as the unknown Other to be feared. I would tend, personally, to conceptualize only two models: the mythic and the anthropological. The proposed chronological order could be maintained if considered as a simple methodological frame. In effect, Herodotus's description of the northern part of Africa (Book IV) participates in both: it presents an anthropological description of communities living between Egypt and the Tritonian lake; beyond the lake, it projects some mythic monsters, dog-headed or headless peoples and humans with eyes in their breasts. The same can be said of Diodorus Siculus's renderings (Book III) and many others.

The general movement in which the reactivation of Greek texts takes place is more than a simple revision of traditional scholarship. It signifies, in fact, a reversal of perspectives, which is the sign of a major epistemological rupture. It means a complete reconversion of guiding concepts, and, more specifically, to borrow Foucault's language, the placement of everything within the order of its system, rules, and norms (1973: 359–61). As a consequence, controversies were suscitated by the new orthodoxy—regarding details, apparently, of major points such as the referent of *melas* in ancient Greek, the scientific credibility of oral tradition, or the precise linguistic relationships between the Egytian Coptic and African languages—because of what made them possible. The paradox—but is it really one?—resides in the fact that this epistemological reversal, which sanctions African histories as recourses to and reflections of their own regional cultures and their cross-cultural contacts, is the same in the West; or, more exactly, it defines a moment in the recent history of knowledge in the West, one that erases dichotomies and whose best symbol may be Freud. In effect, to quote Foucault, because Freud is "the first to undertake the radical erasure of the division between positive and negative (between the normal and the pathological, the comprehensible and the incomprehensible, the significant and the non-significant), it is easy to see how he prefigures the transition from an analysis in terms of functions, conflicts, and signification to an analysis in terms of norms, rules, and systems" (Foucault 1973: 361).

Taken from this viewpoint, the present-day obsession of some black intellectuals with ancient Egypt and Greece becomes quite intriguing. It poses an interesting problem by suggesting that philological or historical power is not transcultural but that it nevertheless treats well-known and perfectly spatialized old texts as a virgin domain awaiting a new mastery. One can see how psychoanalysis would be a silent companion to such enterprises, to this new will to truth searching for its foundations. However, this is not the place to analyze this passion and its ambiguities.

Among the most original adventures in this sense, I shall refer, chronologically, to four books.

(1) Drusilla Dunjee Houston, *Wonderful Ethiopians of the Ancient Cushite Empire* (1926, last edition 1985), celebrates the founders of a bright civilization. Houston (1876–1941), a self-trained historian and philologist, demonstrates an impressive encyclopaedic knowledge of her subject. Her research would have been a first-rate contribution if it were more critical of sources and more rigorously applied the norms of historical and philological methods.

(2) Grace Hadley Beardsley, *The Negro in Greek and Roman Civilization: A Study of the Ethiopian Type* (1929), is considered a classic in the genre. A former professor of Latin and history at Goucher College, Beardsley combines impeccable information with sharp skills in literary analyses (chapter 1, on the Ethiopian in Greek literature, and Chapter 11, on the Ethiopian in Roman literature); history (as in chapter 2, on the Ethiopian in Greece); art history, with the study of plastic vases (chapter 3), vase paintings (chapter 4), terra cottas (chapter 7), Hellenistic bronzes (chapters 8 and 9), and Roman art (chapter 12); and even what today we may label socio-psychology, with her exploration of the Ethiopian type in the fourth century (chapter 5), the Ethiopian in the Hellenistic world (chapter 6) and the character of the Ethiopian (chapter 10).

(3) Frank Snowden, Jr., a professor of classics at Howard University, in *Blacks in Antiquity* (1970), offers a study more oriented toward literature and attempts to prove that "the Greco-Roman view of blacks was no romantic idealization of distant, unknown peoples but a fundamental rejection of color as a criterion for evaluating men" (Snowden 1970: 216).

(4) Engelbert Mveng, *Les Sources grecques de l'histoire négro-africaine depuis Homère jusqu'à Strabon* (1972), is the most philological of all. A Jesuit priest, and a scholar from Cameroon, Mveng, offers a synopsis of his doctoral thesis presented at the University of Paris, which is primarily an analysis of written documents and archaeological data (epigraphic and iconographic) attesting to the Greek knowledge of Africa. The ensemble is organized clearly: (a) the presentation of sources,

(b) a critical exposé of problems concerning the sources, (c) an analysis of the content of the sources.

Martin Bernal, in his *Black Athena,* which I analyze extensively in chapter three of this book, referring to Jacob Carruthers's classification of black scholars interested in the African presence in Greco-Roman antiquity and in Egyptian history, distinguishes three main groups: the first comprises "the old scrappers," who, "without any training," dedicated their talents to the cause of black history and black contributions; the second, "which includes George Washington Williams, W. E. B. Dubois, John Hope Franklin, Anthony Nogueira, and Ali Mazrui," would have, according to Carruthers, "argued only that Blacks had a share in building the Egyptian civilisation along with other races;" a third group, in which one finds Cheikh Anta Diop, Ben Jochannan, and Chacellor Williams, gives an essential importance to the African initiative. Rightly, Bernal notes:

> Thus, at the end of the 1980's, I see continued struggle among black scholars on the question of the 'racial' nature of the Ancient Egyptians. On the other hand, there is no serious division among them on the question of the high quality of Egyptian civilization and of its central role in the formation of Greece. (Bernal 1987: 436)

Naming and Metaphorizing

In most dictionaries of the sixteenth century, it is Latin nomenclature that reproduces itself. *African* is the equivalent of *Afer,* as substantive as well as adjective, and simply designates any person from the continent regardless of his or her color. It literally translates *Africanus.* The renowned Roman Scipion, who was not black, is historically known as Africanus Scipio, as is Augustine of Hippo. The latter, should he come back, would most probably, and much to his surprise, pass as a black man for the U.S. immigration system of racial classification. But that is another problem. For the Romans, *Africa* designates properly one of their provinces, and *Africans,* the *Afri* or *Africani,* its inhabitants: "populi partis Africae, quam dicimus septentrionalis, exceptis Aegyptiis, Numidiis, Mauris, ei maxime qui sub Carthaginiensium imperio tenebantur" (*Thesaurus Linguae Latinae,* I, 125, 53 sq.). Yet, in technical and literary works one finds another[1] meaning, that of a third part of the world (*tertia orbis terrarum pars,* e.g., Pliny, Natural History 2, 123) and which in this sense is the equivalent of the classical Greek *Libya.* The concordance is still perceived in the sixteenth and seventeenth centuries as Robert Estienne indicates it: Africa or Libya, *"Libya et Hesperia a Graecis appellata,"* named Libya and Hesperia by the Greeks (Estienne 1740, I, 1156).

Aethiops, the proper name of Vulcan's son in Greek mythology, is the generic qualification of any dark-skinned person (Estienne 1816–18). The word, as noted in the *Thesaurus Linguae Latinae* (I, 1554, 62), presents an impressive number of variations of its sounds (*ae-* and *e-*; *-th-* and *-t-*, *-i-* and *-y-*).

The signification, however, has been constant throughout ancient Greek history (see Beardsley 1929). On the other hand, *Aethiopia,* says Isidorus, qualifies the continent: *dicta a calore – colore – populorum quos solis vicinitas torret (Orig.* 14, 5, 14). The reference murmurs a singularity: the land or the continent is called *Aethiopia* because of—and here it is a textual confusion that raises an image—the heat *(calore)* or the color *(colore)* of the people living near the sun that burns them. In this perspective, we can thus understand an old distinction between the eastern and western Aethiopia: "Aethiopia duae sunt una circa ortum solis, altera circa occasum in Mauretania," there are two Ethiopias, one in the east, the second in the west, in Mauretania (Isidorus, *Orig.,* 14, 5, 16; *Thesaurus Ling. Lat.,* I, 1157, 4).

Despite this definition, which clearly distinguishes a western Aethiopia from an eastern one, the notion has been confused from the very beginning. Homer, for example, localizes his Aethiopians along with the other Libyans (*Odyssey,* IV, 84 sq.). In Herodotus's text, the notion seems really polysemic. As opposed to the northern part of the continent, inhabited by Libyans, Aethiopia is described as the country beyond Egypt, at the end of the world (III, 25), and also as the southernmost inhabited region (III, 114). Diodorus Siculus (III, 8–9) actualizes the same variation of meanings in describing Aethiopians. He situates them in "the lands lying on both banks of the Nile and on the islands in the river;" he notes "those dwelling above Meroë" and he even refers to those Aethiopians who, according to Strabo (XVII, 2, 3), inhabit the area near the torrid zone. In any case, it is clear that by the first century A.D. the continent as a whole has been divided into three main parts by geographers: Egypt, Libya, and Aethiopia, the last corresponding more or less to sub-Saharan Africa (see Mveng 1972).

The declining use of Aethiopia as the name of the continent begins with the European explorations in the fifteenth century, which promote, among other curiosities, *Nigritia* as a name for the continent. *Nigritia,* from the Latin *niger,* was already known to ancient geographers, and its inhabitants were called *Nigriti* (e.g., Pomponius Mela, I, 4). The Latin *niger* corresponds to the Greek *melas* and, insofar as the color of human beings might be concerned, it strictly translates the Greek *Aithiops,* that is, a face burned by the sun (see, e.g., Mveng 1972), a neutral value that one can find as late as in the 1611 dictionary of Cotgrave: "neigre adj., de la couleur d'un nègre." It is interesting to note that the Richelet dictionary had already introduced, in 1566, *nigritude,* a feminine substantive, which signifies those of "black color."

From the European eighteenth century springs a clear and strong connection between the African continent and the concept of primitiveness, and thus of savagery. "Primitive," etymologically, simply indicates the originary, and, in the strictest sense, Africa is, probably, the originary locus of humankind. "Savage," from the late Latin *silvaticus,* as shown in the reading of Burton's treatise, is equivalent to marginality and, from a cultural normative space, designates the uncultivated. For example, in French, from the medieval period to the seventeenth century, *savage* often means simply "stranger," or, as defined by Dubois, Lagane, and Lerond for eighteenth-century France, "asocial."

There are immense problems involved in designating the eighteenth century as the moment of strategic articulation of the concepts of primitiveness and savagery. Indeed, the great era of explorations took place between 1485 (Bartolomeu Diaz's voyage around Africa) and 1541 (the end of Jacques Cartier's mission). Information and descriptions about the newly discovered "savages" found their way into the European consciousness, which strives to assert its *Cogito* toward what "it" defines as radically different.

But most of the theoretical debates and hypotheses—for example, those of Joseph de Acosta, Pedro Mexia, Sir Walter Raleigh, Pierre Viret—about this new "other," from the fifteenth to the eighteenth century, share two main characteristics: they depend, essentially, upon a religious and moral argument, and they remain strictly in the domain of a static philosophical anthropology (see Pagden 1982). Thus, theories on diffusion, degeneration, or environmentalism work around, and, in any case, give witness to, a predicament: how can one account for the truth of Genesis if humankind does not descend from one people? On the other hand, if geography, as a hypothesis, can explain the varieties of human cultures, can one accept it and its implications without opposing Genesis? (See Hodgen 1971.) The debates and theories led to propositions that hierarchized humans in the natural chain of being. They contributed to static, immobile philosophical anthropologies and not to a possible temporalization of natural and cultural differences. They thus also led to the conception of a historical anthropology, which, because of its spatial displacements, would have to face the problem of cultural relativism. As Hodgen relates:

> The break came in the eighteenth century with Leibniz and Erasmus Darwin. "The different classes of being," said the great German philosopher, "the totality of which forms the universe, are in the ideas of God, who knows distinctly their essential gradations. . . . Accordingly men are linked with animals, these with plants, and these again with fossils. . . . All the orders of natural beings must necessarily form only one chain, in which the different classes, like so many links, are so closely connected . . . that it is impossible for sense or imagination to determine where any of them begins or ends; . . . [and all are] pregnant with a future state . . . [or] orderly change." Dr. Darwin went further, in comments that would have filled earlier zoologists and botanists with horror. Anticipating Lamarck by fifteen years, he remarked that "when we revolve in our minds . . . the great changes, which we see naturally produced in animals after their nativity . . . we cannot but be convinced, that . . . all animals undergo perpetual transformations . . . and many of these acquired forms or propensities are transmitted to their posterity." Nevertheless, during the lifetime of Linnaeus and for many decades thereafter a belief in the fixity of species was as respectable among scientists as a belief in God. God was still thought of as the personal fabricator of every kind of gnat and bramble. (Hodgen 1971: 470)

More important, let us note that, in historicizing human cultures, the Age of Enlightenment inscribes itself on and revitalizes a Cartesian horizon: "If God be the source of natural laws, then it may be said that the world was not 'produced at once in a finished and perfect state,' but came gradually into existence." The importance of this view, writes Margaret Hodgen, quoting one Dr. Bock, "lies in the fact that a deity, whose ways are perhaps mysterious and beyond the grasp of human reason [. . .] was now replaced by an inexorable regularity and legality operating 'uniformly in all times and places.' It was this principle of legality and uniformity which was used by the Moderns to demonstrate the inevitability of progressive change in knowledge" (Hodgen 1971: 449–50). Evolutionism stems precisely from this epistemological locus, which, at the same time, locates its own misfortune. Insofar as the Enlightenment historicizes human cultures, and, specifically, wishes to arrest their growth and diversification (see Duchet 1971), could this trend have still operated without (principally) dwelling on the historicity of its own civilization? In any case, the new order of knowledge, which could have led to the creation of an immense table of historical systems of differences, turned out to be the basis for a highly controversial hypothesis (see Lévi-Strauss 1952 and 1976): a scale of civilizations held to be the signifying parameter of human merits, cultural values, and, indeed, technical progress. Cultural anthropology, in its worst expressions, became then the mirror reflecting "primitive" societies, focusing on their particular positions on the linear chain of civilizations, and, later on, as a service to colonial enterprises, analyzing the conditions for converting these societies.

Such is the context which metaphorizes the names of Africa. To concern myself with only the discourse produced (see also Bhabha 1986), which endlessly repeats itself in the books of the "colonial library," the context—or more exactly its will to truth fissures ancient words—constructs stereotypes, allocates remarkable adjectives to Africans and other "primitives," and finally establishes its civilizing mission. It is thus the late eighteenth- and early nineteenth-century conjunction of anthropology and colonial projects that hones the concepts and actualizes, in the image of the colonized, all the negative metaphors worked out by five centuries of European explorations of the world (see, e.g., Hammond and Jablow 1977).

The explorers and navigators of preceding centuries met Africans and described them, sometimes without sympathy at all. They did so in the name of a difference and not necessarily because of an intellectual politics of prejudice. The paintings they make are, visibly, culturally autocentered. But it is important to know that, contrary to Greek realism for example, the sixteenth- and seventeenth-century representations, most generally, "Westernize," or more specifically, as illustrated in Willy Bal's anthology (1963), "Italianize" black bodies according to principles of similitude. That this drawing together does not exclude antipathy means simply that the individuality of beings and things, their differences, should be preserved (see, e.g., Foucault 1973: 17–23). The seeds of prejudice are already there. Vigorous ideologies are constructed which ceaselessly expound the logic of differences and which ultimately will serve slave traders. But there is not yet, properly speaking, a "science." As a consequence, all paradoxes seem possible: the scandalous slave trade, on the one hand; on the other, events like the meeting of Vasco da Gama and the Hottentots in 1497. To salute the Portuguese voyager, the Hottentots play their flutes, sing, and dance. When they have finished, the courteous da Gama orders trumpets from the ships and invites his men to sing and dance in order to thank his hosts. Only from the eighteenth century on is there, thanks to the Enlightenment, a "science" of difference: anthropology. It "invents" an idea of Africa. Colonialism will elaborate upon the idea.

But one could continue the declension. Out of the idea, Africa has become a metaphor. For example, in Michael Burn's *The Modern Everyman* (1948), the principal character explodes at one moment and illustrates it well: " . . . Our son shall follow Learning beside Life,/ Like an explorer, like a colonist,/ For ever landing on fresh continents,/ For ever opening fresh Africas/ Of thought, experiment, imagination,/ following springs to find their final sea,/ Ascending rivers to their primal source,/ A Livingstone of the Laboratory./ A Cortez of the mind, the brain's Magellan!" (Burn 1948: 14)

Romanus Pontifex (1454) and the Expansion of Europe

In his 1493 *Inter Coetera* bull, Pope Alexander VI states:

> Among other works well pleasing to the divine majesty and cherished of our heart, this assuredly ranks highest, that in our times especially the Catholic faith and the Christian religion be exalted and everywhere increased and spread, that the health of souls be cared for and that barbarous nations be overthrown and brought to the faith itself.

This statement, as well as the general meaning of the bull, has two important implications. First, it signifies that as the successor of Saint Peter, the pope is a visible representative of God himself, and thus above kings, and can, as he does in *Inter Coetera*, "give, grant and assign forever [to European kings] countries and islands [newly] discovered." Second, non-Christians have no rights to possess or negotiate any dominion in the then-existing international context, and thus their land is objectively a *terra nullius* (no-man's-land) that may be occupied and seized by Christians in order to exploit the richness meant by God to be shared by all humankind. Thus these colonizing Christians will be helping the inferior "brethren" to insert themselves in the real and true history of salvation.

Inter Coetera is just one of the official papal letters giving these rights to the newly joined houses of Aragon and Castille. It was signed on May 3, 1493. More followed: a sequel, *Inter Coetera (II)*, is dated June 28, 1493, and another, *Eximiae devotionis*, July 1493 (which, for political reasons, was dated as if issued on May 3); these were followed by *Dudum siquidem* (September 25, 1493), *Aeterni Regis* (June 21, 1497), and *Eximiae devotionis (II)*

(November 16, 1501), all by Alexander VI. To these bulls of the Spanish pope to his king, one should add Julius II's *Universalis Ecclesiae* of July 28, 1508. Apart from giving the king of Spain absolute power over newly discovered lands, these documents also gave him power over ecclesiastical structures in the New World. The king was to pay for the processes of evangelization, the building of churches, and organization of the new Christianity. And he had a say in the designation of bishops. *Inter Coetera II* (June 28, 1493) confirmed that all lands discovered or to be discovered beyond 100 leagues west and south of the Azores would belong to Spain. The Tordesillas Treaty (June 7, 1493) pushed the line of demarcation further, 270 leagues west of the original. It made Brazil "Portuguese" instead of "Spanish" and divided the world between Portugal and Spain.

Alexander VI gave to the "Kings of Castille and Leon, all singular the aforesaid countries and islands [. . .] hitherto discovered and to be discovered." Note that *Inter Coetera I* and *II,* as well as the other documents mentioned, were prefigured by a lesser-known bull of Nicolas V, pope from 1447 to 1455 and the founder of the Vatican library. It has been said that, with him, the Renaissance "occupied the papacy," although usually the expression is meant to designate the pontificate of Leo X (1513–21), a Medici.

Romanus Pontifex (1454) is one of a number of papal bulls that document the Portuguese "ius patronatus," which also include *Dum Diversas* (June 18, 1452) *Ineffabilis et summi* (June 1, 1497) of Alexander VI, *Dudum pro parte* (March 31, 1516) of Leo X, and *Aequum reputamus* of Paul III (November 3, 1534), which codified the dispositions and rights defined in *Dum Diversas, Ineffabilis et summi,* and *Dudum pro parte.* These papal bulls stipulate rights, privileges, and obligations of the House of Portugal in the colonization of newly discovered countries.

Romanus Pontifex (1454) is a five-page letter in the 1730 version of *Magnum Bullarium Romanum seu ejusdem Continuatio* that I consulted. The beginning is interesting for it mentions recent history, but its overtones allude to ancient times:

> Alfonso Lusitaniae Regi cujus Filius Henricus studio iter in Indiam Orientalem aperiendi usque ad Guineam et Nigrum Fluvium penetraverat, et insulas varias detexerat.

The address to Alfonso pertains to historical events: the discoveries made by the *Infante* Henry the Navigator (1395–1460) in his explorations. *Inter Coetera* of Calixte III (March 13, 1456) gave the *Infante* of Portugal, who was also the grand master of the Military Order of Christ, the *ius patronatus* over all the countries discovered and to be discovered in Africa en route to South Asia. Henry, or, more specifically, his executant—the grand prior of the Military Order of Christ residing in the convent of Tomar, Portugal—had absolute civil and religious power over these countries. In 1514, the jurisdictional power would pass to the bishop of Funchal and the *ius patronatus* would be given back to the king. The second part of the quotation praises Henry for opening up the route to "Oriental India"—Henry had penetrated Guinea up to the Black River *(ad Guineam et Nigrum Fluvium penetraverat)*. This geographical reference also has classical overtones. In the first century, Pliny *(Natural History* V, 8, 44) spoke of the *Nigri fluvio eadem natura quae Nilo,* the Black River, which had the same features as the Nile.

The second paragraph of *Romanus Pontifex* establishes the political and theological authority of the letter. Its author states his official title: *"Romanus Pontifex Regni coelestis clavigeri successor; et Vicarius Jesus Christi"* (Roman Pontiff, successor of the holder of the key to the celestial kingdom, the Vicar of Jesus Christ). It is in this capacity that Nicolas writes to Alfonso V, backed by both a religious and a political history of the papacy, invoked in the contro-verted bull *Unam Sanctam* (July 11, 1302) of Boniface VIII, in which was affirmed the primacy of the spiritual power (of the pope) over the temporal one (of kings): "It belongs to the spiritual power to institute the temporal one and judge it if it is not good. [. . .] We say, declare and define that to be submitted to the Roman pontiff is for any creature a necessity for salvation."

In the second paragraph of the bull, Nicolas specifies the mission of the colonization: to expand Christianity. And he invites the king to follow the tradition exemplified by the royal House of Portugal: a commitment to spread the name of Jesus to the most remote territories of the world.

> Catholicus et versus omnium Creatoris Christimiles, ipsiusque fidei acerrimus ac fortissimus defensor, et intrepidus pugil.

The mission is detailed in the third paragraph, and is directly linked to Portu-guese explorations. An explicit reference, another one, is made to the achieve-ments of the *Infante* Henry, who brought the name of Christ to India and to Guinea: "usque ad *Indos, qui Christi* nomen *colere dicuntur* navigabile fieret [. . .] *ad Ghineam provinciam tandem pervenirent."* The Guinea referred to is unclear, but might be the Ethiopia of ancient geographers, since the naviga-tors had reached the source of the Nile *(ad ostium cujusdam magni fluminis Nilis communiter pervenirent).*

Paragraph four of the bull is terrifying. In the name of God, it gives the King of Portugal and his successors the right not only to colonize but also to convert forcibly to Christianity and enslave *"Saracenos ac paganos"* (Saracens and pagans) in perpetuity. Here is the central statement:

> Nos praemissa omnia et singula debita meditatione pesantes, et attendentes, quod cum olim praefato Alfonso Regi quoscumque Saracenos ac Paganos ali-osque Dominia, possessiones, et mobilia et immobilia bona quaecumque per eos detenta ac possessa invadendi, conquirendi, expugnandi, debellandi et subju-gandi, *illorumque personas in perpetuam servitute,* ac Regna, Ducatus, Comita-tus, Principatus, Dominia, possessiones et bona sibi et successoribus suis applicandi, appropriandi, ac in suos successorumque usus et utilitatem conver-tendi, *aliis nostris literis* plenam et liberam inter cetera concessimus facultatem. [my emphasis]

The concept of *terra nullius* resides in the right to dispossess all Saracens and other non-Christians of all their goods (mobile and immobile), the right to invade and conquer these peoples' lands, to expel them from it, and, when necessary, to fight them and subjugate them in a perpetual servitude *(debellandi et subjugandi illorumque personas in perpetuam servitude),* and to expropriate all their possessions.

In the last two paragraphs, Nicolas reinscribes his letter in the tradition of his Church's politics and the spiritual power of the papacy.

The *Romanus Pontifex* makes several points. First, all non-Christian peoples have no ownership rights to the land on which they are living. Second, when Christian Europeans—namely, Spanish and Portuguese people—met natives, they would invite the local king or chief and his advisers to a meeting. They would present to them a Christian interpretation of history that closely followed the Old and New Testaments. At the end of the meeting, the natives were invited to pledge submission and to convert. If the natives failed to accept the "truth" and, politically, to become "colonized," it was not only legal but also an act of faith and a religious duty for the colonizers to kill the natives. The philosophical system underlying the *Romanus Pontifex* and its explanation of how to deal with non-Westerners was Aristotelian, which, as we know, also justifies slavery. Whereas for the "liberal" Father Las Casas (1951) the two *Inter Coetera* bulls signified that Spain had the right to expand Christianity in America but without taking the Indians' lands, for Father Sepulveda, a rigorous Aristotelian philosopher, "all natives were meant to be subjugated." According to Sepulveda, God created natives for a purpose, and it was morally wrong to oppose the enslavement and exploitation of natives because such opposition thwarted that purpose.

A comprehensive study of the *"terra nullius"* politics by Keller, Lissitzyn, and Mann (1938) indicates that between 1400 and 1800 not one non-European nation was considered to have the right "to possess or to transfer any dominion in the international law sense." Keller, Lissitzyn, and Mann provide concrete illustrations of European techniques for creating rights of sovereignty in newly discovered lands. About the Portuguese practice, they record the following:

In 1419, Joâo Gonzalves Zarco discovered Madeira. In accordance with the instructions he had received from Prince Henry, he took official possession of the island through three symbolic acts: first, he erected a cross; secondly, a mass was celebrated; thirdly, clods of earth from the island were taken and brought back to Portugal, given to Prince Henry. The island was colonized after and became part of Portugal.

In 1494, Diego Caon discovered the mouth of the Congo River on the west coast of Africa. Diego Caon erected "a pillar of stone with the royal arms and letters of Portugal" on it. In the same manner, on his trip to India, Vasco da Gama stopped in the Kingdom of Melinde, on the East Coast of Africa.

In the Kingdom of Melinde, on the east coast of Africa, Da Gama and his company struck up a very cordial friendship with the King. The Portuguese mentioned to the King a certain "mark," the name of the King of Portugal written upon a stone, their King's sign, placed in the countries of all his friends in commemoration of his sincerity. The King of Melinde was highly pleased at this intelligence, and wanted to have the pillar placed at the gates of his palace, but the Portuguese replied ingenuously that it would not be very easily seen by those entering the port, and that it should be displayed in a more prominent location. The King agreeing to this, a tall column of white marble, bearing the two escutcheons mentioned above, with the name of King Manoel I engraved on the base, was set up on a high hill overlooking the harbor, visible far out to sea. Correa adds that Da Gama had six of these pillars, already suitably engraved, with him, ordered made by his King, who commanded that they be set up in countries where friendship was established, so that the remembrance of it might last forever, "and that they might be seen by all nations that might come later." (Keller et alii 1938: 25)

A more elaborate ceremony occurred in 1481, when Don Diego took formal possession of the Guinea Coast in West Africa.

There the cavalcade proceeded [. . .] to a large tree at no great distance from the village Aldea, as the most desirable situation for their intended fortress; the royal arms were immediately displayed upon the tree and an altar raised beneath; the whole company proceeded to join in the first mass that was celebrated in Guinea. (Keller et alii 1938: 24)

The Spaniards were even less informal. Their usual practice generally included a formal declaration of taking possession of the *"terra nullius,"* a physical sign symbolizing the act, and a symbolic acting out of the new sovereignty. A 1514 royal instruction to the explorer De Solis specifies the steps:

The manner that you must have in the taking of possession of the lands and parts which you shall have discovered is to be that, being in the land or part that you shall have discovered, you shall make before notary public and the greatest possible number of witnesses, and the best-known ones, an act of possession in our name, cutting trees and boughs, and digging or making, if there be an opportunity, some small building *(edificio),* which should be in a part where there is some marked hill or a large tree, and you shall say how many leagues it is from the sea, a little more or less, and in which part, and what signs it has, and you shall make a gallows there and have somebody bring a complaint before you and as our captain and judge you shall pronounce upon and determine it, so that, in all, you shall take the said possession; which is to be for that part where you shall take it, and for all its district *(partido)* and province or island, and you shall bring testimony thereof signed by the said notary in a manner to make faith. (Keller et alii 1938: 39–40)

Indeed, the formal statement stipulates that the new country is taken in "the name of the king of Spain." Thus, for example, Columbus, during his first trip in 1492, took possession of islands in the West Indies "in the name of the Spanish monarchs by public proclamation and unfurled banners." And Spanish explorers usually put up crosses, as did Columbus on his third and fourth voyages and Vicente Yáñez Pinzón and Diego de Lepe in 1500 in South America at the sites where the ceremonies of taking possession took place. Sometimes, the physical ceremony amounted to simply erecting a pile of stones, as Balboa did in 1513 on the Pacific Coast. Finally, the new jurisdiction and control over the land was symbolized in various acts, such as cutting trees and drinking water, as Pinzón did on the northern coast of South America. Diego de Lepe also cut down trees, but in addition marked his name on other trees. On his second trip, Columbus took possession of new territories by means of a legal ceremony similar to that by which Unamuno took possession of parts of the coast of California, as described in a report of 1587:

> Having left orders aboard ship as to what was to be done, and having elected *alcaldes* and *regidores,* that there might be some one to take possession of the port and whatever else might be discovered, I landed with twelve soldiers. . . .
>
> When we reached this hill, as it seemed to be a suitable place to take possession in His Majesty's name of the port and the country, seeing that I and the rest of the party had landed and traversed the country roundabout and the port quietly and pacifically, as in territory belonging to his domain [*de la demarcacion i Corona del Rey*], I did so in the name of King Philip our master, in due legal form, through Diego Vasquez Mexia (one of the *alcaldes* elected for this purpose) in his capacity of *Justicia,* setting up a cross as a sign of the Christian faith and of the possession taken in His Majesty's name of the port and the country, cutting branches from the trees which grew thereabouts, and performing the other customary ceremonies. (Keller et alii 1938: 40)

The Spanish taking possession of a *"terra nullius"* and its symbolism often included a recitation known as the *Requirement,* although it was seldom performed to the extent specified in the instructions. Fundamentally, it was a systematic presentation of the Christian philosophy of creation and history to the natives. At the end of the recitation, the natives were invited "to pledge allegiance to the pope and the king of Spain." If the natives refused to make the pledge, it was legal to occupy the natives' land by force, if necessary.

The French practice before the end of the seventeenth century was rather simple, compared with the Spanish or the English ceremonies. It was almost as informal as the Portuguese practice. It then took on a highly structured form in the last quarter of the seventeenth century, as exemplified by the ritual of June 14, 1671, during which Daumont de Saint-Lusson—representative of Jean Talon, Intendant of Canada and personal representative of the king of France—took possession of the Lake Superior region. Leading his men, de Saint-Lusson marched to the top of a hill where Indian chiefs and representatives were already assembled.

> All around the great throng of Indians stood or crouched or reclined at length, with eyes and ears intent. A large cross of wood had been made ready. Dablon

[one of the Jesuit missionaries in the party], in solemn form pronounced his blessing on it, and then it was reared and planted in the ground, while the French, uncovered, sang the *Vexilla Regis.* Then a post of cedar was planted beside it, with a metal plate attached, engraven with the Royal Arms; while Saint-Lusson's followers sang the *Exaudiat,* and one of the Jesuits uttered a prayer for the King. Saint-Lusson now advanced, and, holding his sword in one hand, and raising with the other a sod of earth, proclaimed in a loud voice:

"In the name of the Most High, Mighty and Redoubted Monarch, Louis, Fourteenth of that name, Most Christian King of France and Navarre, I take possession of this place, Sainte Marie du Saut, as also of Lakes Huron and Superior, the Island of Manitoulin, and all countries, rivers, lakes and streams contiguous thereunto,—both those which have been discovered and those which may be discovered hereafter, in all their length and breadth, bounded on the one side by the seas of the North and the West and on the other by the South Sea: declaring to the nations thereof that from this time forth they are vassals of His Majesty, bound to obey his laws and follow his customs; promising them on his part all succor and protection against the invasions of their enemies; declaring to all other potentates, princes, sovereigns, states and republics,—to them and to their subjects,—that they cannot and are not to seize or settle upon any parts of the aforesaid countries, save only under the good pleasure of His Most Christian Majesty, and of him who will govern in his behalf; and this on pain of incurring his resentment and the effort of his arms. Vive le Roy!" (Keller et alii 1938: 125)

From the sixteenth century on, the British practice was a highly elaborate procedure, which, like the Spanish, included specific steps: the first was to obtain letters of patent. Then various rites were performed in taking possession of a territory in the name of the king or the queen. These included at least the following three: the erection of a symbolic sign, a formal declaration proclaiming that the land was under English sovereignty, and the promulgation of a set of laws. The voyage of Sir Humphrey Gilbert provides a typical example. Letters of patent, a royal grant of exclusive privilege for his discoveries, were given to him on June 11, 1578. The queen gave him "free libertie and licence [. . .] to discover, find, search out [. . .] barbarous lands, countries and territories not actually possessed by any Christian prince or people."

In 1583, Gilbert anchored in St. John's Harbour, Newfoundland. The official ceremony of taking possession was organized on August 5, 1583, "in the presence of the entire company and some 'strangers.'" After the ritual, Gilbert, in the name of Queen Elizabeth's right of sovereignty and of his own lordship, promulgated a code of three laws that (a) established the Church of England in Newfoundland; (b) made punishable as high treason any acts prejudicial to the Queen's right of possession; (c) made punishable any words of dishonor to the Queen, for which the penalty was to have one's ears cut off and one's ship and goods confiscated.

In conclusion, the *Romanus Pontifex* of 1454 shaped all subsequent agreements concerning rights to newly discovered lands. It not only laid the foundation for the succeeding papal bulls, but throughout the years its basic tenets were faithfully maintained even as its politics were modified and transformed to fit concrete demands in the expansion of European projects. Despite the great number of agreements and contracts that were made in this connection, no European power considered the natives to have any sovereignty or any accepted rights over their lands, except in a few rare instances in territories of Southeast and Eastern Asia, notably China. These agreements were, in their intent and in their form, devices allowing the Europeans to enter the country and build *avant postes*.

The *Romanus Pontifex* philosophy also reflects two fundamental concepts that were to guide colonization. First, it affirmed the primacy of the papacy over the Christian kings, going back in its most explicit and extreme expression to Boniface VIII's bull, *Unam Sanctam* of November 1, 1302. In the mid-fifteenth century, the spiritual primacy and rights were, as we have seen, objects of political negotiations. Second, it provided the basis for the *"terra nullius"* concept—that is, the concept of the European right of sovereignty outside of Europe, and ultimately the right of colonization and the practice of slavery. This philosophical position was said to spring from "Natural Law." Thus, just as in a forest where there are stronger and weaker essences, the latter living and developing under the protection of the former, the human "races" would observe the same rule. It would be the "mission" of the stronger race to help their inferior "brethren" to grow up; and in any case, according to the doctrine, it was up to the most advanced race to make sure that all goods made by God for the whole of humankind should be exploited. In 1526, Francisco de Vitoria justified colonial conquests on the basis of Christian trade rights, explaining that it was God's intent that all nations should trade with each other. His contemporary, Sepulveda, invoking Aristotle's lesson, maintained that natives were meant by God to be dominated. In sum, from a Christian point of view, to oppose the process of colonization or that of slavery could only be morally wrong.

II.

WHICH IDEA OF AFRICA?

Si les discours doivent être traités
d'abord comme des ensembles
d'événements discursifs, quel statut
faut-il donner à cette notion d'événement
qui fut si rarement prise en
considération par les philosophes?

—M. FOUCAULT, *L'Ordre du
Discours*, 59.

The reactivation of Greek texts, the reversal of perspectives in history, bears witness to an epistemological transformation. Knowledge about Africa now orders itself in accordance with a new model. Despite the resilience of primitivist and evolutionist myths, a new discourse—more exactly, a new type of relation to the African object—has been established. Anthropology, the most compromised of disciplines during the exploitation of Africa, rejuvenated itself first through functionalism (during the colonial period), and, toward the end of the colonial era, in France, transmuted itself into structuralism. In so doing, anthropology, at least theoretically, revised its own connection with what it was supposed to serve from its institution as a scientific discipline. In any case in the mid-1950s it fused with other disciplines (economics, geography, history, literature, etc.), thus constituting a new vague body known as Africanism or knowledge about Africa. Bound together in the same epistemological space but radically divided by their aims and methods, these disciplines, apropos of the idea of Africa, were caught between very concrete demands for the political liberation of the continent, the designation of their own scientificity, and their philosophical foundation. The African figure was an empirical fact, yet by definition it was perceived, experienced, and promoted as the sign of the absolute otherness. To dramatize this point, I quote a passage from the *Order of Things*:

> In this figure, which is at once empirical and yet foreign to (and in) all that we can experience, our consciousness no longer finds—as it did in the sixteenth century—the trace of another world; it no longer observes the wandering of a straying reason; it sees welling up that which is, perilously, nearest to us—as if, suddenly, the very hollowness of our existence is outlined in relief; the finitude

upon the basis of which we are, and think, and know, is suddenly there before us; an existence at once real and impossible, thought that we cannot think, an object for our knowledge that always eludes us. (Foucault 1973: 375)

From this quotation—a commentary on the figure of madness as the truth and the alterity of modern Western experience—I would like, paradoxically, to suggest that, in general, truth has been the aim of "Africanism"—which I understand to be the body of discourses on and about Africa. Is it really a paradox when one pays careful attention to exotic figures of Africa that, since the fifteenth century, testify to a conjunction of the continent with folly? (See Hammond and Jablow 1977; Mouralis 1988.) Yet, as strange as that might appear, methodical shifts, transformations, and conversions within such technical discourses as African anthropology and history have been predicated by criteria on how to attain the truth about Africa and express it in "scientifically" credible discourses. In its demands, the search would, for example, account for the existing tension in anthropology between evolutionism, functionalism, diffusionism, and structuralism.

It appears to me that the various methods of Africanism have carried with them another issue, which is a major one. It bears on how the empirical aspect witnesses to the truth of theoretical discourses and vice versa. Indeed, this problem largely goes beyond the modalities of Africanist methodological schools. In a paper on "The Search for Paradigms as a Hindrance to Understanding," Albert Hirschman notes that "a recent journal article argued forcefully against the collection of empirical materials as an end in itself and without sufficient theoretical analysis to determine appropriate criteria of selection." Immediately after this, Hirschman specifies his own project: to evaluate "the tendency toward compulsive and mindless theorizing—a disease as prevalent and debilitating [. . .] as the spread of mindless number work in social sciences" (Hirschman 1979: 163).

Taking seriously Herskovits's cultural relativism, I would suggest that the real issue is not one of theory versus empirical collection. It is rather about the silent and *a priori* choice of the truth to which a given discourse aims. In this context, I understand truth as a derivative abstraction, as a sign and a tension. Simultaneously uniting and separating conflictual objectives of systems constituted on the basis of different axioms and paradigms, truth is neither pure idea nor a simple objective.

"Whatever may be the case in respect to [a] wish for unity, it is at the beginning and at the end of truths. But as soon as the exigency for a single truth enters into history as a goal of civilization, it is immediately affected with a mark of violence. For one always wishes to tie the knot too early. The *realized* unity of the true is precisely the initial lie" (Ricoeur 1965: 176). Thus we have for example, the challenge of Christianity linking its fate in A.D. 313 to that of the Roman Empire; the paradoxical power of a European expansion outside its borders, which, almost exactly five hundred years ago, invented and organized the world in which we are living today on the basis of the concept of natural law; and the lie that justified slavery and, apropos of all non-European territories, the idea of *terra nullius,* thanks to which America, Australia, and South Africa are what they are today. The representations and signs that gave the hidden and violated memory of these countries their right and pertinence as a beginning seem to have disappeared.

These types of "paradoxical" signs may be less interesting. They unveil their own internal contradictions too easily. But can I anchor this statement about truth as fault, give it a philosophical basis in a reflection dealing with the tasks of Africanists?

Let me elaborate my hypothesis. I think that in the brief history of Africanism it has become obvious that beyond the dichotomy between rudimentary and scientific knowledge, illusion and truth—a dichotomy entertained by evolutionists Lévy-Bruhl and his disciples, including Evans-Pritchard—there is a major problem concerning the very conditions of knowledge. Most of us would agree with Michel Foucault that some distinctions should be made. On the one hand, there is the fact of necessary distinctions about the truth itself. One: there is *"a truth that is of the same order as the object—the truth that is gradually outlined, formed, stabilized, and expressed through the body* and the rudiments of perceptions"; two: there is *"the truth that appears as illusion"*; and three: concurrently *"there must also exist a truth that is of the order of discourse*—a truth that makes it possible to employ, when dealing with the nature or history of knowledge, a language that will be true" (see Foucault 1973: 320; my emphasis). Such distinctions should have a universal application. On the other hand, there is an important question that concerns the status of a true discourse. As noted by Foucault, "either this true discourse finds its foundation and model in the empirical truth whose genesis in nature and in history it retraces, so that *one has an analysis of the positivist type* [. . .]; or the true discourse anticipates the truth whose nature and history it defines [. . .], so that *one has a discourse of the eschatological type"* (Foucault 1973: 320; my emphasis).

These methodological separations—about types of truth, the conditions of possibility of a true discourse, and the tension between the positivist type and the eschatological type—make sense. Is there really a way of conceptualizing rigorously the reality of Africa as long as we have not faced these separations?

In order to clarify some of the theoretical consequences of the preceding remarks, I would like to focus seriously and at length on cultural relativism as expounded by Melville Herskovits, the founder of African Studies in the United States; and then briefly bring into the discussion a contemporary and percussive argument made by Jean-Loup Amselle, a French scholar, who is a *maître de conférences* at the Ecole des Hautes Etudes en Sciences Sociales in Paris.

Herskovits's Cultural Relativism

Let us begin with a simple inquiry. Herskovits's questions about ancient civilizations will speak even to the most skeptical. How true is our knowledge about them? He writes:

[...] one may well ask, is not our knowledge of the civilizations of the palaeo-
lithic at best too scanty? Do we know too little of the actual life of the people
to judge it? In what sort of dwellings did these men live from the earliest times?
What sort of language did they speak? What was their religion and their social
organization? What clothing did they wear? What foods other than the meat
of the animals whose bones we find in the refuse heaps did they eat? These and
numerous other questions will occur to one; it is unfortunate that most of them
cannot be answered with anything more than guesses, shrewd though these be.
(Herskovits 1929: 121)

The predicament (as well as the real significance of the so-called crisis of
social sciences in general and African Studies in particular) might be stated
here. As Benoît Verhaegen (1974) saw it, the predicament resides in the tension
between the claim and the will to truth of empirical discourses (in which,
supposedly, reality determines the credibility and objectivity of the discourse)
and the claims of eschatological discourses (in which a promise and the value
of a hope are supposed to actualize a truth in the process of fulfilling its
being). As noted by Foucault, in this tension, from a contemporary viewpoint,
Marxism comes in contact with phenomenology and posits the human being
as a disturbing object of knowledge. More simply, one discovers that both
Auguste Comte and Karl Marx witness an epistemological configuration in
which "eschatology (as the objective truth proceeding from man's discourse)
and positivism (as the truth of discourse defined on the basis of the truth of
the object) are indissociable" (Foucault 1973: 320–21).

This awareness should impose itself as an intellectual demand. Most African
Marxist projects in the 1960s ignored the complexity of their own epistemological roots and thus erased the paradoxes of their own discourse and practice. On the other hand, non-Marxist works, by ignoring history (as
framework of their own discourses) and the conflicting historicities of their
"objects" of knowledge, tended to privilege the allegory of closed, inexistent
societies reduced to mythical pasts, or, as in the case of Mbiti's project (1971),
postulated a subjunctive mood accounted for by an uncritical leap out of
history into a Christian eschatology. In all cases, it is a past, a history, or,
more exactly, histories of Africa that were erased, and the idea of Africa was
reduced to a potentiality. Here we may remember Herskovits's advice:

[...] make no mistake, cultural relativism is a "tough-minded" philosophy. It
requires those who hold it to alter responses that arise out of some of the
strongest enculturative conditioning to which they have been exposed, the eth-
nocentrisms implicit in the particular value-systems of their society. In the case
of anthropologists, this means following the implications of data which, when
opposed to our enculturated system of values, set up conflicts not always easy
to resolve. (Herskovits 1972: 37)

I question Marxist lessons on Africa. Yet, the Marxists seemed somehow
right in insisting that there is a relation of necessity between the practice of
social science and of politics, and thus that of ethics. One might oppose their
political deductions, but, with respect to the idea of Africa, there is no way

to ignore their significance and the evidence they unveil. In terms of the future, the cost (or the price) of social mythologies (development, modernization etc.) invented by functionalism, applied anthropology, and colonialism is such that a redefinition of the "Africanist" discourse and practice should be isomorphic with that of our political expectations. In terms of the past, the same holds true: what is the price to be paid for bringing back to light what has been buried, blurred, or simply forgotten?

Let us dwell on the Marxist project and its implications. From the 1950s, from the political awakening of Black Africa onward, Marxism appeared to be the inspiration for the renewal of the continent. A remarkable apotheosis, to the extent that the promises implied were, from the onset, given as concrete expressions of the life of real people and as a negation of the exile which had held them captive, Marxism seemed to be the exemplary weapon and idea with which to go beyond what colonialism incarnated and ordained in the name of capital.

From this stemmed also, and without a doubt, the new inflection brought, right after the last European war, to African Studies by Marxist concepts whose explicit intention and theoretical framework clearly impugn the dogmatism of colonial sciences and its cultural programs in regard to non-Western societies. The debates on the Asian mode of production, on the lineage mode of production, and on the concepts of oral tradition and *"pensée sauvage"* opened new horizons. In any case, with Yves Bénot, Endre Sik, Jean Suret-Canale, and many others, these concepts become facets of a militant Africanism which progressively transforms the aims and methods of anthropology, sociology, history, and political economy.

On the other hand, during the same period, political men of action in Africa, sensitive to this power of conversion of Marxist thought and seduced by the metaphors of an egalitarian society organized on the basis of economic registers in the service of the betterment of people, of all people, conceived the political liberation of new African countries in terms of Marxist revolution. This political plan, in fact, unfolded the generosity of Marxist Africanism and submitted itself to the same norms: the evidence of a common human condition; a shared opposition to the privileges of history, race, or class; and a negation of the equivalence of property and political power. And, in order to desacralize the civilizing assumptions of the colonial violence, this was the era of African socialisms. Often formally brilliant, these socialisms, generally speaking, functioned and lived as texts marked by fantasies of an illusory new beginning of history. Within their concrete articulations in social formations, over the years they revealed themselves to be nothing other than deviations of the Marxist projects they were claiming to establish. The rigor of the materialist discourse of Nkrumah was matched by one of the most mediocre political dictatorships; the socialist test of Sekou Touré turned out to be, across the years, only an autocratic order whose effort, in the final analysis, jumbled all investments and Marxist figures that it had initially justified; the *Ujaama* of Nyerere unveiled nothing but the contradictions of bureaucratic mechanisms that asphyxiated the disfranchised classes whose State socialism was supposed to improve; finally, the elegance of Senghor's readings of Marx and Engels is, following the examples of Althusser or Jean-Yves Calvez, a simple object of scholarly exegeses for erudites.

This failure, contrary to the racist clamor and to the theses that issue forth from facile analyses, does not seem to me to be solely a failure of African intelligence. Indeed, one can link this failure to that of Marxist Africanism and its epistemological incoherences. In any event, it should be noted that the myths of African socialism originate in the same place as those of Marxist Africanism: that precise space which, in Marxian thought, determines and celebrates the powers of "revolution," determines the rights and the conflicts of the real individuals who make up this totality, that is the faceless proletariat, and, above all, organizes its missions. It is from this place that dreams and systems were established that, in order to prescribe African culture autonomy and economic and technical progress, insisted—and, alas, sometimes continue to insist—solely on the right to be different and on the virtues of otherness. For example: the respectability of an African history reconquered by Africanism from the margins of the primitiveness into which colonial science had inscribed it today authorizes shaky accounts of the Pharaohs. Similarly, the often absentminded and, in any case, guilty contempt of a political economy that invokes relativist curves as working principles explains the methodological impatience which becomes the rule and in which, without any epistemological precaution, metaphors on African tradition are substituted for the constraints of history. This simplification does not stop at a philosophy that, "Africanized" thanks to some missionaries and their disciples, forgets the metaphors of concepts and analogies they allow in expressions such as "Bantu ontology" or "Dogon metaphysics," and operates more and more in a relation of necessity between the significant and the signification that it manipulates.

At the same time, there is the bringing into play of key words that, for thirty years, have dominated the scene in African Studies—negritude, black personality, authenticity, etc.—which all hail in one direct line from the Marxian presupposition of the centrality of the individual as historical actor. It is true that the Marxian paradigm has crossed idealistic temptations of the missionaries, who, in order to better assimilate, were the first to establish adequate methods for rendering their messages indigenous. It is also true that the Marxian paradigm sprang up in the 1950s in a space that had already been conquered by a critical but liberal Africanism: that of a Georges Balandier, with the colossal provocation of his "sociology of Black Africa," or that of Jan Vansina, who, with his concept of oral history, imposed an ordeal by fire upon institutional ideology. These crossings do not invalidate my thesis. On the contrary. They have contributed to putting the credibility of colonial science off-center. In the space thus left, the Marxian invitation would become a wish for the possibility of a new beginning; and Marxism, both in the social sciences and in politics, would be established as providential coincidence and sign of liberation. New signs, methodological displacements, and an ideological commotion, surely of a discreet but efficacious nature, were being born. They were to open a historical process. I believe that they made their mark on it. Indeed, in the 1960s the vocabulary of the criticism of colonial ratio was Marxist, that of the African independences as well as of the nonalignment programs was Marxist. The regimes, the progressive movements, and their leaders were Marxist. Similarly, the *interlocuteurs valables* ("authorized representatives") in Africa were Marxist or, at least, wielded a syntax that had a Marxist aspect; the Africanists who were respected and accepted, both by Africa and by the West, were, more often than not, Marxists or, at the very least, Marxist sympathizers; the discipline of the future that attracted or terrorized, political economy, was Marxist. What this adjective crystallizes in these expressions, as in the attitudes that it covers up, shows nothing in common except for a garrulous will to be itself and the obscure recourse to a primordial astonishment: we are, fundamentally, all equal on the strength of our birth, as in death. In short, we are, all of us, marionettes in an absurd puppet theater whose elementary rationality could, at least theoretically, make the communality of our destiny and the precariousness of our common human condition a reality.

The remarkable failure of the Marxian paradigm can be explained. The body of the innovating discourses was a vague object, unsettled, proposed but never really named; indicated but always absent; dramatized but, at every turn, covered by confusing adjectives that kept it veiled. There is something here that sounds simply like a mystification. Granted, some African political leaders could have been led astray or, more precisely, they could have believed that the arrangement of the grids of a racial otherness might, just as it stands, be a Marxist claim and bring about a socialist society on the level of the organization of power and production. I find it hard to believe that the majority of Africanists—African as well as Western—would have fallen into that abstruseness. Directly concerned with the experiment that the conquest of Africa by a socialism "of human countenance" would be, extolling society in the name of the rights of subjectivity, they could not be unaware that the endeavor, the result of their good offices and the collection of their purposely technical formulas, was muddling up something essential. The subjective moment in Marxian thought is necessarily canceled out by an other, which is objective and, at the same time, a memory of history and dialectic sequence. To be precise, and referring to what Marx himself said in 1879 to the German Social Democratic party, which had found refuge in Zurich, I contend that the class struggle is the propulsive force in history, but it is neither chance nor the hazards of the condition of individuals, singular members of that class, that signifies history. Historical materialism is neither subjective figuration nor a demand for individual, psychological attitudes, but rather, and much more so, it is a law and a focus of pressure and configuration coercing each other on history's ladder.

Jean-Paul Sartre quickly understood that and stated it clearly: first in *Black Orpheus,* in which he shows that the desire of the Negro for difference, although established as a denial of the thesis of white supremacy, is made to self-destruct in the name of dialectics; then in *Critique de la raison dialectique*, in which he rewrites the setting of the limits of liberty, radically correcting the romanticism of absolute choices which were displayed as exemplary value and insolvency of the individual in *L'Etre et le Néant*. In Africa, Léopold Sédar Senghor is very likely the only theoretician who, from the very start, has been attentive to the contrasts of the two moments of the Marxian thesis: the decisive crudeness of the right to otherness, the subjective moment par excellence, and immediately afterwards its absorption into the brilliancy of objectivity and the abyss of history. The violence implied by the passage from the first to the second moment, as well as the force of reduction of the latter, would account for reasons that made Aimé Césaire decide to leave the French Communist Party.

Thirty years after Aimé Césaire's resignation, the tensions probably seem more clearcut. And, on the other hand, Césaire's choice and Senghor's have become question marks. For the same reason, the order of Africanist discourse appears ambivalent: has it not, then, covered the same body? If the subjective condition of the African subject which Senghor and Césaire incarnated seemed, in the 1960s, happy and respectable, is it only because it necessarily had to make place for the violence of objectivity that would inflame to the quick and destroy it? Innocuous questions? Absolutely not! Generous and naive Africans have read books by Marxist Africanists, or have reread Marx, Engels, Mao, often in cheap editions that came from the Soviet Union. A fair number among them, between 1955 and 1965, found reasons for ecstasy in these silent discussions. In reality, these "dialogues" were nothing but the echo of explicit incitements to the violence that had been proposed by the works which had awakened these Africans to political awareness in the name of cultural otherness. In short, from the very start, their reading had been falsified by the "bad faith"—in the Sartrian sense—of the invitations to historical and cultural alterity. Some of them, in the name of an unconditional faithfulness to Marx, took up arms to fight against the neocolonial state, or to undermine the African socialisms, and have obviously lost.

Then, as if in response to these missed bets, new and vehement calls repeated the Marxist lesson in its irreducible objectivity. There were political regimes—such as those in Angola, Benin, or the Congo—and new associations, such as those that reunited the African Marxists. These calls were being mobilized against political commentaries and attitudes that gave value to subjectivity and the idealistic signs of difference, and, on the other hand, claimed to concentrate on a strict and rigorous application of the socialist code. In short, we had passed from the questionable variations around the theme "Marx, the European of the nineteenth century, did not know Africa" to another one: "Marx, the universal guide."

This shift was important. It appeared to have informed the most aggressive orientations of contemporary research as well as of the most fruitful ideological debates, such as those raised by Paulin Hountondji in philosophy, Majhemout Diop on the notion of class, and A. Dieng on the Marxist question as African problem. It has also been said that this shift or this conversion would signify, in the final analysis, a remarkable recapturing of Western historicity. The colonial period had founded this historicity as availability of capital. In the name of the universality of Marx, it was being established, in clear daylight at last, after all the hypocritical vocabulary of the last thirty years, as a requirement of Marxist and socialist codes. What a symbol!

It is toward this major point among all the others that Bogumil Jewsiewicki offers us his *Marx, the West, and Africa*. In their saturation and their opacity, what these three terms are saying, the relationships within which they mutually define themselves, the theoretical or concrete architectures they have authorized, are neither obvious nor simple. It was time that someone describe the theatrical nature of these concepts, decipher their polysemy and the values they take on or lose depending on the context. Jewsiewicki does it well and with a mastery gained by long years of study of what these concepts signify as resources and as patience. The attentive reader of his monograph will feel it as well. Jewsiewicki brings us a study which is also an intoning of the intellectual contradictions and inconsistencies that are, in part, responsible for the present crisis in Africanist science, and of the failures in renewing the African political space as it came out of the colonial experience. He forces us to rethink, as I have tried to do in the preceding pages, the African history of Marxism and oppose it to the principles of relativism.

Perhaps it is now time that we reread carefully Herskovits's *Economic Life of Primitive Peoples* (1940) and reanalyze its basic opposition between life before and life after the machine, between the "foreign" and the "familiar."

Herskovits stresses, in his well-known volume on *Cultural Relativism* (1972), that cultural relativism—that is, an anti-ethnocentric approach to otherness—should be understood as a method, a philosophy, and a practice.

> As a method, relativism encompasses the principle of our science (i.e., anthropology) that in studying a culture, one seeks to attain as great a degree of objectivity as possible; that one does not judge the modes of behavior one is describing, or seek to change them. Rather, one seeks to understand the sanctions of behavior in terms of the established relationships within the culture itself, and refrains from making interpretations that arise from a preconceived frame of reference. Relativism as philosophy concerns the nature of cultural values and, beyond this, the implications of an epistemology that derives from a recognition of the force of enculturative conditioning in shaping thought and behavior. Its practical aspects involve the application—the practice—of the philosophical principles derived from the method, to the wider, cross-cultural world scene. (Herskovits 1972: 38–39)

The project thus explicitly promotes the necessity of making statements which fall within the context of the actor's perceived and understood terms and experiences. Most clearly it denounces the partiality of prejudice. The exigency of such an orientation in Africanism actualizes a hermeneutical task, that of interrogating the reality of "temporal distance" and "otherness" with a rigor similar to that proposed by Hans-Georg Gadamer apropos of historical consciousness:

—We must raise to a conscious level the prejudices which govern understanding and in this way realize the possibility that "*other* aims" emerge in their own right from tradition—which is nothing other than realizing the possibility that we can understand something in its *otherness.*

—[. . .] what demands our efforts at understanding is manifest before and in itself in its character of otherness. [. . .] we must realize that every understanding begins with the fact that something *calls out* to us. And since we know the precise meaning of this affirmation, we claim *ipso facto* the bracketing of prejudices. Thus we arrive at our first conclusion: bracketing our judgements in general, and naturally first of all our own prejudices, will end by imposing upon us the demands of a radical reflection on the idea of questioning as such. (Gadamer 1979: 156–57)

The identity of tasks that I am postulating by bringing Gadamer's meditation on the problem of historical consciousness into Herskovits's relativism can also be reflected in similarities existing between history and anthropology. Claude Lévi-Strauss has put them forth and used them to posit the two disciplines as two faces of the same Janus:

[. . .] the fundamental difference between the two disciplines is not one of subject, of goal, or of method. They share the same subject, which is social life; the same goal, which is a better understanding of man; and, in fact, the same method, in which only the proportion of research techniques varies. They differ, principally, in their choice of complementary perspectives: History organizes its data in relation to conscious expressions of social life, while anthropology proceeds by examining its unconscious foundations. (1963: 18)

Herskovits's cultural relativism bears witness to *Einfühlung,* which basically means "sympathy." This reminds me of a remarkable temptation faced by the Belgian missionary Placide Tempels in the 1940s—an era dominated in anthropology by reductionist models. The temptation was precisely one of fusing—identifying with the other to the point of becoming (at least once) the other—in order to speak sensibly about the other. Yet, such a project and its procedures of *Einfühlung,* while undoubtedly legitimate, at least in principle, are fundamentally difficult to understand. They seem to presuppose at least two ambitious theses. The first concerns the possibility of a fusion of the I and the Other, which, transcending or negating the indetermination and unpredictability of the I, would suggest that the I can really *know* the other. Sartre has indicated in a strong text some of the major and paradoxical difficulties of this thesis (1956: 353).

The second problem stems from the questionable transparency of the object of anthropology. For Herskovits, the human as object of knowledge and science seems an obvious given accounted for by the history and dynamics of a cultural space. Thus, for example, Schmidt's "cultural invariants" from a comparative perspective or Edel's theory of "indeterminacy" matter little for him, "since the difficulty would appear to be no more than a semantic one" (Herskovits 1972: 56–57).

> The problem would rather seem to be analogous to that of ascertaining *the most adequate basis* for deriving general principles of human behavior, in terms of the relation between form and process. Here the issue is clear [...], with the particular experience of *each society giving historically unique formal expression to underlying processes,* which are operative in shaping the destiny of all human groups. (Herskovits 1972: 57, my emphasis)

In sum, Herskovits privileges the centrality of culture as totality, instead of the individual consciousness. Consequently, a collective societal dynamic appears to stand, diachronically or synchronically, as a sort of consciousness of a society. He thus clearly confirms anthropology in its traditional configuration, that is, in the proximity of nineteenth-century biology and physiology. Yet, Herskovits insists that "his cross-cultural approach" studies "*Man in the large* [his emphasis], in the light of differences and similarities between societies, and in the ways by which different peoples must achieve these ends that all peoples must achieve if they are to survive and adjust to their natural and social environments" (Herskovits 1972: 108). A question remains: what is this "*Man in the large*"? How has he been conceived as a possible object for knowledge or for science, and from which epistemological and cultural space?

Focusing on variations of hypotheses about this "*Man in the large,*" Herskovits comments on distortions in interpretations as dependent upon inappropriate attitudes and exemplifies the paradox of the history of anthropology. "Early students of man," he notes, "[...] stressed the concept of 'human nature,' but this was essentially to allow them to bring observed divergences under a single head. Later, more emphasis was laid on these differences, but again this was to show how diverse the manifestations of common human tendencies might be" (Herskovits 1972: 57). Or, as in the case of "Man" before and after the machine, Herskovits antagonizes experiences and brings together cultures in terms of the type of their technologies (Herskovits 1940: 22).

Herskovits's concept of "*Man in the large*" does not seem to rest on a clear distinction between the object and the subject of a culture, a language, a thought, on the one hand, and the subject and the object of the anthropological discourse, on the other. In fact, I would say that the concept, mainly in Herskovits's earlier works, actualizes a truism of physical anthropology of the period: in order to know Man (with a capital M), it is imperative to know man's varieties, differences, and similarities. A concrete illustration can be seen in his contribution to *Man and His World* (1929). In his chapter, entitled "The Civilizations of Prehistory," Herskovits repeatedly uses statements such as: "we cannot say what *type of man* lived at the dawn of prehistory" (1929:

108); "*Man of (the) pre-Chellean epoch* had little in the way of civilization, yet it must have taken hundreds of generations to have brought him to this stage" (1929: 110); "That *paleolithic man* lived in Africa we are certain [. . .]" (1929: 127); "the greatest contribution of *neolithic man* to human civilization was the fact that he learned how to tame plants and animals" (1929: 130, my emphasis).

That Herskovits was aware of the problem (and of the complexity of the question "What is man?"—a fundamental question going back to Kant's anthropology) is obvious when one pays attention to the declension of the concepts of civilization and culture in the singular and the plural; the singular generally postulates the unity of humankind, and the plural its diversity and cultural variation. One gets the clearest picture of Herskovits's art of double-speak in his brief 1961 critique of Henry E. Garret, a psychology professor who argued that racial differences and inequalities are empirical facts that were being opposed by a conspiracy of apostles of "the Equalitarian Dogma." Garret's arguments, published in an issue of *Perspectives in Biology and Medicine* (Autumn 1961), furnish an example of what Herskovits himself calls elsewhere "Classical imperialism" (1972:73). Herskovits's criticism outlines two different and complementary orders of reflection. On the one hand, there is an explicit ethical argument contending in the name of "science" and "reason" that there is a historicity proper to each human group and even each individual. This historicity can account for differences between cultures and between individuals, but "no scientifically valid evidence has ever been produced to show that these differences, either in general intelligence or particular aptitudes, are related to race" (1972: 115). On the other hand, a more discreet order, strongly pressed, yet implicit, alludes to a major epistemological issue that I can illustrate by using one of Michel Foucault's statements: "Western culture has contributed, under the name of man, a being who, by one and the same interplay of reasons, must be a positive domain of *knowledge* and cannot be an object of *science*" (Foucault 1973: 366–67).

Fundamentally a relation to values, cultural relativism, in diachrony or in synchrony, is, as Herskovits aptly put it, "an approach to the question of the nature and role of values in culture" (1972: 14). As such, it defines itself as a vivid interrogation of ethnocentrism:

> The very core of cultural relativism is the social discipline that comes of respect for differences—of mutual respect. Emphasis on the worth of many ways of life, not one, is an affirmation of the values in each culture. Such emphasis seeks to understand and to harmonize goals, not to judge and destroy those that do not dovetail with our own. Cultural history teaches that, important as it is to discern and study the parellelisms in human civilizations, it is no less important to discern and study the different ways man has devised to fulfill his needs. (1972: 33)

Following Kluckhohn, Herskovits believed that "the doctrine that science has nothing to do with values [. . .] is a pernicious heritage from Kant and other thinkers" (1972: 42). *The Human Factor in Changing Africa* (Herskovits 1967), particularly in its two chapters on Rediscovery and Integration, is probably the most concrete illustration of this belief.

Let us now bring into the discussion structuralism, the other major relativist trend in anthropology. In a careful reading of structuralism, after expounding the linguistic model and its transposition in Claude Lévi-Strauss's *Structural Anthropology* (1963) and *The Savage Mind* (1966), Paul Ricoeur turns to the German theologian Gerhard von Rad's *Theology of the Historical Tradition of Israel,* and notes:

> Here we find ourselves confronting a theological conception exactly the inverse of that of totemism and which, because it is the inverse, suggests an inverse relationship between diachrony and synchrony and raises more urgently the problem of the relationship between structural comprehension and hermeneutic comprehension. (Ricoeur 1974: 45)

This statement springs from both a methodological critique of structuralism and a philosophical thesis. The critique, says Paul Ricoeur, shows that "the consciousness of the validity of a method [...] is inseparable from the consciousness of its limits" (Ricoeur 1974: 44). These limits for Ricoeur would seem to be of two types: "on the other hand [...] the passage to *the* savage mind is made by favor of an example that is already too favorable, one which is perhaps an exception rather than an example. On the other hand, the passage from a structural science to a structuralist philosophy seems to me to be not very satisfying and not even very coherent" (Ricoeur 1974: 45). If I understand Paul Ricoeur's critical reading of Lévi-Strauss's *Structural Anthropology* and *The Savage Mind* correctly, the example which permits the first passage is Lévi-Strauss's thesis about kinship as language, or, symbolically, marriage rules as "words of the group," to use Lévi-Strauss's expression (Lévi-Strauss 1963: 61; Ricoeur 1974: 36). As for the second passage, its fragility could be accounted for, according to Ricoeur, by the Lévi-Straussian concept of *bricolage.* Here is Ricoeur's question:

> Hasn't he [Lévi-Strauss] stacked the deck by relating the state of the savage mind to a cultural area—specifically, that of the 'totemic illusion'—where the arrangements are more important than the contents, where thought is actually *bricolage,* working with a heterogeneous material, with odds and ends of meaning? Never in this book is the question raised concerning the unity of mythical thought. It is taken for granted that the generalization includes all savage thought. Now, I wonder whether the mythical base from which we (Westerners) branch—with its Semitic (Egyptian, Babylonian, Aramaic, Hebrew), proto-Hellenic, and Indo-European cores—lends itself so easily to the same operation; *or rather, and I insist on this point, it surely lends itself to the operation, but does it lend itself entirely?* (Ricoeur 1974: 40–41; my emphasis)

The overall effect of this line of questioning is important. It implies two main problems. First, the "unity" supposed by the concept of the "savage mind" is not proven. Thus Melville and Frances Herskovits's *Dahomean Narrative,* for example, would simply be evidence of a well-localized *bricolage.* Second, if the "savage mind" is only a hypothetical construct whose theoretical unity is challenged by a tension between actual well-spatialized and contradictory *bricolages,* how could it be used as a measure for a comparison with the base from which sprang the Western tradition?

Let us pause one moment and reflect on the last phrase of my quotation from Ricoeur. Does the mythical base from which Westerners branch themselves lend itself *entirely* to the same type of operation as does non-Western cultural mythical thought? As hypothesis, we could retain Herskovits's understanding of myth as a cultural narrative, "seen as deriving from human language skill, and man's fascination with symbolic continuities. But as a cultural fact, it also finds dynamic expression in the play between outer stimulus received by a people, and innovation from within" (Herskovits 1972: 240). Furthermore, Edmund Leach has demonstrated in brilliant and controversial studies that biblical narratives can lend themselves to structuralist analysis (1980; Leach and Aycock 1983). Although Georges Dumézil rejected the concept of structuralism and explicitly stated that he was not a structuralist (Dumézil 1980: 11, n.17), his works also convincingly demonstrate that Indo-European historical and cultural experiences submit to typologizations, systems of transformations and patterns similar to those produced by structural analysis in non-Western societies (see, e.g., Dumézil 1980). And Luc de Heusch's *The Drunken King* (1982), one of the foremost systematic structuralist analyses applied to Bantu myths, derives its methodology from both Lévi-Strauss's and Dumézil's lessons. These facts seem, at least partially, to weaken Paul Ricoeur's strong statement.

But in the case of Israel's historical tradition, Ricoeur claims to find a conjunction of historicities that does not seem to exist in totemic cultures and societies (Ricoeur 1974: 45–56). He distinguishes three historicities. The first, that of a *hidden time,* expounds in a mythical saga Yahweh's action as Israel's history. The second, that of a *tradition,* founds itself on the authority of the hidden time. In successive readings and interpretations of this authority, the tradition perceives its past and its becoming, and reflects them as a *Heilsgeschichte.* Finally, there is the historicity of hermeneutics, which Paul Ricoeur refers to, using von Rad's language, as *"Entfaltung,* 'unfolding' or 'development' to designate the task of a theology of the Old Testament which respects the threefold historical character of the *Heilige Geschichte* (the level of the founding events), the *Überlieferungen* (the level of constituting traditions), and finally the identity of Israel (the level of a constituted tradition)" (Ricoeur 1974: 47).

This makes sense. Yet, how can one jump from the founding sagas of Abraham, Isaac, or Jacob to the concept of a *Heilsgeschichte* unless one has already accepted that these founding events do indeed witness such a concept? It is *faith* in the confession, overextended by the narratives and subsequently by the power of commentaries and interpretations, which, accomplishing gradually a minimal confession, justifies a hidden time as sacred, and confirms this time and at once transmutes it first into signs of God's kerygma and then into both history and eschatology.

Here, then, is the paradox: Paul Ricoeur's reading seems pertinent only insofar as it can be understood within the economy of a *tradition* that it documents and explains from the point of view of a Western Christian. On the other hand, it is the very foundation of this tradition, and particularly the posited singularity and specificity of Israel's history, that gives meaning to Ricoeur's hermeneutics and its ambition. We are really facing something like a firmly closed circle which expands by exaggerating its own significance from the internal logic of a dialogue between its own different levels of meaning. In effect, from the margins of Christianity or, more exactly, from the margins of a Western history that institutionalized Christianity, how can one not think that what is going on here is a simple exegesis of a well-localized and tautologized tradition that seems incapable of imagining the very possibility of its exteriority, namely, that, in its margins, other historical traditions can also be credible, meaningful, respectable, and sustained by relatively well-delineated historicities?

It is in Herskovits's philosophical statements that I have found reasons to believe in truth as a goal. Other traditions situated outside of the Western space, Christianity and its institutionalized procedures, and contemporary secularized philosophies, speak also about their own hidden times, and all of them, each in its manner, bear witness to their own historicities. Are these historicities two, three, or four? What really should matter is the challenge that this question implies. As Herskovits aptly put it:

> there remains the challenge to take concepts and hypotheses into the laboratory of the cross-cultural field, and test their generalizing value, or arrive at new generalizations. Perhaps challenge is too austere a word for our implicit meaning. In the tradition of humanistic scholarship, it is an invitation to discover for the world literature and thought vast resources which will inform and delight us. (Herskovits 1972: 241)

If taken seriously, this last invitation cannot but destroy classical Africanism—or, at any rate, conflict with its conceptual frames and boundaries. Jean-Loup Amselle's research confirms this beyond a doubt in the case of African anthropology.

A Critique of "Ethnological Reason"

Amselle's purpose in *Logiques métisses* (1990) is to question the theoretical presuppositions of "ethnological reason" and to imagine the possibility of a reversal of anthropology's perspective. Essentially, *Logiques métisses* is a critique of "ethnological reason," which, by definition, always extracts elements from their context, aestheticizes them, and then uses their supposed differences for classifying types of political, economic, or religious ensembles. Thus, apropos of Africa, one gets such classical oppositions as State vs. segmentary societies, market vs. subsistence economies, Islam or Christianity vs. paganism, etc. To this "reason," which runs through the history of Western thought like Ariadne's thread, Amselle presents an opposing reason, the *"raison métisse."* This reason, instead of distinguishing and separating, would bear witness to the "indistinction" or original syncretism of elements in a social totality and thus at least solve the dilemma opposing "the universality of human rights" and "cultural relativism," a dilemma which, in terms of political values, actualizes the tension and opposition between universality as totalitarianism and cultural relativism as an expression of democracy. Amselle writes:

> Toute notre démarche consistera [...] à montrer que le relativisme culturel suppose l'exercice d'un regard à la fois proche et éloigné sur des entités sociales qui sont en réalité mouvantes et ont été préalablement extraites de leur contexte par l'opération conjointe des voyageurs, des missionnaires et des militaires. (Amselle 1990: 10)

> All our method consists in showing that cultural relativism supposes the fact of a look which is both near and far away from social entities. These social entities have been first separated from their context in the united analysis of travelers, missionaries, and militaries.

The method's strategy is twofold: on the one hand, it refuses to reduce African cultures and the body of its social practices and negotiations to an immobile essence; and, on the other hand, it is a critical reappraisal of the politics of universality.

Logiques métisses, a collection of nine essays, manages to achieve a coherent unity by organizing the material from a thematic pattern based on years of fieldwork and research by the author in West Africa. The first two chapters dwell, respectively, on the very notion of "ethnological reason" and on the reality of internal tensions in all cultures. The focus is successively on the history of "ethnological reason," on its ideological practices, and, in a theoretical and critical reversal, on the fact of cultural conflicts and negotiations which everywhere always bring about transformations in the identity of collectivities. Chapter three illustrates a real system of transformations (Peul, Bambara, Malinke), and chapter four theorizes by questioning some basic concepts of political anthropology as used and applied principally since the publication of the 1940 volume on *African Political Systems* edited by M. Fortes and E. E. Evans-Pritchard. The discussion continues in a more illustrative manner in chapters five and six, in which, using two case studies, Gwanan and Jitumu, the author challenges both typologies of political anthropology and ethnographic classifications. The last three chapters—respectively on White Paganism, Cultural Identity and Cultural Model, Understanding and Acting— bring the debate back to a wider historical framework of political and cultural confrontations: Who is in charge of defining "ethnicities," "identities," "differences"? Where could one find them as pure essences, bearing witness to their own originary being?

A number of major themes are addressed in the *Logiques métisses*. One concerns the efficiency of the universality model. This model posits its rationality as an all-embracing paradigm accounted for by a framework such as that of dialectical sequences in sciences where they seem to be observed facts: action and reaction, in mechanics; differential and integral, in mathematics; combination and dissociation of elements, in chemistry; positive and negative, in physics. From this rigid model, Marxists (e.g., Lenin 1967) postulated the class struggle as the equivalent network in social science, thus expanding the order of efficiency (and necessity) of dialectical connections to the domain of social sciences. Do we deal with a similar move of theoretical expansion when—apropos of the State in Africa—we observe, after Amselle, that the politics of *African Political Systems* first actualizes a transfer of conceptual networks, and second, describes "African systems," producing a model that explains why the colonial order could not but be the fulfillment of these regional systems? Indeed, the masterful distinction between "segmentary" societies and those having a centralized political power or State—to use Amselle's expression: "a reduction and disarticulation of African precolonial types"—might be a key to the understanding of the logics of "Indirect Rule" and other colonial policies. Surely, it would have been pointless, at least for specialists, to reanalyze the theoretical regimes inherent in both the foundation of anthropology and the power of this distinction. Yet perhaps such a review could have shown to nonspecialist readers two things: one, that anthropology and colonialism reflect each other, and, two, more specifically, how African anthropological practices operate in a self-assured method, a method that brings to light the supposedly unknown (the segmentary) in its absolute difference, defines it with concepts such as evolution, and, in the same movement, isolates the African political varieties in a grid framed on the basis of what is already known from elsewhere.

The second major theme posits an alternative. Against the essentialist implications (as well as the totalitarian projection) of the universalist temptation, Amselle suggests a different approach:

> L'analyse en termes de logiques métisses permet au contraire d'échapper à la question de l'origine et de faire l'hypothèse d'une régression à l'infini. Il ne s'agit plus de se demander ce qui est premier, du segmentaire ou de l'Etat, du paganisme ou de l'islam, de l'oral ou de l'écrit, mais de postuler un syncrétisme originaire, un mélange dont il est impossible de dissocier les parties. (Amselle 1990: 248)

> An analysis using the concept of *métisse* logic allows one to avoid the question of origin and to hypothesize on the possibility of an infinite regression. The point then is not to look for what is prior between the segmentary and the State, paganism or Islam, oral or written, but to postulate instead an originary syncretism, a mixture in which it is impossible to dissociate elements.

Thus, he can demonstrate, in the case of West Africa, the presence of the State in the segmentary, of Islam in paganism, and of the written in the oral. The point is well made and convincing. It goes well beyond the context of the mystifying inventions of "ethnic" and "cultural identities" in the intellectual history of West African anthropology. It challenges directly the practice of anthropology itself, specifically its "reason," whose basic categories—such as *ethnos* vs. *polis,* savage/barbarian vs. civilized, primitive vs. advanced, etc.— become totally irrelevant. I would expect some analysts to wonder whether the discovery of "modern" elements in a "traditional" culture is irregular among postmodern intellectuals, particularly those inhabiting transitional societies. This significant question proves that Amselle's argument is basically right, since the question conveys explicitly the violence of the memory of the "ethnological" reason.

Yet, another question remains: the *Logiques métisses* opens up the possibility of an anthropology of powers. Is this really still an anthropology (as the author wishes), or something else like, perhaps, say history?

After Amselle's remarkable demonstration, one could, polemically, say, well, the real task of Herskovits's and Lévi-Strauss's disciples should consist in the struggle for the promotion of cultural relativism. However, I do not think that the illusory harmony and power of a truth negating its own shattered signs and significations deserves in this day and age (or after Derrida), at least in principle, such a radical stance. In effect, Herskovits's lesson has become more constructive, an allegory not only for transcultural dialogues, but also for the designation of possible paths toward levels of truth in one's own culture. Discourses on the empirical, on the eschatological, as well as on conditions for constructing a true discourse partake in the unimaginable unity of an impossible Truth. As mediations, they express and signify the absolute existence and the absolute absence of Truth. Thus, our discourses, in a plurality and ambiguity made possible by Herskovits and others, witness an activity of representation which itself speaks of our collective predicament. As Walter Benjamin once put it, "Es existiert bereits als ein sich-Darstellendes": Truth is always representing itself.

From "Primitive Art" to *"Memoriae Loci"*

As surprising as it may seem, art, specifically so-called primitive art, seems best to reflect in contemporary consciousness the idea of Africa. In effect, the juxtaposition of the two words—"primitive" and "art"—seems to emphasize a paradox, if one agrees with Edmund Leach, who states that "the notion of artist is a European one." But is it possible to conceive of a piece of art without a creator, without an artist who executed it? Let us dwell on the issue.

The concept of primitivism, precisely that of "primitive" art, is linked in a relation of necessity to most non-Western productions and, particularly, to those from Oceania and Africa since the eighteenth century. But why "primitive"? In his 1986 *History of Art,* H. W. Janson could still write:

> "'Primitive' is a somewhat unfortunate word [. . .]. Still, no other single term will serve us better. Let us continue, then to use primitive as a convenient label for a way of life that has passed through the Neolithic Revolution, but shows no signs of evolving in the direction of 'historic' civilizations." (quoted in Price 1989: 1)

However, the impact of this "primitive art" on some modern European artists, such as Gauguin, Klee, Picasso, and others, made possible some curious new usages. Expressions such as "primitive art in Europe," "Romantic," "intellectual primitivism," "subconscious primitivism," popularized, thanks to Robert Goldwater's *Primitivism in Modern Art,* first published in 1938, predicate a complicity between the so-called primitive products and European modern art, a decadent art, according to some critics who did not hesitate to compare it to children's creations. One should mention that, besides a spatial and aesthetic reference to faraway and little-known cultures, the concept was extended to the point of including under its vague caption such diverse things as popular paintings, children's drawings and, indeed, some European trends. As Max Deri put it with some humor, they all bring needed joy to a decadent European culture (Deri 1921).

In sum, it can be said that the concept of primitive art cumulates and simultaneously conveys two orders of meanings. On the one hand, there is the most recent one. It transcends the break between the "civilized" and the "savage," and labels as "primitive" various products of "modern" artistic schools that, supposedly, would have restored a sense of nature, simplicity, and directness to the Western tradition and promoted *oeuvres* which aesthetically present three main features: a symmetrical unity of the totality, a clear stylization, and an emphasis of the surface. From this viewpoint, Constantin Brancusi, Franz Marc, Henri Matisse, Pablo Picasso, André Derain, Maurice de Vlaminck, and many others are without doubt "primitive" artists. Not only did they move in a counterculture circle symbolically analogous to that of "primitive societies," but, more important, they took pride in inspiring themselves from works of these societies, and reevaluated not only traditional Western techniques and styles but also their own perceptions, attitudes, and aesthetics in order patiently to "digest primitive art" and produce a new art (Goldwater 1986). They had, as Kandinsky put it, renounced the importance of the external in the name of "interior truths" (Kandinsky 1914).

The second order of meanings, in fact the primordial condition that engendered the meanings discussed above, comprises at least two complementary sets. The first, clearly, is marked by Darwin's postulates on the evolution of beings (see also Guernier 1952). It is also the most ancient, in which "primitive art" fuses indistinctly with archaic art in the strictest sense of the word. Accordingly, its producers and their cultures would witness the beginnings of

Jacob Epstein, *Mother and Child.* 1913. Marble. The Museum of Modern Art, New York, gift of A. Conger Goodyear.

human civilizations. The following citations, quoted in Sally Price's *Primitive Art in Civilized Places* (1989a: 2), speak by themselves and loudly:

> We are dealing with the arts of people whose mechanical knowledge is scanty—the people without wheels (Hooper and Burland 1953).

> Primitive art is produced by people who have not developed any form of writing (Christensen 1955).

> Now the term . . . has simply come, for lack of a better term, to refer to art of classless societies (Moberg 1984–85).

In the eighteenth century and in the nineteenth, not to speak of preceding centuries, this "art," or, more precisely, the objects meant by the term "art" were generally perceived as constituting a lower level of achievement, as compared to the artistic productions of the West, and made visible concretely the

Joan Miro, *Painting*. 1933. Oil on canvas. The Museum of Modern Art,
New York, gift of the Advisory Committee.

deviation existing between the aesthetic sensibility and creativity of the West
and the rest. Such "art" was belittled because it was "primitive" vis-à-vis the
"civilized" pieces (see, e.g., Tylor 1871). Yet the despised works of "primitivism" were to open up into new aesthetic sequences when, at the end of the
nineteenth century and the beginning of the twentieth, they allowed a radical
revolution in the Western tradition as exemplified by Gauguin and the school
of Pont-Aven, by Picasso's itinerary, and, more generally, by artistic trends
such as Constructivism, Cubism, Purism, and Expressionism.

The "integration" of "primitive" art takes place in two operations. The
first is an "ethnologization" of productions from overseas. Isolated as a deviation, these products are, indeed, different. How do we understand them in the
light of Western tradition? Tylor (1871) is, perhaps, the best illustration of
this "ethnologicist" perspective: he establishes a relation between the technical
development of, among other factors, material arts and that of mentalities
that subsequently confirm the inferiority of the "primitive." The complete
title of his book sums up well his perspective: *Primitive Culture: Researches
into the Development of Mythology, Philosophy, Religion, Language, Art and*

Paul Gauguin, *Offerings of Gratitude*. c.1891–93. Woodcut. The Museum of Modern Art, New York. Lillie P. Bliss Collection.

Custom. The operation of ethnologization consists of isolating a datum from its real context (and references to its background are generally used only to specify the datum as an entity, not as an element of a cultural whole), analyzing it (in fact, differentiating it from everything else), classifying its attributes and its model, and assigning it a label, locating it as such or such from that given latitude, longitude, tribe, etc. As a labeled artifact, the work can be filed, retrieved, and subsumed to the grids of ethnographic study. But another dimension can be insinuated. In the process, from the first phase of analysis to the final phase of signifying, another operation might take place, an aestheticization. In ethnographic studies, a product is granted or denied the status of art on the basis of external criteria; in effect, in order to belong to the realm of artistic achievements, a work needs to produce visibly characteristics and constraints that can, technically, be localized on a chronological scale determined by Western experience. Thus, a distinction appears between art object and ethnographic artifact. Yet we should note that the aestheticization operation might storm upon the "primitive object" with illusions, delusions, or even illuminations of exceptionally sensitive people looking for alternatives outside their own tradition. The "barbarian" becomes an alternative, as in the case of Gauguin, who, seduced by the epiphany of the difference, could proclaim: "primitive art is a nourishing milk"; and, more provocatively: "despite its beauty, the Greek has been the error."

Gauguin was a marginalized figure and, moreover, it is said, unstable psychologically. Most "sensible" people of that period shared Tylor's perspective. Siebold in his 1843 *Letter on the Usefulness of Ethnographic Museums* had

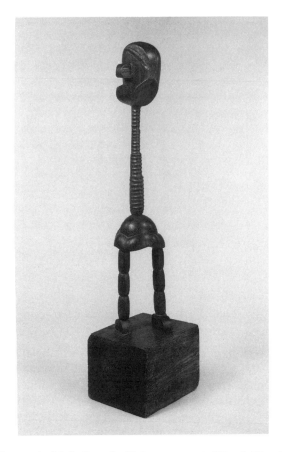

Constantin Brancusi, *Little French Girl.* c.1914–18. Wood. The Solomon R. Guggenheim Museum, New York, gift, Estate of Katherine S. Dreier, 1953. Photo: David Heald © The Solomon R. Guggenheim Foundation, New York.

already perceived a political urgency: objects made by "primitives" were a key to their difference and constituted an efficient means of knowing them in order to dominate them. Siebold's project integrates and justifies an old reductionist view. Putting overseas objects in museums in "ethnographic spaces" in the West imposes itself as a necessity: to exhibit overseas cultures, to introduce them to the metropolitan populace, and to attract the interest of financiers who can invest in colonies. Ethnology's vocation and colonialism are beautifully mixed in the same logic. Siebold did not invent it. His voice shares imperialist assumptions of an intellectual atmosphere which was already present and which, in the second part of the nineteenth century, led to the scramble for Africa.

Ethnology and colonialism articulated themselves in ethnographic museums. They had the same premises cohering in the same objective, that of converting overseas territories to the self and imagination of the West. Ethnographic museums thus constitute the negativity of a dialectic, and therefore the representations they promote should be negated in the long run. The museums and their content remain witness to a "primitive" past, as do cave and rock paintings. And ethnographic museums developed: 1856, Berlin, an ethnographic section is created in the Museum of Antiquities; 1857, Oslo, creation of a museum of ethnography at the University of Oslo; 1866–76 and 1877, organization of the Yale and the Harvard Peabody museums; 1869–74, New York, the American Museum of Natural History; 1878, Paris, Le Trocadéro; 1881, Cambridge, The Cambridge University Museum of Archaeology and Ethnology; 1891, Göteborg, Museum of Ethnography; 1893, Chicago, Field Museum of Ethnography; 1897, Tervuren, the Congo Exhibition; 1899, Philadelphia, The University Museum.

The ethnographic museum enterprise espoused a historical orientation, deepening the need for the memory of an archaic European civilization and, consequently, expounding reasons for decoding exotic and primitive objects as symbolic and contemporary signs of a Western antiquity. In the following years, some European artists question whether "primitive art" was really "primitive" by bringing together in their own creations learned representations of the so-called "primitives," their own historiographical consciousness, and claims to a creative liberty. This signified a reconsideration of, and a protest against, an artistic tradition, and specifically, insofar as the concept of the masterpiece was concerned, "the item of work executed by an apprentice to prove he had adequately learned his craft—albeit accession to 'mastership' brought with it financial and other privileges—; in the modern sense of the word, however, something more than manual skill is connoted" (Burgin 1986: 153). Among many others, Georges Braque, Marc Chagall, Max Ernst, Paul Gauguin, Amedeo Modigliani, Pablo Picasso, while essentially faithful to their "island home" (in terms of references toward a cohering space for their imaginations), separate themselves from the tradition of their artistic birth certificate. And, instead of situating themselves within the authority of a respected and well-individualized master, they reach beyond such ritual worship and suggest the unthinkable as their inspiration, namely, anonymous "primitive" models, silently uniting an unnamed genius and a product.

The challenge in the promotion of "primitive" objects as art is bound up with two main issues: Are they art, in which sense, and from what aesthetic grid of evaluation? Or, cannot they be simply understood as *memoriae loci,* as loci of memory, testifying about and illustrating the space of their origin? For a methodological purpose, the two issues can be framed within the tension between the history of art and anthropology. The former is concerned with its own culture and historical space, the latter with other cultures and societies. Robert Goldwater (1986) has also reminded us that the former, the history of art, promotes itself as a technique capable of analyzing and valuing its objects from within an artistic tradition. It relates to non-Western productions

Pablo Picasso, *Les Demoiselles d'Avignon*. 1907. Oil on canvas. The Museum of Modern Art, New York. Acquired through the Lillie P. Bliss Bequest.

on an analogical basis, such as in the comparison of Western medieval art and African art. Jan Vansina (1984) insists on this fact but does not elaborate on its implications. Just one example: the extension of Morelli's analytical method of evaluating a piece to the study of art in the Congo as expounded by Franz Olbrechts in the 1940s seems to indicate a most controversial thesis: art history methods are universal; their rules have been convincingly demonstrated and illustrated by the Western tradition and therefore can be applied to any existing other traditions.

The ethnologization and aestheticization of these "worked objects" from overseas—from now on the qualification I shall use to designate them—constitute another problem. Received as gifts, often bought, and sometimes simply stolen, these worked objects, acquired in a zeal to know and collect, perhaps even preserve "the primitive," end up in an ethnographical museum. What do they mean in this new environment, apart from the generally negative judgment about the cultures that conceived them?

Looking at art objects with perceptibly different kinds of 'identities,' we detect a tendency for perceived worth (a combination of artistic fame and financial assessment) to be inversely related to the amount of detail on the accompanying

Amedeo Modigliani, *Head.* 1915. Limestone. The Museum of Modern Art, New York.

labels. An 'ethnographic object' in the crowded case of an anthropology museum is typically explained through extensive prose, initiating viewers into the eso-terica of its manufacture, use, role in the society, and religious meaning. If this same object is selected for display in an art museum, it is common for its financial appraisal to rise, for its presentation to become more spatially privi-leged (i.e, for the clutter of competing pieces to drop away), and for almost all of the didactic information to disappear. The isolation of an object both from other objects and from verbose contextualization carries a definite implication of Value. It is no doubt this principle that dealers recognize and exploit when they show their collections with only a small round sticker on each piece bearing a number that customers may use, discreetly, to learn the price of a particular item whose purchase they are contemplating. The continuum from ethnographic artifact to objet d'art is clearly associated in peoples' minds with a scale of increasing monetary value and a shift from function (broadly defined) to aesthetics as an evaluatory basis; in terms of display all this correlates with an increasingly cryptic written contextualization. (Price 1989: 84)

For which memory are these exhibited productions witnesses? They seem to be remnants, as some say, of absolute beginnings. Yet they have obsessed some of the most creative artists of the last one hundred and fifty years. In this specific case, are we dealing with a conscious will for reapprehending a lost past, a will which would want to reactivate prehistoric achievements? Or, from a different and more metaphoric viewpoint, should we say that the "primitivist" revolution in Western art actualized a new perspective, analogous to what Western historians did by shifting from a history written from the aristocratic viewpoint to one emphasizing the common peoples' horizon?

"Art objects" or "ethnographic artifacts," these things belong to specific spaces. What they can mean in their own original context cannot but be incommensurable with what they are supposed to signify from a wall or a pedestal in a museum. In their own context, these objects are, strictly speaking, traces of something else and function as live elements of a "material stock," in sum, the material equivalent of an everyday-life library. I am thinking of some "Alexandrian grotesqueries"—such as, from the Metropolitan Museum of Art in New York, the Marble Hunchback (a sign of luck in both Ancient Greece and Rome) or the Slave Boy with Lantern and, comparing them in my mind to some of the African works reproduced in the book edited in 1985 by Susan Vogel and Francine N'Diaye and particularly to the Dogon (Mali) Hermaphrodite Figure from Yaya Village. What is art and what is not art? Or, more simply, what is beautiful, or feigned, or ugly? Indeed, from the less than innocent position I have chosen, the problems of authenticity and the more ambiguous one of elucidating whether there is an African art become arbitrary. In effect, what is really designated by the concept of art and from what perspective?

In 1986, as a discussant of an African Studies Association panel, I faced the issue and, prudently, decided to reduce it to what it is in actuality: a *simple* question (*African Studies Review*, 23, 1986, 3–4), a question that one can use to interrogate any artistic tradition. In the African case, for example, from a historical viewpoint one would be entitled, for obvious reasons, to ask since when "African worked objects" have become "art objects." But few scholars accept the exigency of meditating on articulations that have first *ethnologized* these "worked objects" and then *aestheticized* a few of them by moving them from natural history museums to art museums, or, in some cases, from the "bush" to the monetary sun of art galleries. These operations and their history have divided and subdivided almost *ad infinitum* processes and methods of classifying these objects. From the period of "fetishes" and other "tomahawks" in the sixteenth century, through that which conceived African "worked objects" as purely functional and described them as simple media witnessing to the transparency of primitive tradition and the representation of its "bodies" (things, totems, symbols, allegories, etc.), down to the present-

Hermaphrodite figure. Wood. Dogon, Mali.
Paulme-Lifszyc expedition, 1935. Musée de
l'Homme, Palais Chaillot, Paris.

day debates, analytical grids and the aesthetics they have produced might have missed, through their emphasis on difference, the originality of these "worked objects." Thus, I am afraid, they may have missed the possible nature of any work of art whatsoever.

Maurice Merleau-Ponty invited us to pay attention to the fact that there exist voluntary and involuntary creations (1973). Examples might be found in poetry, and in the creativity of an improvised automatic writing. Indeed, one could even invoke the beauty (in form, style, and aim) of graffiti (during the French students' uprising of May 1968, for example.). There is also the case of children's drawings, which were, until recently, seen as naive because they do not seem to correspond *significantly* to the "objectivist" perception of adults' "two-dimensional perspective" (which itself, by the way, as Merleau-Ponty demonstrated, "cannot be offered as an expression of the world that we perceive and so cannot assume a privileged conformity with the object"). Interestingly, the so-called "primitive arts" were lumped together with children's productions. We can now decode this aberration. It meant to mark a distinction between "brute" expressions and "art," or "a canonical style" (perceived in a historical continuum and as an expression domesticating and transcending the banality of nature). As attested to by Impressionists and Cubists, to refer to Merleau-Ponty's critique of André Malraux, senses and sense-data varied throughout the centuries, and "it is certain that [European] classical perspective is not a law of perceptual behavior" (1973).

The real problem might be elsewhere: in the artist's dream and language. African or European, the real issue for all of them is the same: they do not have a "master" of truth apart from their perception. They do not have, to use Husserl's word, the *Stiftung,* which Merleau-Ponty notes is a foundation, an institution, indicating "first, the unlimited fecundity of each present which, precisely because it is singular and passes, can never stop having been and thus being universally." Insofar as African creativities are concerned, I would hope that the 1991 exhibition *Africa Explores: 20th Century African Art,* organized by the New York Center of African Art, has, beyond yesterday's preconceptions about the functionality and the anonymity of artistic productions, shown the variety of individual and subjective styles.

> Malraux shows perfectly [noted Merleau-Ponty] that that which makes a "Vermeer" for us is not that this canvas was painted one day by the man Vermeer. It is the fact that it embodies the "Vermeer structure" or that it speaks the language of Vermeer. It observes the system of equivalences according to which each one of the elements, like a hundred pointers on a hundred dials, marks the same deviation. (Merleau-Ponty 1973: 70)

We can, and it is time for us as critics and students of African art to do so, read and try to bring to light the discourses we face on canvases, the contradictory languages of sculptures, the textures of batiks, and, apropos of oeuvres by, for example, Thomas Mukomberanwa, Iba N'Diaye, Trigo Piula, or Twins Seven-Seven, try to decode and publicize the richness of a language that museums might silence, as they do with everything they stabilize. Also, we should face another major problem concerning any work of art, African or European, Asian or Oceanian: the signification of its canonization. Should not we note with Merleau-Ponty that

> The Museum gives us a false consciousness, a thief's conscience. We occasionally sense that these works were not intended to *end up* between these bare walls for the pleasure of Sunday strollers, for children on their free afternoon from school, or for Monday intellectuals. We sense vaguely that something has been lost and that these gatherings of old maids, this silence of the grave, and the respect of pygmies do not constitute the true milieu of art. (Merleau-Ponty 1973: 72)

Thus, in order to decode these objects—an ambitious and, at the same time, completely ridiculous task—let us say that one could refer to at least three minimal criteria. The first, the sociocultural milieu, would identify the worked objects according to their producers: were or are they made by gatherers, fishermen, cattle herders, agriculturalists? The second, the criterion of social relations of production, may within the same culture separate or allow a complementary analysis of palace art and that of, say, blacksmiths, healers, hunters, members of secret societies, women, etc. The third, the criterion of function, could classify these objects according to their use: divination, funerary, entertainment, everyday life, religious, magic, etc. Such a three-pronged approach would account for the objects in the context of their own real background and transcend the shortcomings of anthropologists' ethnologization and aesthetization of the objects. As Robert Brain remarks in a generalizing statement at the outset of his *Art and Society in Africa:*

> Art in Africa has always been very much a part of the people's life, manifest in every aspect of their working, playing and believing worlds; yet almost every general survey by art historian or ethnologist has been primarily devoted to the aesthetic appeal of the work of art or the peculiarities of its style and form. (Brain 1980)

In their original context, contrary to lax beliefs that they are essentially and only functional, these objects, at least in Central Africa, play a more complex role. In effect, they consolidate in their being a heritage. More specifically, they combine in their bodies two spectacular meanings. On the one hand, by the will of the society, they are submitted to a specific duty and thus have a functional, utilitarian dimension. In metal or in wood, highly decorated or not, a chair is a chair, and is made to be sat on. In the same way, the use of a bowl in ivory or in wood, or that of a richly or poorly decorated drum is obvious, even though the item may be reserved for a special category of people, or linked to specific performances, rituals, or sets of symbols. On the other hand, in their materiality, from the most sophisticated (e.g., an Igbo ceremonial vessel, a Dogon wood stool supported by *nommo* couples, or an ordinary Luba chief's stool) to the most apparently banal and simple (e.g., a Kuba mug, a Fulani calabash, a Hausa leather bag), all of these objects speak (to those who can really understand) of the continuity of a tradition and its successive transformations. They are perceived and experienced this way in their milieu, although not explicitly by all members of the community. This fact is not exceptional. How many churchgoing Christians in the West, when they visit ancient basilicas or churches, are capable of understanding some of the paintings in which a fish dominates? Generally, the guide has to explain this mysterious presence by referring back to a very ancient symbol and the Greek word for fish ('Ιχθυς), which when read, letter after letter, is an introduction to a statement of faith: Jesus Christ, God's Son and Savior.

Indeed, African worked objects signify an "archival" dimension with a commemorative function. They impress onto their own society a silent discourse and, simultaneously, as loci of memory, recite silently their own past and that of the society that made them possible. Here is a concrete illustration. Comparing three Central African drums of a similar basic shape—they come from "a village drum of the Kuba, a royal drum of the Kuba, and a village drum of their western neighbors—the Lele"—Jan Vansina notes:

> The difference in execution is striking. The Kuba drum, owned and used by the village, is decorated only with a modest band of decoration. The Lele drum usually shows decorative carving all over in a very fine pattern and exhibits a human face on its side; this rich drum is also only village owned and village used. But Lele villages, unlike the Kuba villages, were sovereign units. They were often larger and always more proud and their drums show it. The Kuba royal drum has deep incised decorative patterns all over and inlays of copper, beads and cowries. It was much richer than the Lele drum and reflected the institution of kingship, even though a dynastic drum such as this one was the emblem of one king only, not the drum of kingship itself. (Vansina 1984: 47)

Independent of what this highly Cartesian perspective suggests—does not the analysis impose upon African objects and their geographical distribution a grid that reproduces its own logical paradigms?—let us note that Vansina's project could, for example, be extended for comparison to Luba, Lulua, Songhye, Sanga, Bemba, and Lunda. With the drum and other objects as commemorative traces, the analysis of distribution of features of style and types of decoration could bring about a map of well-localized cultural traits and a demonstration of how, despite their similarities, these traits have been enclaving themselves in constructed differences (Delange 1967). Such a meticulous reconstruction, if well done, would lead one to useful comparative studies of different "primitive" traditions. It also indicates history as a necessity, or, more exactly, histories as responses to the memories witnessed by the objects. In effect, in each cultural enclave, the worked objects unveil, spontaneously, in their form and symbolism, means, skills, gestures, and rituals passed down to the apprentice by a master. A chronology retraces the origin of a worked object and, often, even the slightest modification produced by an artist testifies to a history.

The concept of apprentice is a delicate one. The disciple is, in effect, generally inscribed in already determined genealogy (Brain 1980). One does not simply decide to become an art worker. Similarly, in a number of West African societies, the profession of blacksmith is determined at birth. Another example: my ancestors, the Songye, fearing the possibility of losing a bulk of knowledge through endemic diseases, war, or natural catastrophes, instead of establishing familial genealogies and thus counting on individuals for the preservation of ancient memories, specialized entire villages: one in the esoteric knowledge of the group, another in carving, a third in something else, and so on. In many societies, a woman, by the very fact of marrying a blacksmith, knows that she will become a potter and an expert in such body operations as circumcision and scarification.

At this point, a reader may react: Did you really say history? Is there such a thing that could rigorously link worked objects to their genesis and, at the same time, integrate their testimonies into a history of the society that produces them? Are not these objects simple remnants of an ancient practice that is disappearing in the bourgeoning of second-rate objects for tourists and airport shops?

I would say, indeed, apart from objects in stone, textile, and nonferrous metals, the media of most worked objects can be dated (Vansina 1984: 33–40) and, thus, situated into a chronological frame. Moreover, local oral traditions and rituals voluntarily situate some of the objects in time. At the level of generalization at which this presentation has been so far restricted, I may add that these temporal indications should be used critically, particularly in conjunction with information coming from archaeological data, in order to allow credible historical constructions. Yet, since many worked objects are in nondurable materials, such as wood, clay, leather, textile, or mat, the challenge becomes different. If one accepts that the object is often an index to its own past, what technical imagination may be capable of both dating the worked objects and tracing as far back as possible its concept? The worked object is, in effect, a live memory, reproducing, in its own successive concrete images, its conceptual and cultural destiny, which, often and explicitly, is a testimony to a will to remember or to forget certain things. To reinvest worked objects with their own past from the context of their own society is, indeed, to revive the historical activity and the reactiveness of a culture with its motions and exemplary beauty.

This reverses Siebold's dream decisively. It indicates also how the "primitives" can digest—and have been, at least intellectually (see e.g., Ajayi 1969; Diop 1960; Ki-Zerbo 1972; Mveng 1965), digesting—the West and its mythologies.

The point I am trying to make is simple: worked objects—be they drawings, scarifications, or even, as in the case of Central and East Africa, painted bodies—perpetuate as memories of a locus the immediacy of a perspective and its boundaries in the strict sense. This preservation function does not exclude revision or the reinterpretation of canons. Specialists of memory create, invent, and transform, yet they also faithfully obey their vocation and responsibility: to transmit a heritage, record its obsessions, and preserve its past. This is what we may call a social practice of history. One could apply to it what Pierre Nora says of *lieux de mémoires:* "fear of a rapid and final disappearance combines with anxiety about the meaning of the present and uncertainty about the future to give even the most humble testimony, the most modest vestige, the potential dignity of the memorable" (Nora 1989: 13).

III.

THE POWER OF THE GREEK PARADIGM

For Jacques and Claude Garelli

> As the Egyptians have a climate peculiar to
> themselves, and their river is different in its
> nature from all other rivers, so they made all
> their customs and laws of kind contrary for
> the most part to those of other people.
>
> —HERODOTUS, II, 35

Amazons, Barbarians, and Monsters

Explaining his intellectual ambition, Michel Foucault wrote that he was "studying statements at the limit that separates them from what is not said, in the occurrence that allows them to emerge to the exclusion of all others. Our task is not to give voice to silence that surrounds them, nor to discover all that, in them or beside them, had remained silent or had been reduced to silence" (Foucault 1982: 119). I wish that I could here reexamine what has been said in the Greek tradition about the so-called *barbaroi* and about *oiorpata*. I am immensely indebted to Foucault for what I am doing, even if I seem more oriented toward focusing on statements that enunciate separations in what they say. Foucault knew quite well that there is no such thing as a history of silence, which does not imply that there is no way of writing a history of silenced experiences. About this he is rather clear: "the description of a statement does not consist [. . .] in rediscovering the unsaid whose place it occupies; nor how one can reduce it to a silent, common text; but on the contrary, in discovering what special place it occupies, what ramifications for the system of formations make it possible to map its localizations, how it is isolated in the general dispersion of statements" (1982: 119).

I choose to look at the "special place" that *agrioi* (savages), *barbaroi* (barbarians), and *oiorpata* (women killers of men) occupy in the texts of some classical writers (particularly Herodotus, Diodorus Siculus, Strabo, and Pliny).

Indeed, in my reading, in my selection of passages, I have tried to avoid the temptation of psychologizing, so that my exegesis "reproduces" almost literally the original and "redescribes" it in its own "textual violence."

Mapping the Margins

Diodorus Siculus explains his objective at the end of the first paragraph of Book III: to describe the Ethiopians, the Libyans, and the Atlantians (III, 1, 3). For their geographical location, one can refer to the statement which opens Book V of Pliny's *Natural History:* "Africam Graeci Libyam appellavere et mare ante eam Libycum. Aegypto finitur." ["The Greeks gave to Africa the name of Libya and they call Libyan the sea which lies in front of it. It is bounded by Egypt."] This indication reproduces a division which goes back to the time of Herodotus (IV, 145–67). During the first century, specifically after Caesar's victory over Pompeius's army at Thapsus in 46 B.C., Africa is the name of Carthage's territory. On the east, it is bounded by the province of Cyrenaica, and to the west by the two Mauritaniae. The administrative reorganization of 27 B.C. integrates *Africa Nova* (Numidia) and *Africa Antiqua* and establishes three main regions: the *dioecesis Hipponiensis,* the *dioecesis Numidica,* and the *dioecesis Hadrumentina.* The first two are under the authority of a *legatus* and the third is governed by a *procurator* (Mommsen and Marquardt 1892, XI, 11; Mommsen 1921).

The Roman African coast is both a culturally strong and a politically weak part of the empire (Benabou 1976). Pliny, in a lively description, situates it. He begins by presenting the two Mauritaniae, Mount Atlas *(fabulosissimum),* the first Roman penetration into the northwest region of the continent under the principate of Claudius, the coast of Tangier and Algeria, Numidia, Africa proper—*regio et quae propriae vocetur Africa est*—the region of Tunisia and Tripoli, the gulf of Cabes and Sydra, the province of Cyrenaica, and *quae sequitur regio Mareotis Libya appellatur Aegypto contermina* ["the following region which is called Libya Mareotis and borders upon Egypt"] (V, VI, 39).

It is interesting to note that Pliny's ethnographical map proceeds eastward, whereas that of Herodotus, written five centuries earlier, goes westward and begins with an ethnography of the Adrymachae, who inhabit the region nearest to Egypt (VI, 168). When closely compared, the two maps reveal striking differences and similarities. Before analyzing differences and resemblances, let us look at Herodotus's ethnographical map. He presents a succession of ethnic groups, characterizing each by particular traits, customs, or stories he has learned about from other people. His account is a detailed one, from the Egyptian borders to the Tritonian lake, and each community is clearly typified on the basis of some major paradigms: habitation, social *locus,* food, physical features, and marriage. Thus, for example, we can derive from Herodotus the following list of sixteen groups.

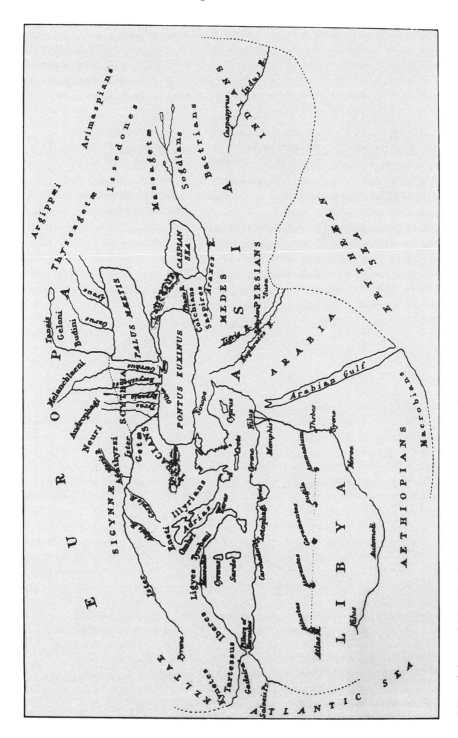

Map of the world in Herodotus's time, 440 B.C. Reprinted by permission of the publishers and the Loeb Classical Library from Herodotus, I, Books I–II, translated by A. D. Godley. Cambridge, Mass.: Harvard University Press.

1. Adyrmachidae (IV, 168)	live near Egypt	wear a sort of Libyan dress; their women wear bronze torques on both legs and their hair is long; the only Libyans who offer the king all virgins who are to be wedded.
2. Gilgamae (IV, 169)	inhabit the country to the west as far as the island of Aphrodisias	this is the country of silphium; their customs are not "extraordinary."
3. Asbystae (IV, 170)	dwell in Cyrenaean territory	they are drivers of four-horse chariots and follow Cyrenaean practices.
4. Auschisae (IV, 171)	inhabit the inland of Barce, touching the seacoast at Euhesperidae	Cyrenaean customs.
5. Bacales (IV, 171)	live in the middle of Auschisae territory	Cyrenaean customs.
6. Nasamones (IV, 172)	are west of Auschisae in a populous country	hunters of locusts and remarkably promiscuous; cult of ancestors; bury their dead sitting.
7. Garamantes (IV, 174)	southward, they dwell in a country of wild beasts	they do not have weapons and do not know how to defend themselves.
8. Macae (IV, 175)	live on the neighboring seaboard to the west; around the river Cinyps there is a thick wood	they shave their hair to a crest, left on the top of their heads.
9. Gindanes (IV, 176)	dwell next to the Macae	women wear as many leather anklets as they have had lovers.
10. Lotus-eaters (IV, 177)	are on a headland jutting out to the sea from the Gindanes' territory	their only fare is the lotus.
11. Machyles (IV, 179)	inhabit the region of the Tritonian lake	Lacedaemonians had a colony here; the Machyles eat the lotus too, but less than their neighbors.
12. Ausees (IV, 180)	dwell on the shores of the Tritonian lake	whereas the Machyles wear their long hair behind their heads, the Ausees have it in front; they are promiscuous.

13. Ammonians (IV, 181)	inhabit inland of Libya, which is full of wild beasts	they follow the worship of the Zeus of Thebes.
14. Garamantes (IV, 183)	are ten days' journey from Augila	have oxen that go backward as they graze and chase the "cave-dwelling Ethiopians," whose speech is like that of bats.
15. Atarantes (IV, 184)	are ten days' journey from the Garamantes	they have no individual names; curse the blazingly hot sun.
16. Atlantes (IV, 184)	inhabit the region of Mount Atlas	they eat no living creature and have no dreams in their sleep.

With its Greek mythic references going back to the Argonauts (IV, 179) and its particular Greek tradition in terms of sacrifice and customs (IV, 189), the Tritonian lake region is Herodotus's *point de repère*. It is "civilized." Curiously with Diodorus Siculus (III, 53, 6) it will signify a region of barbarism inhabited by Amazons. In any case, Herodotus notes about the area that "the inhabitants of the Tritonian lake region mainly sacrifice to Athena, next to Triton and Poseidon" (IV, 188).

For groups west of the lake, Herodotus's account becomes vague. After the presentation of the Ausees (IV, 191), he notes that he has spoken of "the nomad Libyans" who dwell on the seacoast. The locations of the Ammonians, the Garamantes, and others are then measured by the number of days to journey thither. He knows nothing of the peoples living beyond the Atlantes: "I know and can tell the names of all the peoples that dwell on the ridge as far as the Atlantes, but no farther than that" (IV, 185). That given, he portrays in a very careful ethnography the two main groups of Libyans: East and West of the Triton. The first region, which is bounded by Egypt, is low-lying and sandy (IV, 191) and has a great variety of animals. Besides beasts existing elsewhere, there are gazelles, horned asses, antelopes the size of oxen, foxes, hyenas, porcupines, wild rams, jackals, panthers, land crocodiles, one-horned serpents, etc. (IV, 192). The peoples are nomads (IV, 186), live in movable houses (IV, 190), eat meat and drink milk; they do not touch the flesh of cows nor rear swine (IV, 188). Some sacrifice to the sun and moon (IV, 186); others honor Isis and bury their dead in the Greek manner (IV, 190). West of the Tritonian lake the country is hilly, wooded, and full of wild animals and strange creatures ("as say the Libyans").

> In that country are the huge snakes and the lions and the elephants and bears and asps, the horned asses, the dog-headed men and the headless peoples that have their eyes in their breasts [. . .] and the wild men and women, in addition to many other creatures which are not fabulous. (IV, 191)

The inhabitants do have some curious practices, such as burning the veins of the scalps or temples of their four-year-old children with the grease of sheep's wool. They also use goat's urine to heal burns. But they are, on the whole, exemplary healthy people (IV, 187). Among them, Herodotus names four main groups. The Maxyes, "who claim to be descended from the peoples who came from Troy"; they till the soil, possess houses, paint their bodies with vermilion, and wear their hair long on the right side of the head and shave the left (IV, 191). The Zauekes, neighbors of the Maxyes, whose "women drive the chariots to war" (IV, 193). The Gyzantes, who also paint themselves with vermilion; these are makers of honey and eat apes (IV, 194). The Charchedonians, who trade in gold with populations dwelling beyond the Pillars of Hercules (IV, 195–96).

After this broad picture, Herodotus concludes. He notes that he does not know more—"These are all the Libyans who can be named" (IV, 197)—and then he presents a global evaluation of nations:

> I have thus much further to say of this country: four nations and no more, as far as our knowledge serves, inhabit it: whereof two are autochthonous and two are not; the Libyans in the north and the Ethiopians in the south of Libya are autochthonous, the Phoenicians and Greeks are later settlers. (IV, 197)

Pliny's chronicle follows different norms. It proceeds from west to east, specifically from Mauritaniae to the extreme eastern regions of Libya; and south of Egypt to the Ethiopian centers of Napata and Meroe. It is possible to divide the countries, regions, and peoples he presents on his ethnographical map into two main groups: the unmarked (Roman and Greek influenced) and the marked or exotic others.

Unmarked	*Marked*
From Mauritaniae to the river Sebou, the colony of Banasa and the city of Sallee (*NH*, V, i, 1–5): there is a succession of Roman cities, *oppida*, and friendly autonomous towns.	The Atlas region: *incolarum neminem interdiu cerni, silere omnia* ["none of its inhabitants are seen, everything is silent"] (*NH*, V, i, 6). *Spatium ad eum immensum incertumque* ["It is an immense distance, an unexplored country"] (*NH*, V, i, 7). In a westerly direction from Mount Atlas: wilderness and dense forests (*NH*, V, i, 8–16).
The coast: *sita oppidum ex adverso Malacae in Hispania situm, Syphacis regia, alterius iam Mauretania* ["In front of Malaga in Spain there is the royal city of King Syphax and this is the other Mauretania"] (*NH*, V, i, 18).	The Tingitana province, home of Maurusii, Masaesyli, Gaetulae, Baniurae, Nesimi. It produces elephants (*NH*, V, i, 17).

Numidia (or Metagonitis): country of Nomads (*vero nomades a permutandis pabulis, mapalia sua, hoc est domos, NH, V, ii, 22*). [Its people [are called] Nomads from their custom of frequently changing their pasturage, carrying their *mapalia,* that is their homes.] This country produces nothing remarkable apart from marble and wild beasts.

The desert and then the Garamantes' country, beyond the denizens of Phazania and Fezzan in the Sahara: *excipiunt saltus repleti ferrarum multitudine, et introrsus elephantorum solitudines* ["There are forests filled with a multitude of wild beasts, and further desolate haunts of elephants"] (*NH, V, iv, 26*).

Africa proper (Tunisia and Tripoli) contains also the Byzacium region of *fertilitatis eximiae, cum centesima fruge agricolis fenus reddente terra* ["of exceptional fertility, the soil paying the farmers interest at the rate of a hundred-fold"] (*NH V, iii, 25*). *Ad hunc finem Africa a fluvio Ampsaga populus DXVI habet qui Romano pareant imperio* ["between the river Ampsaga and this boundary Africa comprises 516 peoples that accept allegiance to Rome"] (*NH, V, iv, 29*).

The desert coast with its inhabitants: Marmaridae (from El Bareton to the Greater Syrtis), then, Acrauceles, Nasamones, Asbytae, Macae, Amantes in the desert where they build houses of rock salt (*NH, V, v, 34*).

The district of Cyrenaica or *Pentapolitana regio* [the land of five cities] marked by Greek traditions (*NH, V, v, 31*).

Southwest of the Amantes, the cave-dwellers, the Black Mountain, and beyond it the Garamantes' country. *Ad Garamantes iter inexplicabile adhuc fuit* ["Hitherto it has been impossible to open up the road to the Garamantes' region"] (*NH, V, v, 38*).

Mareotis Libya which borders Egypt: *regio Mareotis Libya appellatur Aegypto contermina* (*NH, V, v, 39*).

Peoples in the interior (toward the south): Gaetulii, Egyptian Libyans, White Ethiopians, Perorsi, etc. And eastward: cave-dwellers, Ethiopian tribes, half-animal goat-pans, Satyrs, strapfoots, etc. (*NH, V, viii, 46*).

Egypt: *proxima Africae incolitur Aegyptus, introrsus ad meridiem recedens donec a tergo praetendantur Aethiopes* ["The next inhabited region to Africa is Egypt, which stretches southward into the interior to where the Ethiopians border it in the rear"] (*NH, V, ix, 48*).

Ethiopia: *et de mensura eius varia prodidere* ["Various reports have been made as to its dimensions"] (*NH, V, xxxv, 183*).

The opposition marked/unmarked makes sense when one reads Pliny's account carefully. It refers to his evaluation of peoples and his description of countries in terms of Roman presence or absence. One of the most striking examples might be his remark about Ethiopia and the city of Napata: *nec tamen arma Romana ibi solitudinem fecerunt* ["It was not the forces of Rome that made the country a desert"] (*NH*, VI, xxxv, 182). One also notes that his geographical map details Roman settlements and colonies, and portrays ethnic groups in terms of political allegiance: opposition to, or autonomy from, the Roman power. In a very concrete way, geography here reproduces the expansion of the Roman *Imperium:* conquered kingdoms and colonies of Mauritaniae (Traducta Julia, Julia Constantia, Zulil, Lixus, Babba, Valentia, etc.); cities of Roman culture on the coast of the Mediterranean (Portus Magnus, Oppidum Norum, Tipasa, Rusguniae, Rusucurium, Rusazus, Igilgili, etc.); advanced posts on the margins of the Sahara (Augusta, Timici, Tigavae, etc.); and Roman centers in Numidia, Africa, and Cyrenaica. One also remembers what Pliny writes about the African province:

> Ad hunc finem Africa a fluvio Ampsaga populos DXVI habet qui Romano pareant imperio; in his colonias sex, praeter iam dictas Uthinam, Thuburbi, oppida civium Romanorum XV, ex quibus in mediterraneo dicenda Absuritanum, Abutucense, etc. (*NH*, V, iv, 29)

> Between the river Ampsaga and this boundary Africa contains 516 peoples that accept allegiance to Rome. These include six colonies Uthina and Thuburbi, in addition to those already mentioned; 15 towns with Roman citizenship, among which in the interior must be mentioned those of Absurae, Abutucum, etc.

From the background of this "colonized" space, which symbolically is the equivalent of Herodotus's Tritonian lake region, one perceives a well-specified geography of monstrosity, that is the space comprising unknown places and their inhabitants. In the fifth century, Herodotus could state: "to my thinking, there is in no part of Libya any great excellence whereby it could be compared to Asia or Europe, save only in the region which is called by the same name as its river, Cinys" (IV, 198). Five hundred years later, Pliny describes the region in terms of transformations brought about by Roman presence: Scipio Aemilianus, who placed a fleet of vessels at the service of the historian Polybius (*NH*, V, i, 9), Suetonius Paulinus, who was the first Roman commander to cross the Atlas range (*NH*, V, i, 14), and the expansion of colonies under the first emperors. Yet Pliny's geography of monstrosity faithfully mirrors Herodotus's description, albeit in a more detailed way. To Herodotus's general geographic frame of monsters—dog-headed and headless peoples (IV, 191)—living in the eastern region of Libya, Pliny opposes a curious table of "tribes" inhabiting a vague area around the *Nigri fluvio eadem natura quae Nilo* ["the river Black which has the same nature as the Nile"] (*NH*, V, viii, 44): the Atlas peoples, who have no names; the cave-dwellers, who have no language and live on the flesh of snakes; the Garamantes, who do not practice marriage;

the Blemmyae, who are headless and, as already indicated by Herodotus, have their mouths and eyes attached to their chests; the Satyrs; and the Strapfoots (*NH*, V, viii, 45-46).

As to the Ethopian space and its features, Pliny is not more specific than Herodotus: "The truest opinion is that of those who place two Ethiopias beyond the African desert, and especially Homer who tells us that the Ethiopians are divided into two sections, the eastward and the westward" (*NH*, V, viii, 43).

One of the most systematic ancient texts which addresses the issue of Ethiopians is Diodorus of Sicily's Book III. This work presents in an orderly way the history of the country and some supposedly Ethiopian customs. The history is, in fact, linked to myths and the authority of Greek writers. Ethiopians were, according to such sources, the "first of all humans," (III, ii, 1) and have been called autochthonous. They are the first humans to be generated by the earth, the first to be taught how to honor the gods, "their sacrifices are the most pleasing to heaven," and "from all time they have enjoyed a state of freedom and of peace with one another." Founders of human culture, they sent out colonists to Egypt when "what is now Egypt was not a land but a sea" (III, iii, 2): "[Historians] say that the Egyptians are colonists sent out by the Ethiopians, Osiris having been the leader of the colony" (III, iii, 2). As signs of the Ethiopian influence on Egyptian customs, Diodorus invoked the sacred writing (hieratic), the sacerdotal orders, and the belief that kings are gods (III, iii, 4-7).

Diodorus's ethnography of Ethiopian customs is very selective. It is centered on the king's figure and the absolute powers of priests that the Greek-educated Ergamenes destroyed (III, v-vii). The region on which he focuses is that of Napata, the capital, the neighboring island of Meroe, and the land adjoining Egypt. He adds, "there are also a great number of other Ethiopian tribes" (III, viii, 8) and states that "The majority of them, and especially those who dwell along the river, are black in colour and have flat noses and woolly hair" (III, viii, 2). His general statement is strong, definitive: "as for their spirit, they are entirely savage and display the nature of a wild beast, not so much, however, in their temper as in their ways of living." And he adds, "speaking as they do [. . .] and cultivating none of the practices of civilized life as these are found among the rest of humankind, they present a striking contrast when considered in the light of our own customs" (III, viii, 3). According to Diodorus, some of these Ethiopians gather fruits for food; others eat lotus. There are those who are nourished by the roots of the reeds, and most of them live on the meat, milk, and cheese of their herds. Few are well trained in the use of the bow. With regard to religion, the peoples who inhabit the region above Meroe have two different philosophical positions. Some believe that "the sun and the moon and the universe as a whole" have an eternal and imperishable nature. Others disagree, and a few of them simply do not believe in gods (III, ix, 2).

In Diodorus's text there emerges a tension between his mythical reading of Ethiopian genesis and his ethnographical interpretation of local habits and customs. On the one hand, there is the blessed country of human origin and its "faultless Ethiopians" cherished by gods (III, ii, 3-4), and, on the other, he describes a country whose customs differ immensely from those of the rest of humankind.

In terms of content, there is no complete agreement among the three narratives I have commented upon so far. Yet one observes two remarkable levels of correspondence. First, social signs such as marriage, diet, housing, clothing, naming, or religion allow a sort of table of cultural differences which classifies human societies. Second, there are referential paradigms that serve as *points de repères:* The Tritonian lake region and its Greek culture in Herodotus's narrative, the distribution of Roman settlements in Pliny's, and, for Diodorus Siculus, the intervention of a Greek-educated Ergamenes in the history of Ethiopia. As to the content itself, the subtle integration of geographies of monstrosities witnesses to a search for marvels and to a love of the bizarre. In any case, my comments on these narratives bring to light this notion: the opposition between Greek or Roman civility and barbarianism is concretized by being located on a map. A series of adjectival oppositions, such as those implied by the paradigm of the light (of civilization) versus the darkness (of barbarism), creates and indicates a deviation. The contrast qualifies both a distance and a difficult link. In effect, it often carries a postulation and a strategy—that is, a "manipulation of power that becomes possible as soon as a subject with will and power [. . .] can be isolated" (de Certeau 1984: 35–36)—as in the case of the tension existing between *skotioi* and "adults." In Crete, young men were called *skotioi* because, by age-status, they belonged to the world of women, living "inside" their quarters, and were thus defined as members of an "inside" world as opposed to the "open" world of adult citizens. The basic meaning of *skotios* is "dark" and the word is often found in expressions qualifying persons who are "in the dark," living "in secret," in sum, "in the margin" of the *politeia* or condition and rights of a full citizen.

The Oiorpata's Place and the Politics of Knowledge

The map is a scientific project. It might, occasionally, have political usages. In any case, it is the other side, the technical vision of subjective perceptions. It totalizes knowledge, measures distances, and organizes places according to globalizing schemas. It has also its own history. Anaximander's cosmos is a map. His computation of the Earth's height and his description of its shape and position are reflected in what is commonly known as the Ionian map, which Herodotus completes and supplements, following the frame of one of his predecessors, Hecataeus of Miletus. On the basis of his travels and knowledge, Herodotus mocked the naïveté of ancient geographers, but not the enterprise or its utility. His geography locates *barbaroi* and *agrioi* in their respective "places" and, at the same time, articulates a cultural and metaphoric geography (an arrangement of *muthoi* or stories he heard) on top of the first. His method for this second level of narration is often one of *reservatio mentis*.

Martin de Vos, *Allegory of Africa*. Sixteenth century. Stedelijk
Prentenkabinet (Municipal Printroom), Antwerpen, Belgium.

He notes: "I will not say that this or that story is true" (I, 5). About Egyptian
stories, he insists: "these stories are for the use of whosoever believes such
tales: for myself, it is my rule [. . .] that I record whatever is told me as I have
heard it" (III, 123).

The *barbaroi* and the *agrioi* are part of the general vocabulary of the Greek
politeia. The first basically means "foreigner" and designates a "non-Greek
speaker." The second signifies "wild, savage" and is etymologically related to
agros, "field." As such, *agros* is, specifically, in a relation of opposition to the

household or *oikos*, "a dwelling place" symbolizing family ties and figuratively used for any family, household goods, a reigning house. *Oikos* implies also the meaning of "home city," that of "belonging to a community" (defined by a tradition, a culture, or a condition) well-actualized in one of its parent-words, *oikumene*, which designates the inhabited region of the Greeks in opposition to barbarian countries and, by extension, all the inhabited world known by the Greeks. In brief, in its opposition to the paradigmatic and ethnocentric values of *oikos* (*domus* in Latin), *agros* is the exact counterpart of the Latin *foresticus* and *silvaticus* (Benveniste 1973: 257).

To meditate on the complexity of the dialectic between inside and outside, domestic and foreign, civil and savage, let us begin by focusing on Herodotus's *Oiorpata*. The word is rare in literature, and Herodotus seems to have been the first to introduce it into the Greek. It designates warlike women, known as *Amazons* from the time of the Greeks. Strictly speaking, the concept Amazon is a metonym. The word is composed of the privative *a* and the substantive *mazos* (or *mastos*) "breast," defining therefore a mutilation. According to the legend, such women used to burn off one of their breasts so that it might not incapacitate their handling of the bow and the lance. *Amazonides* is an epithet of the goddess Artemis (e.g., Pausanias 4, 31, 8), the virgin huntress, sister of Apollo, who had at Ephesus a celebrated temple supposedly built by the Amazons. The term *Oiorpata* is also an image. Herodotus explains that it is of Scythian origin:

> The Amazons whom the Scythians call Oiorpata, a name signifying in the Greek language killers of men, for in Scythian a man is *oior*, and to kill is *pata* [. . .]
> (IV, 110)

The story unfolds in three main phases. The first phase consists of the encounter and battle (IV, 110–11) with the Scythians. The peace arrangement that follows (IV, 111) is made possible by a discovery: dead bodies of the Oiorpata on the battlefield have revealed their gender and the Scythians now know that their enemies are women. Finally, a division of place (IV, 112–117) duplicates a specialization of spaces between Scythians and Oiorpata, the latter organizing an intolerant gynecocratic society in which "it is the custom that no virgin weds till she has slain a man of the enemy" (IV, 117).

The fable seems to double here a silent disciplinary model. The Greek order, indeed, has a civil economy in which rights and duties are well-defined. The *politeia* imposes itself as a normative system in which social practices are determined by both traditional and legal procedures. The gender division (in education, initiation, responsibilities) can be used as a key to an understanding of the general economy.

> Jean-Pierre Vernant, using the evidence of the mythical tradition especially, has analyzed a number of different religious festivals, summarizing his results as follows: 'If rituals of status-transition mean for boys entry into the status of warrior, for the girls associated with them in the same rituals, and frequently

themselves subjected to a period of seclusion, the initiation ordeals mean a preparation for sexual union in marriage. Here again the association, which is also an opposition, between war and marriage is evident. *Marriage is to the girl what war is to the boy: for each they mark the fulfilment of their respective natures,* by quitting a state in which each has still some of the characteristics of the other.' (Vidal-Naquet, in Gordon 1982: 174; my emphasis)

Such is the economy that the Oiorpata perturb, not by killing men but more by simply existing. They find their human fulfillment in political autonomy and in war expeditions against their enemies. As such, they negate the Greek paradigm of the status of a "good woman," which, according to Pericles' law of 451, was to be a respectable daughter of a citizen and to become the mother of citizens. Indeed, women did play important roles in important civic rituals such as the *Arretophoria* and the celebrations of Artemis (Vidal-Naquet, in Gordon 1982: 179). They could, even in the *polis,* organize themselves in *politeia gunaikon.* Yet the basic rule seems to be in the opposition between *oikos* and *polis.* The former represents the inside, the feminine, the condition and the possibility of continuity of the *politeia;* the latter, the outside, the masculine, the paradigm of the preservation (and thus the rule of wars) of the *politeia.*

The battle between the Scythians and the Oiorpata dramatizes this tension. Herodotus was a well-educated man. He knew the stories of the Amazons at war (fighting Bellerophon, Heracles, Theseus) and he had in mind the confrontation between Achilles and Penthesileia, the queen of the Amazons, whom Achilles humbled and killed, meanwhile discovering admiration and love for a courageous enemy. Herodotus's careful description of the Scythian battle reproduces a Greek predicament. Only men go to war. Then, what do you do with women who transgress this law, and, in so doing, challenge the order of the *polis?*

Let us look carefully at Herodotus's description of the event. The text describes contexts in which the Oiorpata's practices of life become objects of curiosity and progressively constitute an inventory that signifies an inverted economy of the Greek *polis.* The Oiorpata have been captured on land. They are imprisoned on a ship. They revolt, kill the crew, and, not having the necessary know-how of navigation, leave the ship at the mercy of waves and winds, until it reaches the region of the free Scythians. The description conveys a number of qualfications. The Oiorpata are thus located first on a boat and are characterized as lacking a basic *techne.* They land around the Maeetian lake, and they surprise the Scythians by the strangeness of their speech, their dress, their origin, and particularly their customs. The Oiorpata, having decided to journey toward an uninhabited region, seize a troop of horses, mount them, and raid the country. The Scythians react and there is a war. Herodotus's narrative after the battle organizes the Oiorpata's life and customs in the margin of the Scythians' locality and cultural ways of living. Scythian young men are sent by the elders to seduce the Oiorpata, and their mission is to integrate these "strange women" into the Scythians' continuity; for "this was the project of the Scythians: they wanted that children should be born of the women" (IV, 111). The plan seems to succeed. The youths join the Amazons' camp, having "nothing but their arms and their horses, and live as did the women, by hunting and plunder." An amicable association takes place. The women accept the men and integrate them into their lives and social order. They dwell together, "each man having for his wife the woman with whom he had intercourse at first" (IV, 114).

This narration is most interesting in that it formulates, beneath the setting of a story, a statement about a cultural order. Let us repeat the progression of the story in its symbolic implications. There is, first, a sexual inversion which imposes itself on the reader. The young men have been asked by their elders to encamp on the margins of the Amazons' area and to imitate carefully whatever the Amazons did. "If the women pursued them, then not to fight, but to flee; and when the pursuit ceased, to come and encamp near to them" (IV, 111). The young men have been invited to "feminize" themselves, and the Amazons symbolize what in the *polis* is a normative "masculinity" and here is a *thēlukratēs* or women's rule and dominion (Vidal-Naquet 1986: 209). The tension duplicates other oppositions: the young men *(neotatoi)* are in a situation which structurally is similar to that of *skotioi* (young men not yet adult, seen as still of the dark), the *azostoi* ("those who are without arms"), or the *egdysmenoi* ("those who have no clothes") of Dreros (Vidal-Naquet 1986: 116–17). What the narrative spells out is thus a paradigm. As noted by Vidal-Naquet with regard to the Phaestos festival known as *Ekdysia* ("clothes off"), "the etiology here is a story about a girl who turned into a boy—which forms a link between two sets *boy : girl* and *naked : armed*" (Vidal-Naquet 1986: 117).

The young Scythians have symbolically turned into girls and experience, in the margins of the Oiorpata's place, the reversal of a "law." At this step, marriage is to them (as objective) what war is to the Oiorpata (as vocation). Their integration into the Amazons' life, after the women have tested them and discovered that they represented no danger, functions in the narrative as the end of a status-transition ritual. They are now fully part of a social economy that is an inverted order of the Athenian model of *politeia*. Indeed, the *neotatoi* think of re-reversing that order and invite their partners to join the Scythian tradition and, accordingly, to evolve. "Let us return to our people and consort with them, and we will still have you, and no others, for our wives" (IV, 114), say the young men. The Oiorpata refuse, invoking cultural differences existing between them and the Scythian women: "We shoot with the bow and throw the javelin and ride, but the crafts of women we have never learned; and your women do none of the things whereof we speak, but abide in their wagons working at women's crafts, and never go abroad a-hunting or for aught else" (IV, 114).

The distinction does not refer to physiological characteristics, but to cultural features which distinguish two different modes of life. At the same time, the

Memnon with a Black man. Greek vase, sixth century B.C. Copyright British Museum, London.

Oiorpata radically separate the two communities of women: "We and they therefore could never agree." What is rejected is "a civilization" in its cultural and social practices. The Oiorpata agree to be spouses to the young men and make a proposition: "if you wish to merit the name of just *(dikaioi)* men, go to your parents, let them give you the allotted share of their possessions, and after that let us go and dwell by ourselves." The young men agree. Then another demand follows: "Nay, since you think it right to have us for wives, let us all together, we and you, remove out of this country and dwell across

Memnon with two Amazons. Greek vase, sixth century B.C. Right: detail.
Copyright British Museum, London.

the river Tanais" (IV, 115). And they all move three days eastward and three
days northward.

The negation of "civilization" is now complete. Men have submitted to
women's rule. In Aristotle's perception, this would be equivalent to the master
obeying the slave, or the soul submitting to the body, as, according to Herodotus, Argos is witness to after being defeated by Sparta (VI, 77, 83). If the
Scythian *neotatoi* are called *dikaioi* (just men) it is by women and from within
a *thēlukratēs*. This is the supreme male terror, that is—to use Lacan's concept—the obliteration *(aphanisis)* of a difference which is also a "right to"
one or the other, but not both (as represented in the *vel* (or) used in Symbolic
Logic). To use Aristotle's categories, are they male or female, straight or
curved, square or oblong?

In any case, what the new sociocultural entity constitutes is both the unbelievable and the incredible. The Oiorpata's place on the frontiers of the
Scythian's territory ceases to exist as a geographical location and moves further into the bush, incarnating the absolute *agros* or an area of paradigmatic
monstrosity. That it was in the margins of the Scythians' country that the

Oiorpata were situated was already a sign. For Greeks, Scythians were living at the very limits of the human space. They were quasi savages and thus could have among them both cannibals and vegetarians, monstrous categories which are in sum identical. "The vegetarian is no less inhuman than the cannibal" (Vidal-Naquet, in Gordon 1982: 87). There was, therefore, room for "men killers" and gynecocracy hidden somewhere in the *agros* three days eastward and three days northward from the Tanais.

Let us also note that the ship at the beginning of the story marks a first cut from the Greek place. The connection is erased in the death of the crew and the incapacity of the Oiorpata to substitute themselves as masters of the maritime *techne*. In the Scythian place, the Oiorpata are unveiled as women (and become objects of a collective desire for an ethnic continuity). Yet, it is in this same moment that they affirm their radical difference and choose to maintain their own program by transporting themselves outside of Scythian boundaries. Finally, if the whole movement of the story is to bring to light Oiorpata as cultural delinquents living on the absolute margins of the *oikoumene,* a paradox should be noted: "the men could not learn the women's language, but the women mastered the speech of men" (IV, 114).

Barbarians, Women, and the City

The whole story could be opposed structurally to that narrated by Diodorus Siculus in the first century. His Amazons are based in Africa (III, 52, 4) and we do know that, in terms of information, his narrative is inhabited by a Dionysus, an African (cc 66.4–73.8), and, indeed, on the other hand, by the Greek paradigmatic style. In this context, Amazons seem to originate in Africa: "Now there have been in Libya a number *of races of women* who were warlike and greatly admired for their manly vigour" (III, 52, 4). "They practice the arts of war," are soldiers in the army, and "they went in to the men for the procreation of children." They are in power: adminstrators of the cities, magistrates, politicians in charge of the State. The men, Diodorus, emphasizes are:

> like our married women, spend their days about the house, carrying out the orders which were given them by their wives; and they took no part in military campaigns or in office or in the exercise of freedom of speech. (III, 53, 1–2)

They live in the area of the Tritonian lake (III, 53, 4) which, for Diodorus, is "also near Ethiopia." These Amazons, if we are to believe Diodorus, are "a superior race in valour and eager for war" (III, 53, 6). They seem, according to the account, "here to dominate most of the Northern part of Africa under the leadership of their mythical General-Queen Myrina—she had a treaty with Horus, King of Egypt and son Isis" (III, 55, 4)—before being destroyed by Heracles. And, according to Diodorus, the Amazons' originary space and race in the Tritonian lake area disappeared too (III, 55, 3).

What is remarkable in the case of Diodorus's narrative is that it reverses Herodotus's. Diodorus claims, for example, that his Libyan Amazons "were much earlier in point of time and accomplished notable deeds" (III, 52, 1). Also contrary to Herodotus's Oiorpata, who chose to retire in the bush with their newly acquired men, Myrina conquers until the end the "civilized" space after subjugating most of Northern Africa. Through friendship, diplomacy, or war, she dominates Egypt, Arabia, Syria, Cilicia, Phrygia, etc.; then she attacks and colonizes Lesbos (founding Mitylenê, named after her warrior sister) and, finally, retires, as she has wished, in Cybelê, or "the Mother of the Gods," and gives to the island the name Samothrace, which means, when translated into Greek, "sacred island" (III, 55, 7–9). In brief, Herodotus's Amazons are fugitives leaving Greek culture and choosing primitivity, whereas Diodorus's Myrina and her people move from the margins of Greek culture (the Tritonian) to conquer and civilize the island of "the Mother of Gods," Samothrace.

The model of "primitive" women as described by Herodotus, situated outside the *oikoumene* and closely linked to nature, is also exemplified in Strabo's description of the women of the Samnitae. They are isolated on a small island, northeastward of the river Liger that separates Aquitania from Belgica. Their immediate neighbors on the continent are Celts, who used to practice human sacrifices and other monstrosities, which the Romans stopped (4, 4, 5). According to Strabo, who is quoting Poseidonius, "no man sets foot on the [women's] island, although the women themselves, sailing from it have intercourse with the men and then return again" (4, 4, 6). Unlike the Oiorpata, who are fully in power of their destiny, the women of Samnitae "are possessed by Dionysus and make this god propitious by appeasing him with mystic initiations as well as other sacred performances."

The pattern of these stories is remarkable. It topologizes an itinerary of delinquency, and then metaphorizes it. From the Mediterranean Sea to the Scythians' country and then into the wilderness where the Oiorpata organize their own order, the itinerary traces a departing trajectory, which is both a questioning of the *polis* and a rejection of its history and tradition. Inversely, the women of Samnitae are cultural delinquents from the very beginning of the story. They reveal their delinquency by making it known to those inhabiting the place now pacified and spatialized by Romans: they need men, but not their *politeia*. The physical distance between them and the continent is in itself an objective factor of self-exclusion from a "civilized" map. On the contrary, the Libyan female army of Myrina traces a map and imposes a new cultural order.

Strabo, describing the mountaineers living in the northern part of Iberia (Callaicans, Asturians, Cantabrians, etc.) links distance (from the Roman center) to psychological characteristics of marginals. He notes that only Roman colonial mastery of the geographic distance bettered the Barbarians and introduced them to "sociability" and "humanity":

The quality of intractability and savagery in these peoples has not resulted solely from their engaging in warfare, but also from their remoteness; for the trip to their country, whether by sea or by land, is long, and since they are difficult to communicate with, they have lost the instinct of sociability and humanity. They have this feeling of intractability and savagery to a less extent now, however, because of the peace and of the sojourns of the Romans among them. (3, 3, 8)

The remark would apply *a fortiori* to those humans living beyond the countries of known barbarians. The geographer brings them into a map by naming them or by situating them spatially from a known city. "These are all whom we can name," Herodotus often writes.

Pliny's geography, as we have seen, is a topological list of names that he qualifies in terms of distance from Roman cities, *oppida,* or colonies. He correlates remoteness and savagery in an explicit way. For example, about the town of Meroe and the island of Tados in Africa—a region that had been ruled by several women *(regnare feminam Candacem, quod nomen multis iam annis ad reginas transisset) (NH,* VI, xxxv, 186)—Pliny reports the existence of the race of Aetheria (which afterward took the name, in Greco-Roman texts, of Atlantia and finally that of Aethiops) and then adds: "it is by no means surprising that the outermost districts of this region produce animal and human monstrosities" *(animalium hominumque monstrificas effigies . . .) (NH,* VI, xxxv, 187). In this case, the climate is invoked as a complementary explanation. Yet geographical distance has been, from the beginning, the criterion of measurement and classification. Pliny starts with a statement about the names of communities living in Libya: "the names of its peoples and towns are absolutely unpronounceable for everyone [*nomina vel maxime sunt inneffabilia*], except by the natives" *(NH,* V, i, 1). A similar pronouncement is found in Strabo's description of ethnic groups inhabiting Cantabria and the Vascones in Europe: "I shrink from giving too many of the names, shunning the unpleasant task of writing them down—unless it comports with the pleasure of someone to hear 'Pleutaurans,' 'Bardyetans,' Allotrigans,' and other names still less pleasing and of less significance than these" (3, 3, 7).

It now becomes clearer that the linguistic gift of the Oiorpata as described by Herodotus is ambiguous. In effect, they had to learn the language or, at any rate, to make themselves understood in the great (Greek) or a lesser (Scythian) socio-cultural context. The Scythian *neotatoi* did not have to. They were indeed classified as barbarians living on the extreme margins of the *oikoumene,* but they were still human beings, despite the strangeness of their culture and its customs. For the Oiorpata not to be rejected in the absolute primitiveness of nature and to appear on a map of humanity as conceived by the Greek paradigm, the price to be paid was, at least, a linguistic acculturation.

Acculturation meant, in practice, a radical conversion to the Greek or Roman model of life. Its implications included abandoning one's original language and becoming a member of the Greek or Roman *politeia,* and, if possible, acquiring rights of citizenship in the *polis* or *urbs*. Only such a conversion could bestow on people the virtues of gentleness *(emeron)* and civility *(politikon)*.

About the Cantabrians, Strabo writes that in their culture "there are [...] things which, although they do not mark civilization, perhaps are not brutish." One of them is "the custom among the Cantabrians for the husbands to give dowries to their wives, for the daughters to be left as heirs, and the brothers to be married off by the sisters" (3, 4, 18). This is an obvious picture of a *thēlukratēs,* which Strabo considers not to be a mark of "civilization" (3, 4, 18).

The rule of women constitutes a problem. It can exist only on the margins of the Greek and Roman *politikon,* as could a city with Douloi (slaves) in power. There is the well-known statement by Aristotle in his *Poetics:* "Both a women and slave can also be good; but a woman is perhaps an inferior being—and a slave utterly worthless" (15, 1454a, 20–22). Pierre Vidal-Naquet, who exploits this thesis, masterfully demonstrates two things: first, that in spite of the differences which are involved, "the Greek city in its classical form was marked by a double exclusion: the exclusion of women, which made it a 'men's club'; and the exclusion of slaves, which made it a 'citizen's club.' (One might almost say a threefold exclusion, since foreigners also were kept out; but the treatment of slaves is no doubt merely the extreme case of the treatment of foreigners.)" (in Gordon 1982: 188). Second, "whether we are talking about the Amazons or the Lycians, it is the Greek *polis,* that male club, which is being defined by its historians and its 'ethnographers' in terms of its opposite [...]. There is a splendid example of this technique of inversion, or reversal in Herodotus's statement that the institutions of Egypt are exactly the opposite of those of the Greeks (2, 35)" (in Gordon 1982: 190).

The Oiorpata's gynecocracy and the mythic doulocracy of a slave's city (always situated outside of Greece—see Vidal-Naquet in Gordon 1982: 189) are structural reversals of the Greek paradigm of civilization and organization of power. Two formulas may sum up the basic philosophy: women are to men as slaves are to citizens; a gynecocracy or a doulocracy is to the *polis/urbs* as barbarism or savagery is to the *politikon.*

The *politikon* is a locus of knowledge, says Simonides, giving to the verb *to dokein* a power superior to the traditional and religious *aletheia.* It is the city which constitutes (educates, creates, accomplishes) a man. He writes: πόλις 'ἀνδρα διδασκει. As noted by M. Detienne, "*dokein* is, in effect, a technical term of political vocabulary. It is an exemplary verb of political decision" (1967: 117). Simonides was the first poet to celebrate the achievements of citizens who sacrificed themselves for the city or honored it by their deeds. A new concept was then taking form, that of "a healthy man," exemplified by national heroes, athletes, and indeed by courageous colonists who expand overseas a *politikon* and its values. From the fifth century on, a democratic and highly secular frame defined intellectual norms in which *dokein* is intertwined with its etymological parent, the *doxa,* the only mode of knowing things which, according to Plato and Aristotle, is adapted to a contingent and ambiguous world (see Aubenque 1963; Detienne 1967). The semantic field of the *politikon* specifies the practical space of truth with such concepts as *politikos* (what befits a citizen), *politikos* (way of acting like a citizen), the *politika* (civil affairs), and *politai* (organized social groups of citizens living in a community).

Narratives about the margins and the exteriority of the club of *politai* illustrate differences evaluated from a central canon. As M. I. Finley wrote,

> The history of what is conventionally called Greek "colonization," [is] in reality the history of Greek expansion between about 1000 and 550 B.C., to Asia Minor and the coastal areas surrounding the Black Sea in the east, to Southern Italy, Sicily, and along the Mediterranean in the west. The Greek tradition, scattered in a multitude of writers from Herodotus to Eusebius, consists of a *chronological framework* (and, by the end, in very precise dates), anachronistic propaganda on behalf of the Delphic oracles, and anecdotes. No history of colonization was possible on that basis. (Finley 1987: 95; my emphasis)

Let us now focus briefly on an ancient interpretation examining how knowledge about the margins of the *politikon* is produced. In his *Geography,* Strabo mentions apropos of Spain three major procedures. The first is Homer's method of manipulating historic legendary facts (e.g., the expedition of Heracles and of the Phoenicians to Iberia) and turning them into mythic arrangements, as in the case of the *Iliad* (3, 2, 13). Homer transferred "from the domain of historical fact to that of creative art, and to that of mythical invention so familiar to the poets." The second practice is represented by Herodotus, the recorder (3, 2, 14). Last comes the Roman practice of expanding their own *civilitas* (mode of life, language, and rights; e.g., about the Turdetanians, 3, 2, 15).

Parallel to these concrete practices, Strabo explicitly (3, 4, 19) comments upon the credibility of these cultural discourses and classifies the degree of their pertinence. Hierarchically, there come first the least credible: those of "all the nations that are barbarian and remote as well as small in territory and split up." "Their records are neither safe to go by nor numerous." Remoteness from the Greek patron entails few and unsafe records. In any case, as Strabo puts it himself, "As for all the nations, of course, that are far off from the Greeks, our ignorance is still greater." Then comes a second category of records and discourses, the Roman. Strabo concedes that Romans know how to record and insists on their fondness for self-knowledge, but on the whole he belittles their archival enterprise. It is a poor imitation of the Greek practice. As he says, "The Roman historians are imitators of the Greeks, they do not carry their imitation very far. Hence, whenever the Greeks leave gaps, all the filling in that is done by the other set of writers is inconsiderable—especially since most of the very famous names are Greeks." The only credible and plausible discourse would seem to be and, from Strabo's classification, could not but be Greek. He affirms it rather beautifully: "indeed our ears are filled with these things [i.e., knowledge about regions, migrations, geographical divisions, etc.] by many, and particularly by the Greeks who have come to be the most talkative of all men."

The nameable which circulates in the margins of a spatialized knowledge seems to reflect the unnameable of the everyday existence. The deviation it unveils as knowledge about *agrioi, barbaroi,* or *oiorpata* is already there, simultaneously explicit and negated in the regions where some members of the city are confined or required to withdraw. Aristotle's paradigm on marriage, which is to a girl what war is to a boy, duplicates the servitude of the *doulos* as an antithesis of the freedom of the citizen. In this rationality and its activity, a general classification of the unnameable and monstrosities (living in the darkness surrounding the *polis*) reflects itself in a series of humorous possible transformations.

"Now," says Strabo, "the wanderings of the Greeks to the barbarian nations might be regarded as caused by the fact that the latter had become split up into petty divisions and sovereignties which, on the strength of their self-sufficiency, had no intercourse with one another; and hence, as a result, they were powerless against the invaders from abroad" (3, 4, 5). I read this passage several times to make sure that I really understood it, knowing that in the fifth century the city down the valley from Athens or Sparta was an autonomous state. No, the statement is absolutely correct. It synthesizes well the meaning of "a place" as a reference-schema which haunts a tradition and its knowledge. A space, the Greek, has become, thanks to such articulations, a general organizing principle of knowledge and cultures. Even the procedures of my present reading seem to depend on the explanation of that experience which has invaded our ordinary lives. The wandering Greeks, the Roman conquerors, and then Lafiteau in the eighteenth century faced this very issue of "a science of barbarians" which could not include the Greeks as a comparative category (Vidal-Naquet 1986: 129 ff.; Pagden 1982: 198–209). Applied anthropology in this century has backed up Strabo's analysis, defining its project as a scientific reactivation of the Greek and Roman politics. Apropos of peoples inhabiting the border of the Rhodanus Strabo had this note, which could serve as a concluding metaphor to my reading: "the name of the Cavari prevails, and people are already calling by that name all the barbarians in that part of the country—no, they are no longer barbarians, but are, for the most part, transformed to the type of Romans, both in their speech, and in their modes of living, and some of them in their civic life as well" (4, 2, 12).

Triumph, of the *politikon* and the *politeia* in a conquering cultural action of conversion. Yet is it not really also fear of *agrioi, oiorpata,* and other monsters, that is, the fear of difference?

Black Athena

> Finally, I should like to return to the critical
> issue of the title *Black Athena*. I must admit

> that I did originally suggest it as a possible
> title, but on thinking it through I wanted to
> change it. However, my publisher insisted on
> retaining it, arguing: "Blacks no longer sell.
> Women no longer sell. But black women still
> sell."
>
> —M. BERNAL, *Arethusa*, Fall 1989: 32

Martin Bernal's volumes on *Black Athena,* subtitled *The Afroasiatic Roots of Classical Civilization,* constitute an event. Volume one (1987) is concerned with "The Fabrication of Ancient Greece 1785–1985," volume two (1991) with "The Archaeological Documentary Evidence." Others are to come and should confirm, unless Bernal undergoes a major psychological conversion, the thesis he has been so far expounding about two things: the origins of Greece, and the implications of these origins. Bernal's thesis is based painstakingly on the hypothesis of two conflicting models about Greek origins: an Ancient one, and its reversal, an Aryan one. Under the former, "it was maintained that Greece has originally been inhabited by Pelasgian and other primitive tribes. These had been civilized by Egyptian and Phoenician settlers who had ruled many parts of the country during the 'heroic age'" (1991: 1). And, in the second, or Aryan, model, which emerged at the end of the eighteenth century in European scholarship, "Greek civilization was the result of culture mixture following a conquest from the north by Indo-European speaking Greeks of the earlier 'Pre-Hellenic' peoples" (1991: 1).

The project is ambitious. The 1987 volume begins by distinguishing a *model* from a *paradigm.* The first is artificial and arbitrary, being "a reduced and simplified scheme of a complex reality" (1987: 3). Thus, from this definition, one model might be more productive or more reliable than another "in its capacity to explain the features of the 'reality' confronted" (1987: 3). By paradigm, Bernal understands "generalized models or patterns of thought applied to many or all aspects of 'reality' as seen by an individual or community" (1987: 3). The distinction between *model* and *paradigm* being clarified, let us then face Bernal's central thesis: the overthrow of the Aryan Model. He writes:

> If I am right in urging the overthrow of the Aryan Model and its replacement by the Revised Ancient one, it will be necessary not only to rethink the fundamental bases of 'Western Civilization' but also to recognize the penetration of racism and 'continental chauvinism' into all our historiography, or philosophy of writing history. The Ancient Model had no major 'internal' deficiencies, or weaknesses in explanatory power. It was overthrown for external reasons. For 18th- and 19th-century Romantics and racists it was simply intolerable for Greece, which was seen not merely as the epitome of Europe but also as its pure childhood, to have been the result of the mixture of native Europeans and colonizing Africans and Semites. Therefore the Ancient Model had to be overthrown and replaced by something more acceptable. (1987: 2)

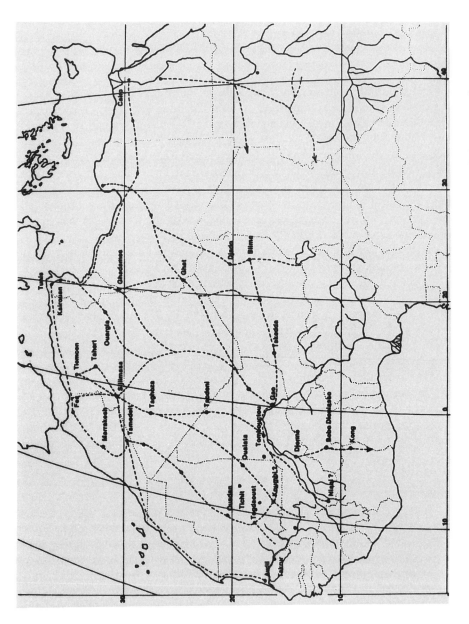

The principal commercial axes across the Sahara Desert between the eighth and the sixteenth centuries and the avenues of Islamic penetration into the *bilad al-sudan,* or "land of the Blacks." Drawing after

Bernal promotes a "Revised Ancient Model" that demonstrates that although "all Ancient Egyptians [did not resemble] today's West Africans, [Egypt is] essentially African" (1987: 437). And he adds: "the fundamental reason I am convinced that the Revised Ancient Model will succeed in the relatively near future is simply that within liberal academic circles the political and intellectual underpinnings of the Aryan Model have [today] largely disappeared" (1987: 437).

The very opposition between Ancient and Aryan models might seem puzzling. As an American graduate student with a Classics background, Denise McCoskey, reminded me after reading the first volume for one of my classes, the tension between the adjectives "Ancient" and "Aryan" is questionable. Her statement was—and she is right—

> Ancient versus Aryan, while politically important for Bernal, however, is problematic from the outset. Most obviously, the tactic implies both that all scholarship in the "Aryan" period was racist and that none of the ancient scholarship was. This very assumption, however, is undermined, though never satisfactorily addressed by Bernal [. . .] who is forced to concede at times both that ancient authors omitted mention of African/Phoenician influences [. . .] and that earlier modern scholars criticized the tenets of the Aryan model during its formulation.

Bernal is admirably clear in noting what he wishes: to rediscover, if he could, a plausible "nature" of Athena by expounding a *revised* Ancient model. His first volume tries to make the point in ten chapters. They can be grouped around three main themes: the existence of the Ancient Model (chapters 1, 2, 3), the rise and triumph of the Aryan Model (chapters 4, 5, 6, 7), the competition of the two models, antisemitism, and racism (chapters 8, 9, 10).

In three concise opening chapters, Bernal seeks to show both the fact and effects of the Ancient Model by taking a historical perspective which begins with two difficult issues: first, that of Pelasgoi or proto-Greeks, who, according to Herodotus, claims Bernal, would have been "colonized and to some extent culturally assimilated by the Egyptian invasions." Bernal defines them as "Indo-European speaking peoples," but overlooks the problem created by Herodotus's statement that marks the Pelasgoi as a "non-Greek-speaking-populace." In any case, Bernal, using startling evidence, insists that they were taught by Egyptians how to worship the gods. They would have mixed with the Hellenes some time during the second millennium B.C. The second issue concerns the Ionians, who were living on the Anatolian shore and whom Herodotus assimilated to Pelasgoi. The two issues combine to show the fact of a (cultural) colonization by Egyptians and Middle-Easterners. Indeed, Bernal focuses on the civilizing roles of such foreigners as Danaos (from Egypt) and Kadmos (from Sidon), and his close reading of Aeschylus's *Suppliants* enables him to make a powerful case for the thesis of an Ancient Model.

Bernal also refers to ancient witnesses drawing, for example, upon the testimony of Herodotus, who "derived Greek customs from the East in general and Egypt in particular" (1987: 100). As Herodotus wrote:

I will never admit that the similar ceremonies performed in Greece and Egypt are the result of mere coincidence—had that been so, our rites would have been more Greek in character and less recent in origin. Nor will I allow that the Egyptians ever took over from Greece either this custom or any other. (Herodotus, II, 55–58)

The nationalism of Thucydides, who rejects all civilizing marks from foreigners such as Danaos, Kadmos, or Kekrops, provides evidence supporting the reality of the Ancient Model. Isocrates admits its reality. Plato, his rival, who spent some time around 390 B.C. studying in Egypt, was profoundly marked by the Egyptian culture. As Karl Marx, quoted by Bernal, put it: "Plato's Republic, insofar as division of labour is treated in it, as the formative principle of the state, is merely an Athenian idealization of the Egyptian system of castes" (in Bernal 1987: 106). Aristotle was fascinated by Egypt and by the power of her priests, the inventors of *mathēmatikai technai,* or the mathematical arts. There is more. Christian factors witnessed *a contrario* to the fact of the Ancient Model's power. Two metaphors: "In 390 A.D. the temple of Serapis and the adjacent great library of Alexandria were destroyed by a Christian mob; twenty-five years later the brilliant and beautiful philosopher and mathematician Hypatia was gruesomely murdered in the same city by a gang of monks instigated by St. Cyril. These two acts mark the end of Egypto-Paganism and the beginning of the Christian Dark Ages" (1987: 121–22). Yet, the Egyptian effect remained till the eighteenth century. The Renaissance was fond of Egypt and thought that it "was the original and creative source and Greece the later transmitter of some part of the Egyptian and Oriental wisdom, and the veracity of the Ancient Model was not at issue" (1987: 160). In the seventeenth and eighteenth centuries, Hermeticism, Rosicrucianism, Freemasonry marked the triumph of the Ancient Model. One of the most significant examples was a Roman Catholic priest, the German Jesuit Athanasius Kircher, an ironic reversal of St. Cyril. An astrologist, Kabbalist, and Hermeticist, Kircher was convinced that the ancient Egyptian culture was both a *prisca theologia* and a *prisca sapientia.* For Kircher, it contained both the announcement of Jesus (in Hermes Trismegistos) and the representation of Christianity in a philosophy that made possible Greek rationality.

Napoleon's 1798 expedition to Egypt monopolized and, at the same time, challenged this heritage. The reasons that justified the project provided also explanations for how the Ancient Model had to be challenged. As Bernal notes:

There is [...] no doubt that [Napoleon] was deeply involved in Masonic affairs, that there were many members of the craft in the higher ranks of his army, and that Masonry 'flourished exceedingly' under his rule. [...]

In many ways the elaborate surveys, maps and drawings, and the stealing of objects and cultural monuments to embellish France, was an early example of the standard pattern of studying and objectifying through scientific enquiry that became a hallmark of European imperialism [...].

On the other hand, there were still many traces of the older attitude towards Egypt, and among the scientific members of the Expedition there was the belief that, in Egypt, they could learn essential facts about the world and their own culture and not just exotica to complete Western knowledge—and domination—of Africa and Asia. (1987: 184)

The expedition symbolizes, in reality, the end of the Ancient Model and, in Bernal's analyses, the onset of the Aryan Model.

The argument for the Ancient Model is complex and dense. By necessity, the demonstration is more historical than philological. Skillfully, it brings together disparate but concordant witnesses for its central thesis. But sometimes it overlooks delicate issues concerning the credibility of the texts used. That Herodotus believed in the Ancient Model might be a good illustration. Bernal relativizes the accusations made against Herodotus by Plutarch's *De Herodoti Malignitate* for magnifying barbarians. We know that Herodotus probably visited Egypt after 460 B.C. and that his histories on the Greco-Persian war respond to *a popular expectation,* that is, he offers a knowledge acceptable and accepted by the people. From the beginning of his reports, he cautions the readers: "For my own part, I will not say that this or that story is true" (Herodotus, I, 5). And in his introduction to his "ethnography" of Egypt he states: "So have [Egyptians] made all their customs and laws of a kind contrary for the most part to those of all other men" (Herodotus, II, 35). Indeed, he claims to distinguish *muthoi* (legends) from facts, distinguishing what he has seen from what he was told. But, as a matter of technique, he also adds the *prosthekas,* or stories, which, although related to the topic, are included in order to please a popular audience. In Book IV, while describing the geography and the people living west of Lake Tritonian, he depicts a museum of monstrosities with dog-headed men, headless people who have their eyes in their breasts, humans who have no names, those who do not dream, etc. (IV, 197 and *passim*). What is the credibility of such a presenter? Against Plutarch, who called him a "master of lies," one may choose to believe Strabo, who describes him as a simple recorder, one who *katagrapsai* (Strabo, 3, 2, 14), writes down everything, even foolish and stupid stories. Herodotus for his part has warned us: "I know not what the truth may be, but I tell the tale as it was told to me." I am thus afraid that Bernal is not sufficiently critical of Herodotus's pronouncements. Dionysius of Halicarnassus, who died in 7 B.C., in his putative defense of Herodotus instead charges him by demonstrating that (a) he was mainly concerned by the choice of topics that could please the public (contrary to Thucydides, who dared to describe a war as it happened); (b) Herodotus knew how to sell his stories by beginning with a nationalist position—the Barbarians are wrong and guilty—and ending with the humiliation of these foreigners (contrary to Thucydides' unpopular but scientifically more exacting perspective, which starts with a description of Greek decadence and concludes by picturing the deadly opposition that separated the Lacedaemonians and the Athenians); and (c) Herodotus was concerned with a popular interest: who is right, who is wrong, and, *a priori,* he knew that he had to demonstrate that Barbarians had been wrong. Thucydides, on the other hand, follows a chronological order in his analysis of the Peloponnesian war in order to produce a *ktema es aei,* a lesson from what happened.

Indeed, the question of Herodotus's credibility is linked to another one, more important—the very practice of history and its philosophy. Thucydides (I, 22) and Polybius (e.g., IX, 2, 5) were convinced that history and its study should have a practical purpose, a position shared by Aristotle. This conception of a *factual* and *didactic* history was not that of Herodotus, and is certainly not that of Isocrates and his disciples. In first-century Rome, apart from such exceptions as Polybius and a few others, historians did not conform to the demands of a Thucydides. History, then, desired to please and generally focused on exciting, exotic, and dramatic events, often inventing them. From Herodotus's practice in the fifth century through Thucydides's objectives of rendering a clear vision of what happened to, say, Diodorus Siculus's first-century narratives, the writing of history was submitted to a series of shifting "philosophies," and these manipulate the information that we get from ancient texts.

Although this angle and my critique do not really weaken Bernal's argument about the Ancient Model, they indicate, at least, that a more careful *critique historique* of texts consulted might be useful. I am not even referring here to present-day exigencies of history but rather to the critical awareness actualized already by such ancients as Thucydides and Polybius. The latter, in his *Histories,* paints explicit requirements: (a) *polypragmosyne,* or a sound engagement to personal enquiry, (b) *empeiria,* or a concrete empirical experience, (c) *emphasis,* or the process of transmitting a given knowledge to the reader.

The second theme of Bernal's book involves the negation of the Ancient Model and the promotion of the Aryan Model. Chapter 6 relates this reconversion to the German "hellenomania" as represented by Friedrich August Wolf, Wilhelm von Humboldt, Hegel, Marx, A. H. L. Hereen, and Barthold Niebuhr. They directly or indirectly participated in the preparation for "a full-out attack on the Ancient Model" (1987: 294). According to Bernal, it is thus in the nineteenth century that the Ancient Model collapses. The Orient became the "childhood" of humankind and Greece a "miracle." It is ironic that Karl Marx, the internationalist, was among those who denied the Egyptian impact on classical Greece. Systematic attacks on the Ancient Model would come from the French scholar Petit-Radel and the German Karl Otfried Müller:

> Niebuhr had made it legitimate to reject ancient sources, and had introduced the French and Indian models of northern conquest in Antiquity. Müller had removed the Ancient Model from Greece. More powerful than either of these, however, had been the work of linguists in relating Greek to Sanskrit, and making it clear that Greek was an Indo-European language. Some historical

explanation of this relationship was necessary, and the model of northern conquests from Central Asia fitted well. Thus a clear distinction has to be made
between the fall of the Ancient Model, which can be explained only in exter-
nalist terms—that is, through social and political pressures—and the rise of the
Aryan one, which had a considerable internalist component—that is to say,
developments within scholarship itself played an important role in the evolution
of the new model. (Bernal 1987: 330)

There is a background to this revolution, says Bernal: Romantic linguistics,
the interest in the birth of Indo-European philology and the rise of India,
particularly the love affair with Sanskrit. "The linguistic relationship meant
that Indian language and culture could now be seen as both exotic and familiar, if not ancestral. [. . .] This tie—and the knowledge, through the Indian
tradition, that the Brahmins were the descendants of 'Aryan' conquerors who
had come from the highlands of Central Asia—fitted wonderfully with the
German Romantic belief that mankind and the Caucasians had originated in
the mountains of Central Asia" (Bernal 1987: 229). This would have been
just a sign and a consequence of "hostilities to Egypt" exemplified by the
marriage of Christianity and Greece against "pagan" Egypt, and illustrated
by such luminaries as Erasmus, who, in the sixteenth century, was in fact
confusing hermeticism and Egypt, and Luther, who opposed Rome with a
"Greek Testament." Then there is the idea of "progress," which Europe identifies with herself, and the race-thinking process, which will lead ultimately to
de Gobineau's thematization of racism. Europe, and thus Greece, could not
have been influenced by Egypt.

This hypothesis brings us directly to the third theme of Bernal's book:
antisemitism and racism. According to Bernal, these attitudes "grew up after
1650 and [. . .] this was greatly intensified by the increased colonization of
North America, with its twin policies of extermination of the Native Ameri-
cans and enslavement of Africans" (1987: 201–02). Concepts such as "racial
inferiority" and "slavish disposition" were not really new. Aristotle used them.
They were simply rethought in a new context. Locke, Hume, Kant, Hegel,
and many others helped provide a justification for them. Intersecting with
Romanticism, racism could be seen, notes Bernal, as one of the "forces behind
the overthrow of the Ancient Model." The quest devoted to authentic roots
would largely account, between 1740 and 1880, for the birth of "Indo-
European" philology, "the love affair with Sanskrit," and Friedrich Schlegel's
"romantic linguistics." During the 1920s and 30s, the Semitic influence was
progressively rejected and a normative Aryanism imposed itself, as exemplified, for example, by Gordon Childe, John Myres, or S. A. Cook, for whom
the Semites were simply "middlemen, copying foreign models . . . , reshaping
what they adopt . . . and stamping themselves on what they send out" (Cook
in Bernal 1987: 390).

Although I essentially agree with Bernal's analysis of the impact of racism
(along with such factors as Christianity, the myth of progress, and Romanticism) for the overthrow of the Ancient Model, I would tend to be more

prudent about the history of racism and I would distinguish "race-thinking" from "racism." The distinction is a crucial one and might have important consequences for Bernal's report of the hostility toward Egypt in the eighteenth century. Let us put aside the difficult question of the Greeks' understanding of races, particularly Aristotle's and its exploitation by Christian theologians until the beginning of the eighteenth century.

There is in eighteenth-century France (to contrast Bernal's focus on Germany) a curious paradigm opposing a "race of aristocrats" to a "nation of citizens." It is promoted, indeed, by aristocrats, who have obvious reasons to oppose the democratic movements. The Count de Boulainvilliers, invoking the eternal right of conquest of Franks, who came from Germany and colonized the romanized and decadent Gallics, was expounding a "race-thinking." On the eve of the French Revolution, Count Dubuat-Nançay was proposing an international society of noblemen and arguing that the real origin of French civilization and culture was German. The Count de Montlosier, in the late 1780s, was opposing the Gallics (calling "them" a mixture of races risen from slavery) so contemptuously that the revolutionary Abbé Sièyes, in his 1789 Qu'est-ce que le Tiers-Etat, suggested that the Count and his followers be sent back to their "original German forests." Arthur de Gobineau, also a Count, belongs to this tradition and, objectively, marks the transition from "race-thinking" to "racism." His Essai sur l'inégalité des races was published in 1853. It integrates the belief that two different "races" live in France, the Gallic (formerly Roman slaves) and the descendants of a German aristocracy. Starting with this premise, he comments on and expands his main theses: (a) there is a connection between the degeneration of a race and the decay of a civilization; (b) in all mixtures of races, the lower race becomes dominant; (c) the race of "princes" or "Aryans" is biologically in danger of extinction. The Essai claims to provide a scientific grounding of racism. The history of "race-thinking" should be divorced from the scientific "racism" illustrated by people such as de Gobineau in the mid-nineteenth century. Ironically, the incredible history of racism took place in France when, under Frederick II, Prussian noblemen fought the rise of their own local bourgeoisie. In the eighteenth century, German Romanticism exploded and with it came such concepts as "original roots," "family ties," "innate personality," and "purity of descent." But, as indicated by Hannah Arendt, in Imperialism, part two of The Origins of Totalitarianism (1968), race-thinking comes from outside this nobility but racism is part of a culture and a civilization. From this viewpoint, nazism was not an accident.

Bernal's second volume provides the foundation for the thesis of the first by adducing "archaeological and documentary evidence" in a manner that does justice to the cause of his "Revised Ancient Model." In brief, Bernal argues, and convincingly, that the "Mediterranean space" was an open one and thus promotes a diffusionist thesis against the isolationist one expounded by the Aryan Model. As signs and proofs, he dwells on the fact that, first, mythological narratives of Egypt and those of Boiotia interconnect (e.g., Se-

mele and Alkemēnē, Zeus and Am(m)on, Athena Itōnia and Athena Alalko-
mena, Poseidon and Seth, the origin of Herakles, etc.). Second, he elaborates
on Egypt's influence on Boiotia and the Peloponnese in the third millennium
B.C. and the relationship that can be established between Crete and Egypt
during the Egyptian Middle Kingdom, from 2100 to 1730 B.C. Third, he
dwells on the meager archaeological and documentary traces about Sesōstris'
campaigns and his son's expeditions to Africa and Asia (as referred to by the
Mit Rahina inscription). Indeed, Bernal seems seduced by the "idea of a 'civilized' African marching in triumph not only across Southwest Asia but also
through regions of a 'barbaric' Europe" (1991: 273). He is more convincing
in demonstrating that some Hyksos, who conquered Crete and possibly Thera,
were Semitic speakers (others, Indo-Aryan or Indo-Iranian speakers), and he
is absolutely luminous in detailing how from the fifteenth century B.C. on
there were economic and cultural contacts between Egypt, Mesopotamia, and
the Aegian. A *Pax Aegyptiaca* would have dominated the eastern Mediterranean during Tuthmōsis III's reign, after 1470 B.C.

> The formative period of Greek culture must be pushed back [...] to the 18th
> and 17th centuries BC, in Hyksos times—the age portrayed in the Thera murals.
> It is most likely that it was in this period that the amalgam of local Indo-
> European with Egyptian and Levantine influences that we call Greek civilization
> was first and lastingly formed. (1991: 494)

Evaluating his own project, and particularly the second volume, Bernal
notes two points that deserve emphasis: first, he writes that "the greatest
single outrage in this volume [...] is the elaborate effort to resuscitate
the northern campaigns of the 12th Dynasty pharaoh Sesōstris [—a 'black
pharaoh'—whose (...)] far-reaching conquests were believed until the late
18th century" (1991: 524). Concerning Egypt's influence, he adds: "the only
controversial aspect of my work [...] is to take the Egyptian claims of
knowledge of, activities in, and suzerainty over the Aegean more literally and
seriously than has been customary" (1991: 526). In promoting this Revised
Ancient Model, Martin Bernal consciously inscribes himself in an intellectual
and recent tradition. As he puts it: "since the late 1960s [...] the Extreme
Aryan Model—which made 'the history of Greece and its relations to Egypt
and the Levant conform to the world-view of the 19th century and, specifically
to its systematic racism'—has been under heavy attack, largely by Jews and
Semitists. The important role of Canaanites and Phoenicians in the formation
of Ancient Greece is now being increasingly acknowledged" (1987: 442). Politically, he claims to situate himself "in the spectrum of black scholarship"
(1987: 437), along with W. E. B. Dubois and Ali Mazrui.

Black scholars have, in general, reproached Bernal for having played down
the contributions of the late Cheikh Anta Diop, a Senegalese nuclear physicist
and Egyptologist. Diop is only mentioned in one paragraph of the 1987 volume as someone who "wrote prolifically on what he saw as the integral relationship between black Africa and Egypt, and in the course of this generally

assumed the Ancient Model of Greek history" (1987: 435). Bernal's project considers diffusionist patterns that originated from Egypt toward the north, the west, and the east, as represented by his maps 1, 2, 3 (1991: 531, 533, 534). Diop, in his controverted publications, was more concerned with the interactions between the south and the north. This difference in perspective might account for the fact that Bernal underexploits other potential powerful "allies" of his, such as Sir James Frazer, and other anthropologists or Egyptologists—such as E. A. Wallis Budge, Charles G. Seligman, and Henri Frankfort, all of whom were baffled by the "'astonishing similarities' in material and spiritual culture between Egypt and some of our African contemporaries" (in Ray 1991: 184).

Benjamin Ray's book *Myth, Ritual and Kingship in Buganda* is important and makes a difference apropos of Buganda. The book is divided into seven chapters. The first analyzes the early ethnography of the nineteenth and the early twentieth centuries. While noting the contributions of travelers, missionaries, and colonial officials, Ray chooses to focus on those of Sir Apolo Kaggwa (1869–1927), the first regent of the kingdom, on the Reverend John Roscoe (1891–1932), a CMS missionary in Buganda, and on the influence of Sir James Frazer. As Ray put it: "taken together, the writings of Roscoe and Kaggwa constituted a unique two-dimensional picture of late-nineteenth-century Buganda, indigenously described in Kaggwa's Luganda works and systematically presented in Roscoe's ethnography written according to Frazer's ethnographic and theoretical scheme" (1991: 23). Ray's first chapter is a fascinating description of how the ethnographic knowledge of Buganda was produced. Frazer, who had never been to Africa, was the master thinker orienting Roscoe (and through him, Kaggwa) and shaping his descriptions and interpretations of ritual practices (birth, marriage, death, etc.), ritual homicide, kingship, etc. In fact, *The Golden Bough* was the mirror from which Buganda ethnography and anthropological knowledge sprang.

Ray moves on to a presentation of the mythological beginning of Buganda with Kintu, the origin of the kingship, and the signfication of the king's body. The progression is exemplary: it goes "from Kintu-the patriarch to Kintu-the-royal founder" (1991: 74), or, let us say, from a reading of mythical narratives to historical interpretations about Buganda, and, in chapter three, to the presentation of a theory of the symbolism of the royal body. In the process of studying the Buganda kingship (or *Kabakaship,* the king being known as Kabaka), Ray provides views of symbolic and historical interactions between the primal ancestor and the living Kabaka. The two orders reproduce also other complementary orders: the myth or legends *(Lugero)* that illuminate the beginnings, and the historical narratives *(Byafaayo)* witnessing to the foundation of the kingdom some time in the late thirteenth century. But in which sense are the *Byafaayo* different from the *Lugero,* and what are the features that allow them to be qualfied as historical?

The rupture from the mythical is interestingly incarnated by the same Kintu who actualized the genesis of a culture. The event is a major one. Let us note that, according to a number of students of Central and Southern Africa (e.g., Alexis Kagame), *Kintu* (designation of a being without intelligence, indeed, as a being-in-itself) is part of a table of basic linguistic categories that would include *Muntu,* or being of intelligence, *Hantu,* which expresses "time" and "place," and *Kuntu,* designating modalities. An examination of linguistic data from the south of Buganda and the area of Great Lakes could have enriched Ray's description of the mutation incarnated by Kintu. As symbol of the State, the *Kabaka* was treated as "most sacred"; hence the ambiguity of his body. Ray offers good descriptions of this ambiguity apropos of codes of etiquette, the royal corpse, the royal mediums, etc. Luc de Heusch has observed and studied the same phenomena in the Bantu-speaking areas, as witnessed to by his *Ecrits sur la royauté sacrée* (1987) and *The Drunken King* (1982).

Ray's ensuing chapters deal with three themes: the royal shrines, regicide and ritual homicide, and Buganda and ancient Egypt. They are interdependent. The royal shrines spatialize a political power whose inscription on earth is linked to the symbolism of the king's body. In the last chapter, the author cautiously analyzes "speculation and evidence" about a connection between Buganda and ancient Egypt. Focusing on E. A. Wallis Budge's arguments concerning the African origin of Egyptian religion and Charles G. Seligman's racial theory, Ray notes "that important similarities do exist between Buganda and ancient Egypt, some of which are quite striking" (1991: 197), and too prudently adds: "the problem with the comparative work of Budge, Seligman, and Frankfort is that it was so entangled with historical, anthropological, and interpretive issues that it was less than illuminating" (1991: 199).

Insofar as ancient Greece and its multicultural experience are concerned, Bernal missed "other allies" such as Engelbert Mveng, a French-educated Jesuit priest from Cameroon and author of *Les Sources grecques de l'histoire négro-africaine* (1972), and a beautiful book by the French scholar Alain Bourgeois on *La Grèce antique devant la Négritude* (1973).

Bernal's enterprise illustrates how a scientific practice is also a political practice. He is explicitly conscious of this. In his response to criticisms from some classicists, he candidly confessed in the 1989 special fall issue of *Arethusa* that his project was made possible by "the recession of antisemitism" and he adds:

> [. . .] if a Black were to say what I am now putting in my books, their reception would be very different. They would be assumed to be one-sided and partisan, pushing a Black nationalist line, and therefore dismissed.

> My ideas are still so outrageous that I am convinced that if I, as their proposer did not have all the cards stacked in my favor, I would not have enjoyed even a first hearing. However, being not only white, male, middle-aged, and middle-class but also British in America, has given me a tone of universality and authority that is completely spurious. But it's there! So, I must thank my lucky stars, rather than any talent that I may possess for having got this far, even if this is as far as I go. (*Arethusa,* Fall 1989: 20)

I have noted some of my disagreements with Bernal's readings, interpretations, and method. Although I understand the political significance of his work, I am also worried by the fact that his project and its usefulness might, and very probably will, be manipulated by both the oversophisticated and the least critical of his constituencies for reasons that have nothing to do with science and the search for truth. That said, I have to recognize that, whether we like it or not, Bernal's enterprise will profoundly mark the next century's perception of the origins of Greek civilization and the role of ancient Egypt. Indeed, his project witnesses to a reversal of what made possible and founded the slave trade since the fifteenth century: imperialism and colonialism, with their triumph in the nineteenth century and in this century, so well exemplified in the 1930s and 1940s by nazism, their natural product.

IV.

DOMESTICATION AND THE CONFLICT OF MEMORIES

> ... sound humanism does not begin with
> oneself, but puts the world before life, life
> before man, and respect for others before
> self-interest: and [...] no species, not even
> our own, can take the fact of having been on
> this earth for one or two million years—
> since, in any case, men's stay here will one
> day come to an end—as an excuse for
> appropriating the world as if it were a thing
> and behaving on it with neither decency nor
> discretion.
>
> —CLAUDE LÉVI-STRAUSS, *The
> Origin of Table Manners*, p. 508

A meeting on international geography took place in 1876 in Brussels, Belgium. Among its objectives, it stipulated three main projects: the exploration of Central Africa, the introduction of European civilization in the area, and an explicit commitment to oppose the slavery practices still going on.

Leopold II, king of the Belgians, was then interested in Egypt, for he considered it to be an excellent entrance to Africa. During the convention, many people referred to activities of the explorer Colonel Gordon in the region along the Nile, and one of his statements, made in October 1876, lingered in the conference's rooms: a good road from Khartoum to Cairo is the best way to stop slavery practices and also "to bring light" to these areas. An aide to Leopold II, Lambermont, probably at the instigation of the king, tried to reach the colonel. In the meantime, the Belgian Committee of the Association Internationale Africaine (AIA) launched exploratory expeditions in Africa via the east coast. In 1877, the Comité d'Etudes du Haut Congo organized, with the approval of Leopold, an expedition led by the American Henry Morton Stanley. It would create the first outposts of a nascent empire. In 1882, supplemented by a number of Belgians, Stanley occupied the whole region along the Congo River from Uele to Kasai. From the east, other AIA caravans—such as those conducted by Dhanis, Chattin, Ponthier, and Lothaire—explored the

Great Lakes region, attacked Arab positions, and conquered their native friends, known as *"les Arabisés,"* those assimilated to Arab ways. When the AIA was finally officially recognized by the Berlin Conference (1884–85) and Leopold II became the sovereign of the Etat Indépendant du Congo, a huge part of Central Africa had already been conquered and combed by Leopold's mercenaries.

The Vatican followed the AIA's activities carefully. On October 14, 1876, Pope Pius IX (1846–78), the pontiff who saw the end of papal states, had already expressed his benevolent and sympathetic attention for the *oeuvre civilisatrice* of Leopold II in writing to the Baron d'Anethan, the Belgian representative in the Vatican (*Corres. Dipl.,* 1876–78: 27). In fact, the Vatican, after losing its temporal power in Europe, still wished to expand Catholicism elsewhere, and in Africa it relied on Leopold. Since 1848, there had, in effect, existed an "Apostolic Vicariate of Central Africa," organized and staffed by Italian missionaries from Verona with Bishop Comboni as their leader. From the Vatican's point of view, it was clear that "Comboni's and his colleagues' apostolate was going to benefit from the AIA and, on the other hand, the Pope thought that missionaries could contribute to [Leopold's] oeuvre" (Roeykens 1957: 60).

Cardinal Franchi, the prefect of the Sacra Congregatio de Propaganda Fide, was a strong believer in the usefulness of a collaboration between the Church and Leopold's colonial project. In 1878, a young and ambitious man, Bishop Lavigerie, sent a secret "mémoire" to the Vatican on this very issue. Pius IX had passed away on February 7 of the same year. A politician of fortitude, he had been described by Metternich, the Chancellor of Austria, who knew him well, as "warm of heart, weak of heat, and lacking utterly in common sense." Was he the one who encouraged Bishop Lavigerie to dream about the possibility of building a Christian kingdom in Central Africa? The successor, Leo XIII, read Lavigerie's "mémoire." It is said that Leo XIII possessed enough intelligence to be able to imagine the world by looking through a window in the Vatican instead of confronting the real thing directly. At any rate, impressed by the "mémoire," he blessed Lavigerie's project, and, by a decree of February 24, 1878, put him in charge of evangelizing and converting equatorial Africa. The missionary saga begins immediately: on April 22 of the same year a first contingent of "White Fathers"—the disciples of Lavigerie, known by this name because of their white habits—departed from Marseilles. Nine months later the team reached Ujiji, exactly on January 22, 1879, and, in July, King Rumoke of Burundi offered them a friendly reception and authorized the opening of a Catholic mission. On November 25, on the western coast of Lake Tanganyika, near the mouth of the Luwela River in Masanze, the first Catholic mission in the Congo was established.

For political reasons, Leopold would like to have had only Belgian missionaries in his African kingdom. Presumably, they would identify more easily with both Catholicism and Belgian nationalism. Lavigerie, who was by then a cardinal, accepted such a perspective. Another caravan of White Fathers, this time Belgians, left Marseilles in July 1891 for the Congo. A young and articulate man, Victor Roelens, was in the team. This first "holy" Belgian expedition was soon followed by others whose mission was similar: to work, along with Leopold's colonists, for the conversion of Central Africa, transforming its space, its inhabitants, and their cultures. To cite only those missions that reached the area before 1911, let us note the Scheutists in 1888, Sisters of Charity from Ghent in 1892, Jesuits in 1893, Trappists of Westmalle and the "White Sisters" (the female equivalents of the White Fathers) in 1895, Franciscan Missionaries of Mary in 1896, Fathers of the Sacred Heart in 1897, Norbertines from Tangerloo in 1898, Redemptorists in 1899, Spiritans in 1907, Christian Brothers in 1909, Benedictines and Capuchins in 1910, and Domincans, Salesians, Marists, and the Sisters of the Cross from Liège in 1911. Numerous other religious Orders would follow this holy army. At any rate, the number of missionaries increased. In 1909 there were 191 Catholic priests in the Congo. There were 471 in 1920, plus 11 Scholastics, 175 brothers, and 13 lay auxiliaries. By 1930 the number was up remarkably: 639 priests, 16 Scholastics, 252 brothers, 27 lay auxiliaries. Furthermore, Orders of brothers which did not have a priestly component counted 59 members in 1920, 101 in 1930, and 701 in 1939. For the nuns, the quantitative progression is also remarkable: 283 missionaries in 1920, 618 in 1930, and 1,631 in 1939. (See de Moreau, 1944.)

These figures show an amazing movement: a will to convert, to transform, to change radically a space and its inhabitants. In the name of faith (Catholicism) and a nationalist call (to expand Belgium), young Belgian men and women moved to Central Africa convinced that they could engineer a historical rupture in the consciousness and the space of Africans. Terming this "imperialism" does not and cannot account completely for the event. One can dwell, effortlessly, on the curious conjunction of the Vatican's calculations (including frustrations after the loss of pontifical States under Pius IX) and Leopold's expansionist ambitions. Such a logical empiricism seems to confuse *doxa* (yes, missionaries were part of the colonizing process, as shown by the waves of their integration in the building of a Belgian Congo Inc.) and *episteme*, or a general intellectual configuration (indeed, the whole process could also be understood as a historical necessity in the sense that the necessity reflected itself back on dubious principles of "Natural Laws" that, in turn, justified it). Most missionaries did not have the education, much less the time, to ponder such paradoxes flawing their generosity. At any rate, as I shall demonstrate by focusing on Victor Roelens's actions, what such a paradox illustrates is very simple: history, in our case colonial history, exploits so-called scientific laws in order to formulate its practice, but it refers to them only when they can be invoked as causes, as legality, justifying divine parameters. In brief, as Paul Veyne put it: "to bring experienced causality and scientific causality to the same logic is to affirm too poor a truth; it is to fail to recognize the abyss that separates *doxa* from the *episteme*" (1984: 166).

The arrival of all these missionaries in the Congo went along with the refinement and elaboration of an ecclesiastical administrative organization. A papal decree of May 11, 1888, erected a Vicariate of the Belgian Congo independent from that of the Higher Congo created on December 3, 1886. By 1911, there were already ten ecclesiastical regions divided according to religious Orders working in the Belgian Congo: 1. Vicariate of Congo (Scheutists, Trappists of Westmalle, Fathers of Mille-Hille); 2. Vicariate of Stanley-Falls (Fathers of Sacred Heart); 3. Vicariate of Higher Congo ("White Fathers"); 4. Prefecture of Matadi (Redemptorists); 5. Prefecture of Kwango (Jesuits); 6. Prefecture of Higher Kasai (Scheutists); 7. Prefecture of Ubangi (Capuchins); 8. Prefecture of Uele (Norbertines and Dominicans); 9. Prefecture of Northern Katanga (Spiritans); 10. Prefecture of Katanga (Benedictines).

Whenever possible, each feminine Order works with its male counterpart. Thus one finds Benedictine, Franciscan, Trappist women, or White Sisters working with their male equivalents in the same ecclesiastical areas. Exceptions exist though, as in the case of the Sisters of Charity from Ghent, who were working in the Vicariate of Congo with Scheutists, in the Prefecture of Matadi with Redemptorists, and in Katanga with Benedictines.

In brief, the separation of Orders and thus the specialization of regions means something important: the necessity of respecting, at least in principle, specific charismas and vocations as postulated by a religious tradition. One might describe stereotypically some of the vocations: a Benedictine, in principle a contemplative, submitted to the rule of prayer and work, lives in a monastery far away from the world; a Dominican, although a monk, is a man of action, well drilled in Christian philosophy and theology in order to defend and illustrate intellectually the pertinence of Christianity; a Franciscan, in the tradition of St. Francis, tends to witness to the magnificence of God's creation and by the poverty of his or her life illumines the glory and liberty of God's children; Jesuits, as they have been rightly perceived, are soldiers who, *perinde ac cadaver,* use the best of themselves to foster Catholicism; Scheutists, organized in the nineteenth century, constitute a community of men who rigorously prepare themselves as missionaries in foreign countries, as do the White Fathers and Sisters. Most of these Orders are known as religious Orders, according to the Canon Law and the Tradition, and differ from the secular clergy, which in Europe is normally in charge of the spiritual life of Christians, animating parishes and most of the works of Catholic dioceses. The Orders intervene in worldly affairs only by an exceptional mandate given to them by a local bishop. In a normal Catholic space, these Orders in principle follow their own missions and are part of the Church in the practice of specialized ministries: Benedictines are cloistered monks; Dominicans are respected as theologians; Jesuits are excellent pedagogues and scientists; Redemptorists are preachers and specialize in retreats (until recently their style was rather outrageous: they were known as specialists in verbal and visual representations of hell, which were supposed to re-animate the faithful). In sum, the ordinary life of the Catholic Church in the West, at the parish level, was not in the hands of religious Orders or, to use the technical expression, of Regulars; rather, the secular clergy, the clergy who do not submit to monkish vows and who depend directly upon the local bishop, attend to parish matters.

Here, then, is the Central African political nightmare. In 1911 the Belgian Congo was divided into ten ecclesiastical regions, as listed above. Let us note three things: First, the distribution covered a political geography which coincided with Leopold's kingdom in Africa. Second, those acting as missionaries were Catholic; they were dependent spiritually on Rome. At the same time, almost all of them were Belgians. Thus both Rome and Leopold expected them to carry out in Central Africa the obligations of the Church and the political objectives of the Belgian king, who happened also to be the sovereign of the African state. Third, the African territory was submitted analytically to spiritual representations of religious Orders and thus forced into constraining patterns: the Catholic converts of Kasai identified with a Scheutist referential horizon, those in Kwilu with that of a Jesuit, those in the northeast with that of a Dominican, those in the east with that of a White Father, and those in Katanga with a Spiritan in the north, a Benedictine in the south, and so forth.

This is a major point because, contrary to what one might think, it touches an essential axis of the politics of conversion. The act of conversion manifests itself in a number of stages, of which we will identify at least three: (1) There is a referential symbol, in this case a human being, who speaks in the name of both political power and absolute truth. (2) The speech communicating this has an edifying style, a spirituality, and, at any rate, refers itself to an absolute truth; its efficacy might be political and Catholic (which makes it credible, convincing); yet it ascribes itself into a style which makes the speech specific, seducing, and thus spells out its power. Attempts to elucidate the specificity of these various speeches result in the imposition of what can only be some poor symbolic and controversial passages: brilliance is Dominican; efficiency, Scheutist; resourcefulness, White Father; patience, Benedictine; intellectual power, Jesuit, etc. (3) The alienation process is the phase where the convert, individually a "child," assumes the identity of a style imposed upon him or her to the point of displaying it as his or her nature; the conversion has then worked perfectly: the "child" is now a candidate for assimilation, insofar as he or she lives already as an entity made for reflecting both a Christian essence and, say, a Domincan or a Franciscan or a Jesuit style.

These three stages are only theoretical constructs and are in conflict with other factors such as the area of birth (rural or urban), ethnic origin, and type of education. The startling thing is, however, that in order to understand the politics of African independence in the 1960s, one should still look carefully at these three stages of conversion and their symbolic patterns. It has been said, and rightly so, that most of the politicians of the 1960s throughout Central Africa were former seminarians. Political scientists have, however, emphasized "tribal" factors. It may be that other factors were also playing a different game, and an important one. The Congo was, in any case, an interesting experiment. Its geography had been turned into a kind of spiritual checkerboard on which each unit or square was occupied by a definite religious style.

How real was the impact of these "idiosyncrasies"? At least let us note one intriguing political coalition that seemed to spring from a socioreligious context. During the first Congolese Republic, some of the most powerful politicians of the moment, such as Joseph Kasa-Vubu, head of the state, Joseph Ngalula, Albert Kalondji, Joseph-Albert Cardinal Malula, and Auguste Mabika-Kalanda, were former students of Scheutists. They used to meet on a regular basis as "former students of Scheutists" and shared between them a "common" language, despite their ideological differences. On the other hand, how is one to account for the fact that when, under the sponsorship of the United Nations intervention in the Congo, the Adula government was constituted, several of its members happened to be former seminarians who had been inducted into the Rosicrucian movement?

Victor Roelens as a Paradigm

Nothing, absolutely nothing, at least at first sight, would have prepared Victor Roelens to become a historical monument anywhere. He was born on July 21, 1858, near the Château des Comtes de Jonghe d'Ardoye, where his father was a gardener. Victor learned at a young age where he came from. He was poor, had to work hard, and yet very early managed to reconcile an acute sense of not belonging with a style of composedness and his attraction for nature. One of his admirers, N. Antoine, wrote of him that "from his youth, he kept till his death a passion for rustic life and work, love of flowers and he cultivated them fondly." Roelens went to the College of Tielt. After one year at the seminary in Roulers, he moved, in 1880, to the novitiate of White Fathers in Algeria, at the Maison-Carrée. By then he was twenty-two years old. On September 8, 1884, at twenty-six, he was made a priest by Cardinal Lavigerie. Then Victor Roelens began a nomadic life. Successively, he assisted Cardinal Lavigerie in anti-slavery committees, worked at the organization of a White Father pedagogy at Woluwé-Saint-Lambert, and taught theology at Saint Ann, a major seminary in Jerusalem. In 1891, Roelens became a member of the caravan that left Marseilles on July 4 for Central Africa via Zanzibar.

"White Fathers" were by then firmly emplaced in East Africa. The AIA had even made possible the foundation of their first missions: Karema and Mpala. Another caravan was that very year traveling to the area and was composed of former pontifical Zouaves converted by Lavigerie to his African cause. They were going to the Tanganyika region to fight the Arab slave trade. On January 27, 1890, Captain Joubert, whose basis was Mpala, had militarily confronted Katele, the chief of Murumbi and an ally of the Arabs. The first anti-slavery expedition directed by Captain Jacques arrived in Mpala just a few weeks before the group of Father Marquès, apostolic adminstrator, which included Victor Roelens. On March 16, 1892, Roelens, accompanied by an aide, Brother Stanislas, founded Saint Louis of Kimbaka. The following year, due to a confrontation between the Independent State and the Arabs, the two missionaries moved to Kirungu, where they created Baudoinville. Roelens, named in the same year an apostolic adminstrator of the Vicariate of Higher Congo by Rome, would be a bishop in 1896. By then, the general activity of his Order had already, at least statistically, made a difference. The area counted two mission-parishes, 750 Christians and 4,771 catechumens.

Roelens noted everything, explicated and justified everything. The complex is well-known. An insecurity of origins is compensated for by a systematic affirmation of competence. Roelens identifies via a projected competence: he must be perfect, or, at any rate, conform to the demands of being a civilized person, a good priest, and an exemplary missionary.

In 1893, Bishop LeChaptois, Roelens's boss, had invited Roelens to move from Kimbaka to a plateau in the Marungu mountains. Kimbaka was too insecure, too often attacked by slave traders. Baudoinville, the new base, named after the Belgian prince who had just passed away, was not very far—in fact only a few kilometers—from Saint Louis du Murumbi, where Captain Joubert, a former Zouave now serving as the secular arm of the White Fathers, lived. On May 8, 1893, Roelens and his new assistant, Brother François, spend their first night on the Marungu plateau. They get up the following morning completely surprised: the climate, fresh and somehow maritime during the night, has won them over. They begin building the mission. In three weeks, the essential is established, consisting of the residence, an orphanage, and a church that can contain eight hundred people. This leads the missionaries to take responsibility for the fate of the village and its life by opening up workshops, farmyards, and various projects.

Village life was now subordinated to the missionaries' schedule. After the space, which they reorganized according to a new memory exemplified by the Church, the missionaries rapidly command time and its categories. There will be a religious economy of days, weeks, months, years, espousing a liturgical calendar, and also specific new daily ritual arrangements. As an entity, the village comes to life at dawn, morning prayers follow the mass, and immediately after comes "Christian instruction." Men, women, children, Christians, catechumens, each group has its program, its teacher, and its message. The afternoon is devoted to a different labor—agriculture or construction, depending on seasons—till 6:00 P.M., the moment of a compulsory evening prayer. A dinner follows and then, till 9:00 P.M. curfew, recreation. The missionaries have regulated everything. In actuality, a lot of smoking and dancing go on, but, to prevent "moral problems" (remarkable naïveté), men and women cannot dance together.

In 1898, five years after the arrival of Victor Roelens, Baudoinville was a small city, with imposing buildings for the clerics, a dispensary, two orphanages, five schools for boys and four for girls. The missionaries still spent much of their resources "buying" the freedom of slaves. Officially, for the government, slave trade had not existed since 1894. But the reality is different and much more complex. Roelens writes, for example, that 50 francs are enough to take care of a young woman slave and that he needs 10,750 francs for 250 former young slaves.

> They live very poorly, our little woman protégées. Every two months, we give to each one of them 1.50 to 2.00 meters of white cotton fabric. The most skilled among them succeed in clothing themselves more or less pretty well. [...] For food, they get every day at noon some sweet potatoes or cassava roots [...]. It is their first meal. In the evening, they get an individual bowl of corn meal or of manioc that they eat with beans. Twice a week, they are given some salt. For important festivities, we try to give them a few small fishes and they love them.

Is such a life a blessing, even for someone coming out of slavery? The new order that the gardener's son expounded theoretically and actualized in his diocese obeyed complex grids. Thus, for Victor Roelens the place of anyone in the church should correspond to his rank. The altar and its space—*terribilis locus*—should be reserved for the clergy; then comes the space reserved for white people; after this is the greater nave, that of black Christians; finally comes the lower nave for the catechumens so that, as Victor Roelens puts it, "they can feel excluded from the celebration of the most sacred mystery and thus experience better their inferiority vis-à-vis the Christians."

This quotation illustrates the project of conversion. It is not only a dream, but a politics that disciplines beings, space, and time in the name of unspoken models. Victor Roelens offered the following significant statement: "Mpala as well as Baudoinville, at this moment, makes me think of a good parish in the Flanders." Here then dreams, models, politics fuse simply. Why should they be separated? The apparent excessive investment in one direction can be considered as a lack in a different system. Anthropology can speak to natural history and to Catholic theology; on the other hand, the right to colonize, as Roelens lived it, brings together theories about the evolution of species, natural law, and imperialism.

Two additional examples witness to the paradoxical and surprising coincidence of the two different orders. First, in 1895, Roelens, accompanied by Father De Beerst, some twenty assistants, and a dozen seamen, left Baudoinville. His objective: to explore the Kivu region, penetrated for the first time by a European, the Baron Von Götsen, that very year. After one week of navigation on the Tanganyika, Victor arrives at Uvira, a military post of the State. From there he walks with his people toward the mouth of the river Udjiji and then sets out to reach the mountains separating the Kivu area from Tanganyika. Unfortunately, the daily contacts with local peoples are not very good; moreover, mutineers storm the region between the Maniema and the Tanganyika. Exhausted, his aides decide not to continue the expedition. It is an overt rebellion. Physically sick, feverish, Roelens capitulates and the caravan returns to Baudoinville. Victor Roelens and his little army were only thirty kilometers from their objective, and had already covered six hundred kilometers when they decided to give up.

A second example illustrating Roelens's political complexity may be derived from a letter. A member of a scientific mission, the Belgian Charles Lemaire, wrote to Victor Roelens in April 1900 to thank him for their stay in Baudoinville. The letter celebrates Roelens and his collaborators. Their collective works incarnate something very exceptional: they are wonder-makers (farmers, builders, architects, lawyers, doctors, etc.). Makers of monuments, such as the Mpala Roman Church, builders of cathedrals, these White Fathers are also gardeners, excellent cooks, and, indeed, good companions. They have converted an African space to the point of reproducing the Flemish land:

> Ce sont des jardiniers modèles. Le potager de la mission de Baudoinville est unique; on y trouve tout ce que l'on désire, même des pommes de terre d'Europe. C'est là que fut planté le premier caféier. Les Pères se font d'ailleurs un plaisir d'envoyer leurs produits aux avoisinants de l'Etat Indépendant. Aussi faudrait-il entendre parler d'eux les agents de l'Etat. J'ai mangé à Baudoinville du pain gris délicieux, de ce savoureux pain flamand, large comme deux, et ferme.

> [The fathers] are exemplary gardeners. The kitchen garden at the Baudoinville mission is unique. One finds in it whatever he may desire, even potatoes from Europe. It is there that the first coffee shrub was planted. The Fathers delight maliciously in offering their products to the Independent State agents. One should then hear these State agents speak of the Fathers. I ate in Baudoinville a delicious brown bread, a tasty Flemish bread as big as two, and very firm.

The work force is cheap, in fact free: former slaves are put to good use, so to speak, and in return they get a religious education that leads them, after some years, first to a Christian baptism and, after the rite, to becoming citizens of the mission-city. The oeuvre praised by Lemarie expands. Since 1877, White Sisters parallel the work of their male counterparts, caring for native women and staffing dispensaries and hospitals. From 1899, the western region first and then the northern are systematically explored by Victor's priests. New missions are opened. Between 1908 and 1916, Roelens directs his efforts toward the Maniema. His men build new missions there: Katana in 1908, Lulenga in 1910, Bobandana in 1912, Nyemba in 1913. With their architectural investments and projects—the church, missionary residences, schools, hospitals, etc.—they reenact a medieval pattern: a religious center is called to transform an area. It signifies and projects an idea, a vision and its values. The history of a conquest becomes African history, expounding itself as both providential path and replication of civilization.

In 1898, Victor Roelens had invited Father Huys, then director of the school system of his vicariate, to organize a minor seminary to prepare native candidates for the Catholic priesthood. It was located in Lusaka. A second seminary was opened in 1929, at Mugeri. In the meantime, on July 21, 1917, a Congolese, Stefano Kaoze, was ordained the first Catholic priest from Central Africa. African conversion could, from that time on, be thought of in terms of collaboration between White Fathers and their black pupils and, in the long run, as a matter of succession: natives becoming their own agents for spiritual transformation.

Did Victor Roelens succeed in his mission? Let us focus on the man. A photograph from the early 1940s when Roelens decided to retire and was replaced by his coadjutor, Bishop Morlion, unveils an ambiguous personality. This son of a Flemish gardener poses as if he were an old aristocrat. The hair is sparse. The eyes vague, contemplating the camera. He has discreet wrinkles on the face, and dark concentric shadows circle the eyes. Old age—Victor is then more than eighty—has inflated his aquiline nose. The mouth and the lips are almost invisible because of the bushy, long, white, and indeed very mission-ary beard. Victor wears the habit of the White Fathers with its typical North African gandoura. Five medals hang on his chest competing for attention with his rich pectoral cross. The man displays himself majestically and the general ensemble witnesses to the air of conquistadores.

Roelens retired as bishop in September 1941. He was then eighty-three. His successor inherited a powerful enterprise that, despite the fact that an im-portant part of it had become an autonomous vicariate, still numbered, in terms of human resources, 97 missionaries (36 priests, 13 brothers, 48 sisters); 620 local collaborators (18 priests, 11 sisters, 539 male catechists, and 52 female catechists); 13 major seminarians and 86 minor seminarians; 53,349 Christians and 14,084 catechumens. By June 1945, the vicariate included more than 700 schools, 16 dispensaries, 6 hospitals, 3 maternities, 5 asylums, and 2 orphanages. Retiring, Victor reminisced:

> I do not think that I have ever had in my poor head an original, personal idea. Since my early age, I have always been very curious: I wanted to see everybody, to know everything. I have listened to and watched carefully everything, and ideas that I discovered elsewhere and which I found practical for this country, I have asked my collaborators to actualize them by adapting them to the milieu.

Tactics and Strategies of Domestication

Leopold's wish was to domesticate his African state with the help of Belgian Catholic missionaries. Even so, he had to take into account other programs, such as those devised by some of his Protestant friends who participated in the Brussels Conference (see Roeykens 1957). There was also in Belgium itself a solid anti-Catholic movement, represented by, among others, the Association Libérale de Bruxelles, fighting against the transplantation of religious ideol-ogies to Central Africa. The Free Masons were also following the colonial enterprise carefully. According to Victor Roelens, Free Masonry was a militant opponent of the missionary enterprise. One A. Sluys, a former director of the Ecoles Normales de Bruxelles, is said to have declared during an international Masonic conference in Paris that "the worst enemy of people is clericalism and [that] if it is not destroyed in its roots, there will not be a solution to the social question" (*Grand Orient de Belgique,* 1900, fasc. III: 217). In 1897, through an indiscretion, missionaries in Central Africa learned about the Masonic initiation of a candidate explorer during which the necessity of providing a Masonic impact upon "moral actions and projects" of candidates for positions in the Congo was emphasized. Their panic intensified when they learned of the December 25, 1900 meeting of the Grand Orient of Belgium presided over by G. Rogers, the Grand Maître. One of the items dealt with how to slow down Catholic missionary activity in the Congo. According to Roeykens, the minutes contained such statements as: "the conversion of Negroes to Catholicism is not, from the viewpoint of real civilization, a real progress, nor a necessary step"; "Dogmas of the Church or Rome do not constitute, in terms of belief, a superior state and they should not replace Negroes' superstitions"; "Morally, one should not have to choose between [black superstition and the Roman Catholic priest's superstition], they equal each other and must all of them be opposed" (see Roeykens).

Victor Roelens believed in a Masonic conspiracy. In 1913, he carefully studied the list of appointees in Belgian Congo courts and concluded that most of them, apart from three Catholics, were anti-Catholics. Three scandals convinced him that he was right. The local colonial administration had introduced three legal actions: one against the Apostolic Prefect of Kasai, a bishop, for infanticide; two others against two priests, a Redemptorist and a Jesuit, for sexual misconduct. Roelens commented upon what he believed to be a persecution and an "insulting war" (1913: 15). The Church was persuaded that the scandals and attacks came from Masonic nuclei already existing in Léopoldville, Elisabethville, Stanleyville, and Boma. In Brussels, the minster of colonies avoided antagonizing its administration with the Church. Roelens went public on February 5, 1913, attacking the government in *Le Patriote* on the theme that official governmental goodwill does not protect missions against everyday colonial vexations and humiliations. The following day, the Belgian minister responded in the same paper and challenged the accuracy of Roelens's statements. On February 7, Roelens counterattacked, maintaining the essence of his accusations. The debate became a public scandal. On February 12 and 14, the minister had to defend his position in parliament. Four days later, in *Le Matin,* an Antwerp paper, Roelens made his frustration more explicit, focusing on what he considered to be the hostile atmosphere existing in the Congo against Catholic missions. In *La Presse* of February 23, and *Le Patriote* of February 27, he continued his campaign, demanding "la liberté de l'apostolat au Congo," the freedom for converting. The confrontation between Roelens and the then minister, Renkin, had turned personal.

In the Church as well as in political spheres, many people tended then to dismiss both protagonists. Happily for Roelens, the Superiors of Catholic Orders and Congregations working in the Congo collectively backed his positions on March 1 and explicitly referred to the existence of a Masonic conspiracy. In vain, in a response published in *Le XXᵉ siècle,* the minister tried to clarify controverted issues, distinguishing colonial policies, administrative

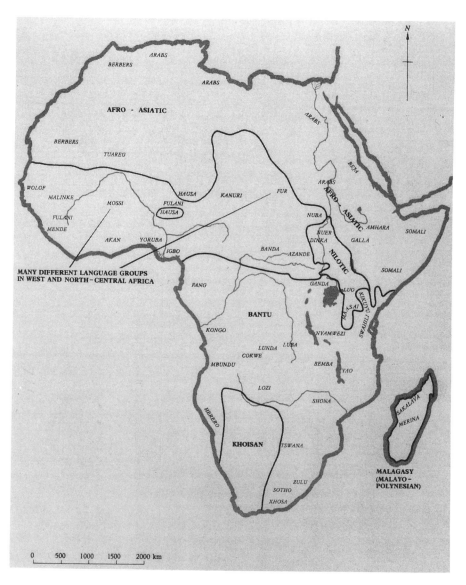

Precolonial Africa. From M. Kwamena-Poh, J. Tosh, R. Waller, M. Tidy, *African History in Maps*. UK: Longman, 1982. Permission the Longman Group UK Ltd.

problems of organizing a colony, and his politics for a collaboration with Catholic missions. Incensed, Roelens responded on March 6, in *Le Patriote*. The whole affair had become excessive. Rome intervened discreetly to calm down both camps. Yet, it was then that Father Thydrat, the Provincial of Jesuits, entered the debate publicly with a pamphlet "defending the missions of Kwango" and criticizing the adminstrative colonial legality which turned

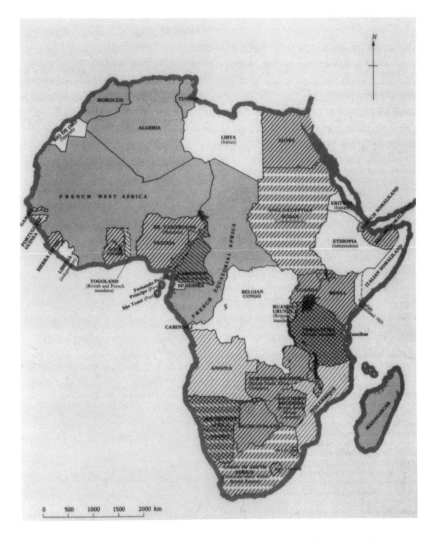

Colonial Africa. From M. Kwamena-Poh, J. Tosh, R. Waller, M. Tidy, *African History in Maps*. UK: Longman, 1982. Permission the Longman Group UK Ltd.

out to be "an anti-religious hostility." The minister reacted by publishing his own booklet in which he, in turn, explained the exigencies of a colonial policy.

Underlying the whole debate is the question of what the right to colonize means. Specifically, is there objectivity or an impartial, truthful background permitting a clear distinction between real, founded, justified "knowledges" and simple opinions? Concretely, should the demands of efficiency in colonizing recognize the possibility of alternative policies, ones competitive ideologically, justified in the "conversion" of the colony? The State did not seem to fear the possibility of judgmental relativisms and, consequently, would accept

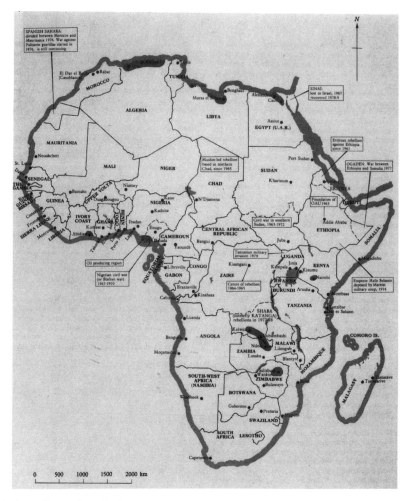

Independent Africa before 1975. From M. Kwamena-Poh, J. Tosh, R. Waller, M. Tidy, *African History in Maps*. UK: Longman, 1982. Permission the Longman Group UK Ltd.

the contribution of Masons, for example, as long as the right to colonize and its basic postulates remain pure references. The Church, on the other hand, saw in such a position an explicit challenge that might undermine its totalitarian priciples. For the most part, its agenda can be summed up in a phrase: conversion to the West is isomorphic with a conversion to Christianity, and therefore to accept non-established Christian ideologies in the colonizing practice would mean to question the very basis of the right to colonize.

The question is important. It precisely demonstrates that the colonial practice was supposed to be guided by a "scientific" and neutral objectivity existing outside of the agents. Colonialism is thus presumptively a science. The debate between Roelens and Renkin demonstrates and actualizes itself as a product of a tension that one can observe in philosophy of sciences between a project of "justified beliefs" and that of "opinions." Sandra Harding has noted recently that

> Insistence on this division of epistemological stances between those that firmly support value-free objectivity and those that support judgmental relativism—a dichotomy that unfortunately has gained the consent of many critics of objectivism as well as its defenders—has succeeded in making value-free objectivity look much more attractive to natural and social scientists than it should. It also makes judgmental relativism appear far more progressive than it is. Some critics of the conventional notion of objectivity have openly welcomed judgmental relativism. Others have been willing to tolerate it as the cost they think they must pay for admitting the practical ineffectualness, the proliferation of confusing conceptual contradictions, and the political regressiveness that follow from trying to achieve an objectivity that has been defined in terms of value-neutrality. But even if embracing judgmental relativism could make sense in anthropology and other social sciences, it appears absurd as an epistemological stance in physics or biology. What would it mean to assert that no reasonable standards can or could in principle be found for adjudicating between one culture's claim that the earth is flat and another culture's claim that the earth is round? (Harding 1991: 139)

Yet, and paradoxically, in the colonial library, as in most social sciences, the absurdity described by Harding has not been seen as such, but, from colonialism to postcolonialization, it is celebrated as a progress, more precisely as an epistemological rupture. But let us focus on Roelens's objectivism and its implications for the conversion of the African space and African minds. At its basis, there is an unshakable belief in the absolute truth incarnated by the Church, and this truth subsequently justifies the usefulness and coherence of an applied science of conversion.

A concrete example might illustrate this. In 1932, Monsignor Dellepiane, just designated by Rome as Apostolic Delegate in the Congo, convoked the first plenary meeting of the *Ordinaires des Missions du Congo-Belge et du Ruanda-Urundi,* that is, of all the bishops in charge of a vicariate or a prefecture. Under the leadership of Victor Roelens, at the news of having in Léopoldville a permanent representative of the Pope, the Catholic missions had decided to build a palace for the Apostolic Delegate. On October 18, 1932, the *Ordinaires des Missions,* as a body, met with the Apostolic Delegate for the first time in Léopoldville. In the address that he made in the name of his colleagues, Roelens, the dean of the group, begins by presenting his submission to the representative of the Pope, then he states their collective "profound veneration" and "filial affection" for the "illustrious King Pontiff" and offers the residence to the Delegate as a sign of the respect that the population, black and white, has for the Pontiff (Roelens, 1932, *Actes:* 20). Moved, Dellepiane honors the bishops for their fidelity to the Church and accepts the gift in the name of the Vatican. Three days later he will interrupt one session of the

Ordinaires to communicate an official message of gratitude from Rome signed by Eugenio Cardinal Pacelli.

Roelens also opened up the sessions of this first meeting of the *Ordinaires* with a substantive report on how to build a "Clergé Indigène," a Catholic local clergy. The document for years had a tremendous impact on official policies for educating Central African clergy. In itself, the expression "Clergé Indigène" seems neutral and implies nothing more than a local, indigenous clergy. It belonged to the missionary language of the area and had found tacit acceptance since 1898 when Roelens ordered Father Huys to organize the first minor seminary. The first member of the "Clergé Indigène" was ordained on July 21, 1917. In itself, the date is a symbol. July 21 also marks the Belgian Independence Day and, as such, could not but mean something special in the mind of Roelens: an integration in the order of Catholic priesthood displays also an assimilation to the political dominant order: the two processes cannot be antithetical. The symbolism of the date of the consecration of the first member of the "Clergé Indigène" is thus simultaneously an accelerator for social and religious transformations and a radical and ambiguous brake. The concept of a "Clergé Indigène" attributes clearly, in effect, specific virtues, unity, and didacticism to all its members: they all shall be black, united under the sponsorship of their educators, and dependent, in principle for centuries to come, upon white superiors and a foreign *magisterium* bearing responsibility for their conversion and guaranteeing their orthodoxy.

That is the project that Roelens elaborates in front of his peers. Christianity as a source and means of salvation and Christianity as a source and means of African renewal cannot be separated, since they aim toward the same objective: Christian life and universal civilization. The rigorous education and promotion of a "Clergé Indigène," of "natives" who can incarnate in their bodies and spirit this didactic program, seem thus a *sine qua non* of the conversion mission.

How was the system to engineer socially the members of this future group? Roelens, (*Actes,* 1932), on the one hand, expounds norms for selecting young boys on the basis of their intellectual, moral, and spiritual orientations and capabilities. They were to be observed, carefully studied, and selected very early. The chosen ones submitted to a new system of life, completely isolated from their ordinary milieu. Then followed three main steps: the minor seminary, eight years (more or less), or the equivalent of the last two years of primary school plus the six years of secondary school; the major seminary, six years (more or less), including two years of philosophy and four of theology; finally, a one- or two-year internship in a Catholic community under the sponsorship of European priests. The first phase of education, the minor seminary, had to conform to three main principles:

(a) Its location and spatial arrangement were to be "adapted" to the "psychology" of the Central African (which, in fact, meant a stylization and a "reconstructing" of a supposedly traditional way of life, submitted to Christian imperatives and surveillance). The seminary buildings were not traditional, but they were not modern either, since they combined, for example, mud buildings and electricity. The seminarians lived in complete isolation and may have had, some kilometers away, a post office or a train station; The rhythm of everyday life submitted to a schedule that had nothing to do with rural or urban life.

(b) This minor seminary, in fact a boarding school, had to be located far from modern life ("éloigné de 'tout centre européen et en dehors du grand mouvement commercial et industriel'"); the aim was to domesticate the students by using the "givens" of their nature and completely converting their behavior to new habits, because, Roelens thinks, "seule l'habitude est stable chez nos Noirs," only habits are stable in "our" blacks. This prescription goes along with very specific strategies of domestication, on which I shall elaborate in the coming pages.

(c) A general policy of acculturation situated these chosen ones between their black brothers and the white colonizers, without reducing them to one or the other group. If their status and behavior were reduced to that of the average black, the project would produce frustrated beings who might develop a negative philosophy ("ce qui les rendrait mécontents de leur situation"); and if they were assimilated too early into the white community, they might become pretentious, demanding, and marginalized ("ce qui les rendrait préten-tieux, exigeants et en ferait des déclassés").

Throughout this long period of acculturation, an average of fifteen years, the candidate learns, in the Foucauldian sense, how to become "a docile body." The seminary structures itself as a "panopticon" through three main factors: the space, which reproduces a monastic model, the repartition of time, and the constitution of transparent consciousnesses.

First, the space. The seminary is a nowhere, situated in the bush. In the Congo, Kabwe, Kafubu, Lusaka, Mayidi, Mugeri, for example, are on colonial maps as ecclesiastical entities. Geographically they are localized outside of real life, constituting themselves as systems in their own right; they are a monastic or carceral order, in their architecture as well as in the orgainization of their buildings, which generally include five main distinct components: the chapel, an area for classes, the professors' residence, refectories, and dormitories. Closed unto itself, without contact with the external world, the seminary is moreover a male and Spartan space. In this respect, it subdues by vocation any dissonance, and only that which is strictly necessary is admitted.

Second, the time. The repartition of time is based on the golden monastic rule of eight by three: eight hours of prayer, eight of sleep, and eight of profane activities such as study, manual labor, sports, and recreation. Seminarians are not monks and their schedule reflects their status. Here is a model based on the normal daily activities realized in most Congo minor seminaries between 1930 and 1960: 5:30 A.M., getting up; 6:00, meditation in the chapel; 6:15, mass; 6:45, studying; 7:30, breakfast; 8:00, class; 12:00 noon, *angelus* and conscience examination; 12:30 P.M., lunch; 1:00, recreation; 2:00, class; 4:00, manual labor; 5:00, studying and spiritual direction; 7:00, dinner followed by recreation; 8:00, evening prayer and last examination of conscience; 8:30, studying; 9:30 P.M., bedtime.

Finally, the transparency of consciousnesses. The seminary pursues the complete deconstruction of an individuality in order "to invent" a new one through three main techniques: (a) thrice-daily self-examinations, before the meditation every morning, after the *angelus* at noon, and just before the evening prayer; (b) an elaborate system of spiritual auto-surveillance, including a weekly confession (during which the candidate supposedly faces his own sins and confides them to a confessor), and a fortnightly spiritual direction, in which the candidate shares with a "spiritual master" his doubts, temptations, and weaknesses and, in return, gets advice; (c) two other systems of regular spiritual renewal: an annual retreat, at the beginning or at the end of each academic year, that forces the students to think about their vocation, and, in the winter, for Advent, and in the spring, during Lent, an explicit invitation for a personal systematic change in response to both the message and the symbolism of the Nativity and the Resurrection of Christ.

The examinations of conscience, the confession as well as the daily mass in the morning and the evening prayer, all begin with the recitation of the *Confiteor*. The recitalist confesses, to God, the Omnipotent, to the Virgin Mary, to Angels and Saints, but also to *vobis fratris*, to "you my brothers," that he is guilty because *peccavi nimis cogitatione, verbo, et opere*, "I have sinned much in thought *(cogitatione)*, speech *(verbo)*, and act *(opere)*." The coherence demanded by this spiritual deconstruction is total: the supplicant exposes himself completely. He has sinned in intentions, in speeches, and in acts; he then submits himself to a perfect and public humiliation: *mea culpa, mea culpa, mea maxima culpa,* "it is my fault, my real fault." And this ritual of self-denigration happens at least three times every day.

Thus space, time, and transparency of consciousnesses are "essential" parts of a plan of domestication. Is the operation different from that which takes place in Europe for the education of Catholic priests? No, in the sense that European seminarists belong to an established order of Christianity, and thus the techniques for their confirmation in the sacerdotal model are organizationally different: if they are submitted to a monastic space and a quasi-identical colonization of time, these are already situated somewhere in their past experience; they are incarnating a tradition which is theirs. At any rate, they are allowed to get out of the seminary space at least for vacation; furthermore, the European procedures of education do not mean, as in the case of their African counterparts, a necessary and absolute conversion of individualities and their psychology, but rather a simple conformation to a paradigm which is part of their culture.

Roelens, in the presentation of his politics of promoting a "Clergé Indigène," stresses this point. He thinks that the expectation of equal performance and determination cannot but be naive. In 1893, "thirteen candidates began studying for the priesthood. Each year after, new ones came. We persevered. Of about two hundred who began studying for the priesthood, only ten have succeeded. 'It is too little' would say those who know Blacks only superficially. 'It is a lot' one would say who knows intimately. 'It is a miracle of grace [. . .]'" (1932: 44). Indeed, it is a perfect miracle when one keeps in mind that these candidates were taught arithmetic, geometry, philosophy, etc. in Latin.

An image might sum up Roelens's politics of conversion. According to many witnesses, he was proud in narrating the advice that King Albert gave to Stefano Kaoze, the first "native" priest, whom Roelens introduced to the Belgian king as his secretary: "Now you are a priest in the evangelizing Church, return there in your country to serve; Blacks are waiting for progress and truth from the Clergé Indigène" (Masson 1936: 80).

Conversion as a Program

The year is 1947. The Right Reverend Father Bernard Mels is the Provincial of the Scheutist missionaries in the Congo. He belongs to a new generation of missionaries. We are in the aftermath of World War II. The *effort de guerre,* which had been imposed upon the inhabitants, has strained the country. The Luluabourg riots, repressed by the colonial administration, have left vivid and haunting memories. A protest letter written by a group of *évolués* (a Westernized middle class sociologically between the white masters and the African masses) explaining the meaning of this exceptional political disturbance circulates secretly within the black and white milieux. Despite the apparent monolithic structure of the adminstrative ideology and policy, new voices begin to be heard. They are mainly surreptitious and critical of most of the methods used for the transformation of the country. Concerning its own politics of creating a middle class, the administration has finally agreed to give to the *évolués* a toy for expressing themselves: *La Voix du Congolais.* They can write to their heart's content; their texts—generally dealing with apparently inoffensive matters such as traditional life and customs, the politics of assimilation, or fiction—are, indeed, when accepted, carefully checked and edited by an editorial board, and then published. The journal has no ambition to call for the questioning of present rulers in the country but, instead, is to be the sign of a Belgo-Congolese community yet to come. Nevertheless, its very possibility is both an interference with, and a partial revision of, long-established ancient policies. From now on, it is accepted, often grudgingly, as a matter of principle, that blacks might become interlocutors. But what kind of blacks?

In the Kasai Catholic vicariate, Christianity had been implanting itself firmly since the last decade of the nineteenth century. After the war, missionaries begin to take into account a dissatisfaction of their followers: Did something go wrong? and what is to be done to correct it? It is in this context that, between September 1946 and February 1947, Bernard Mels gave a series of lectures to his fellow Scheutists, analyzing the political crisis syndrome in the colony and its impact on the evangelizing program.

One could focus on two main issues in Mels's thinking: the necessity of a reconversion of the missionary philosophy, and a new pedagogy that should consider seriously a psychology of culture contact. His leitmotif is the concept of crisis and its historical relativism:

> [W]hen one reads the annals of different peoples' history, it is striking that all historians consider their time as one of crisis, as a historical rupture. This fact is not difficult to explain: in effect, every community, every country constantly evolves and there are always serious problems arising or excesses leading to troubles. Here in the Congo, we are nowadays talking of "evolution," of "revolution" and sometimes the impression given is that things are going upside down and that one should expect worse times coming. There has been always difficulties, and we shall have them always. (Mels 1946–47: 1)

For Mels, the concept of crisis in its most general form is not even a scandal. On the contary, it is part of history and attests to the history of colonization. The European presence in Africa would refer to it explicitly in the transformations that it made possible: an evolution, insists Mels, did take place, creating or furthering social ruptures that might appear revolutionary: "a community begins to agitate, upsetting signs of an old physical and spiritual slavery" (Mels 1946–47: 2). The process seems unavoidable to him, since for its understanding one cannot pretend to oppose science to history. Indeed, riots, the pamphlets of *évolués*, or colonial policies are individualized facts, and knowing them well demands a solid comprehension that cannot but relate them to a universal order of knowledge.

Then Mels focuses on the reasons for the general social malaise in the Congo, pinpointing three main factors. First, there is the distance existing between blacks and whites. Second, he cites the breaking up of African traditions under colonization, which, by expanding new ways of life, would account for a state of insecurity in the minds of many blacks. And, cynically, Mels adds that this situation has probably been achieved thanks to missionary work: "We missionaries can be proud [of what we have done], despite the alarms of certain anthroplogists and bureaucrats who go into ecstacies in the presence of the so-called 'beautiful ancestral customs'" (1946–47: 4). The third factor noted by Mels concerns the distance existing between the rich *(Beati possedentes)* and the poor, those in power and the powerless, which directs the issue toward the problems of new social classes and, more specifically, the problem of the social organization of production under colonization.

For Mels, these three factors or explanations are essential for an understanding of the social crisis. They also justify a change in the policy and strategies of missionary action; to put it in programmatic terms, how should one continue evangelizing without jeopardizing the investment of the past? The easiest temptation would be, according to Mels, to withdraw from the general sociopolitical context and to confine one's activities to priestly and religious commitments. On the contrary, asserts Mels, missionaries should remain active in programs for human promotion by cultivating an interest in the people they serve, by adapting missionary activities to new sociological conditions and following carefully the progressive constitution of the new social group of *évolués,* and by actualizing concretely the official Church doctrine concerning the working class.

Yet, for Mels, the real problem resides in the tension and separation between blacks and whites; in sum, it is a question of racial difference. His speech accepts this as an obvious given, as a fact that only Christian grace can transcend, and, from this viewpoint, he invites the missionaries to inscribe themselves in a perpetual sacrifice and self-denial. He adds also: "we easily become dominators in the Congo, [what appears to be] the servility of Blacks, our own arrogant nature incite us constantly to such a state" (Mels 1946–47: 12). By emphasizing the tension between the black and white communities, Mels wants both to preserve the initial coherence founding the sense of mission and to correct its concrete procedures and practices. The new operation, he suggests, should depend on the originary experience but ought then to reorient the perspective of the mission. In the panoply of new schemes of action, one finds propositions for a new style of Sunday school that would focus on self-promotion of the students, regular meetings for youngsters as a diversionary practice in order to implement the fundamentals of Christian ethics, sessions for *évolués* in which the missionary would play the role of equal partner working for a new society, and monthly or trimestrial retreats for the members of "Catholic Action."

The instructions by Mels indicate a new way of operating. Let us keep in mind that these new ways of operating—or, if one prefers, of reconversion— "are similar to 'instructions for use' and they create a play in the machine through a stratification of different and interfering kinds of functioning" (de Certeau 1984: 80). In effect, the instructions insist on two complementary actions: on the one hand, the necessity of maintaining and spreading the basics of the Christian tradition and, on the other hand, the usefulness for the missionaries in becoming, along with the *évolués* as partners, seekers of a new future: "We cannot let go such an occasion; let us take it with our two hands if we do not want to have regrets someday [. . .]. It is also our duty as missionaries. We are to be the educators of 'our' people" (Mels 1946–47: 6). But on whom is one to act? First of all, on the children, says Mels, because they are "easy to lead" and a "strong personality" can influence them. A normalizing project, a panoptic organization, could, according to Mels, transform children's inherited tendencies (1946–47: 43–44). There are, secondly, the school teachers, important collaborators who should not be confused with cooks and other servants: they should be associated in all scholastic, and parascholastic enterprises but are not to be trusted. The missionary, insists Mels, should be a "father" for the native teacher. Finally, there is the vague and general class of Christians waiting for a new type of dynamism, a fragile body, according to him, in which two main groups cannot be trusted—the old people, because they are too superstitious, and the women, because they are "without will."

We are presented with a panorama disfiguring itself: the mission rationalizes its new role and reformulates new tactics: "they" are, after all, our brothers and sisters, and how can we lead them to salvation without humiliating them? A vocation confronts itself in this question, which is clearly about an entirely new kind of cultural production: what is the *new* idea of Africa to promote? The mission activity and its theoretical postulates invert the past. The colonization and conversion of a space and its inhabitants maintain the objective: civilization. But the methods refigure themselves, constituting new strategies preparing a *succession:* "they" might have to continue our mission; what do we do to ensure an orthodox path? The response, for Mels, is simple: self-conversion and authenticity. He insists: "we [missionaries] scandalize the Blacks more than we imagine. To check this should be easy: just get their impressions about us: and, unfortunately, these are not always false" (1946–47: 34). The missionary thus becomes the object of conversion. He or she has the truth and traces spiritual trajectories. But now, notes Mels, the missionary has to relearn not his or her basic material but the syntax and the vocabulary conveying it.

Linguistic and sociological conversions take place. The missionary begins to speak less and, most important, to listen to the convert and surely to the *évolué,* now an *interlocuteur valable.* What is important here is not only *what* is transmitted, but also *the way* it is communicated, the latter being more important than it was before. Indeed, one can see here the weakness of the whole colonial enterprise. In effect, what Mels teaches his fellow Scheutists is a tactic—nothing less than the art of the weak: how can we survive? how can we maintain the legitimacy of our presence and its vision? The adaptation techniques he suggests witness to a general colonial predicament.

> The more a power grows, the less it can allow itself to mobilize part of its means in the service of deception: it is dangerous to deploy large forces for the sake of appearances; this sort of "demonstration" is generally useless and "the gravity of bitter necessity makes direct action so urgent that it leaves no room for this sort of game." One deploys his forces, one does not take chances with feints. Power is bound by its very visibility. In contrast, trickery is possible for the weak, and often it is his only possibility, a "last resort": 'The weaker the forces at the disposition of the strategist, the more the strategist will be able to use deception.' I translate: the more the strategy is transformed into tactics. (de Certeau 1984: 37)

By what he represents and symbolizes, Mels is in power. He does not need any demonstration of its efficacy, since he knows quite well what he embodies as a white, as a colonial, and as a missionary. The tactics he elaborates in his instructions fit a very practical policy: how to articulate the primacy of the mission in a new manner. Thus, new rules emerge, new norms on how to relate to blacks in general are enumerated, and new tactics are deployed on how to speak and behave with "*évolués,*" whom, despite their sociological position, or perhaps because of it, he seems to despise. The process, as he himself says, is "humiliating," but, he adds, "let us be objective, we should not be guided by our feelings [. . .] towards these arrogant [blacks]. It is our mission to teach them [. . .] and we should not build up the antipathy we sometimes instinctively experience about them [. . .]" (1946–47: 27–28).

Mels is a "modern" compared to Roelens. Let us briefly describe their missionary geographical contexts and then compare the instructions of Mels to those of Roelens written many years earlier during the conquest period.

White Fathers were already working in the east of the Congo when the Scheutists began implementing their missions in the west. A pontifical decree of May 11, 1888, created the Vicariate of Belgian Congo, staffed by Scheutists. Between 1888 and 1908, the mission lost thirty-eight members who could not adapt to the milieu and died. In the meantime, it successfully expanded and built Berghe-Sainte Marie, Nouvelle Anvers, Kalala Merode Salvator, Tshilunda Hemptinne Saint Benoît, Lusambo Saint Trudon, Thielen Saint Jacques. Morever, as did the White Fathers in the east, the Scheutists fought slave traders and "bought" orphans and former slaves. These, converted, constituted the nuclei of missionary posts. In collaboration with the colonial State, Scheutists opened in Boma and Nouvelle Anvers in 1892 specialized institutions for children without families.

Let us keep in mind that, unlike the White Fathers, the Scheutists, of whom thirty-three were missionaries in 1903, were, all of them, Belgians. They actualized the dream of King Leopold II, who, in 1876, invited this young Belgian Order, oriented toward the Far East, to be involved in the colonization of the Congo Basin. And it was in Mongolia, under the governance of the Abbé E. Verbist, the founder of the Order, that Scheutists decided to become colonizers in the Congo.

The privileged collaboration between the State and the Order had a major impact on the politics of evangelizing the Congo Basin. Missions for example, did not have to pay taxes. A decree of December 26, 1888, stipulates the norms of cooperation between the State and the missions. Leopold II himself is quite explicit about the missionaries he prefers: "the State," he writes to Lambermont, "should favor as much as it can Belgian missionaries" (Cuypers 1970: 33). And on July 16, 1890, a decree confirms this privileged status (*Bulletin de l'Etat Indépendant du Congo*, 1890: 13). Three main types of advantages are given to missions, preferably Belgian missions. There are, first of all, at least at the beginning, special allowances given quarterly by the State. Thus, for example, Scheutists, from 1888 onward, receive a regular quarterly subsidy in compensation for the work they do in Congolese schools. In 1890, the exemption of taxes is confirmed, and the State, depending on particular situations, agrees to cover all the costs—for combating the slave trade and for the education of orphaned children (Cuypers 1970: 36). The second type of commitment is more significant: the State promises to build the first "mission" for all the Orders. But, in practice, there is no uniformity. For example, in 1892, Jesuits expect from the State not only the building but the furnishings too. Yet, the Trappists get more than the Jesuits. Finally, there is a third advantage: the State, in principle, takes responsibility of covering all the traveling costs of Belgian missionaries from Europe to their African post.

Such is the background from which to understand Mels versus Roelens. They were both Belgians, yet they belonged to slightly different times in the process of colonization. They were both Belgians, yet one, Roelens, was a leader in an Order that had non-Belgians, and for the other, Mels, the issue of having only Belgians as missionaries no longer seemed to be pertinent. There is a final difference: Roelens spoke at the foundation of a project and Mels, years later, tried to revise it in order to play the game of what seemed the "inevitability" of history: blacks were demanding dignity and equality.

In his *Instructions,* Roelens presented the perception of an era: a psychology of blacks based on "our experience and the experience of others who have especially applied themselves to the study of Blacks." Yet, his "Black" confirmed the stereotype: a being immersed in nature, bad by essence, lazy, impulsive, superstitious, submitted to passions, incapable of reasoning, whose *ultima ratio rerum* would be the habit as both custom and nature. Roelens observed, however, "natural" qualities on which the missionary should work in order to transform the blacks. These qualities include he claimed, a natural sense of honesty, justice, politeness, attachment to the family, generosity, and respect toward those in power.

These are, indeed, easy and controversial generalizations coming from the colonial library. They justify colonization as exploitation and as *mission civilisatrice.* In actuality, with respect to the project of the Christian mission, they found it: as an *a priori* assumption of the enterprise, such generalizations demand a strategy for a radical transformation of a corrupted nature which faces Christianity as a waste (an excess and a sin), a challenge (the unimaginable), and a crime (the negation of civilization). It is thus a didactic strategy for a "domestication" of minds and a social engineering aimed at the production of "new" beings that Roelens unfolded in the *Instructions,* emphasizing five main points: (1) the application of an appropriate method (in effect, "they" are supposed to be simultaneously children—and thus innocent—and completely corrupt "primitives"); (2) a focus on "their" reason in order to adapt it to "their" behavior; (3) a manipulation of the imagination and affective power in order to create a new will to knowledge; (4) the promotion of new "collective" and "personal" types of habits; (5) the routinization of principles of constant and regular work. These points collaborate in a global strategy of colonial practices intended to create a conversion. They convey implicit postulates (e.g., the superiority of a mode of being, the primacy of reason, etc., which manifest the rationality of the conversion program) and explicit principles (the use of imagination to change practices of reasoning or to develop new habits based on an economy of expansion).

Mels's apparently liberal *Instructions* do not contradict Roelens's problematic positions. They seem to inscribe themselves in the same policy of conversion and clearly do so. Strategies, in effect, "do not 'apply' principles or rules; they choose among them to make up the repertory of their operations" (de Certeau 1984: 54). One could analyze Mels's surface modification of the stereotyped language of Roelens by paying attention to the use of such procedures as *polytheatism* (what was "paganism" or "savagery" in Roelens's vocabulary adapts to Mels's new context and is often metaphorized through concepts such as tradition, custom, ancient practices); *substitutability* (as witnessed in the idea of *évolués,* which ultimately will lead to that of *interlocuteurs valables* in the late fifties); *euphemism* (indeed, Roelens did not hesitate to use such words as "primitive," "savage," etc., and to situate them in a strategy of domestication as if he were speaking of animals; Mels, at the end of the 1940s, although sharing the essentials of Roelens's philosophy, had adapted his language and avoids expressions that might seem insulting); and *analogy* (which allows regular refounding of orders of comparison: for example, for Roelens colonization and evangelization were cast in an elementary evolutionary grid while, on the other hand, Mels knew how to use postulates and metaphors propagated by diffusionist and functionalist trends in anthropology).

In sum, to refer to Michel de Certeau, who has, from the work of Pierre Bourdieu, synthesized these practices well (1984: 45–60), Roelens and Mels were strategists in the politics of both domesticating African minds and creating a new idea of Africa. Intelligent and intellectual (thanks to their education and experience), multilingual (by necessity and ambition), and powerful (by status in their Order, in the Church, and indeed in the Congo), they knew which tactics to use and how to implement their strategies to invert African cultural orders. In effect, strategies simply "'play with all the possibilities offered by traditions,' make use of one tradition rather than another, compensate for one by means of another. Taking advantage of the flexible surface which covers up the hard core, they create their own relevance within this network" (de Certeau 1984: 54).

Geography and Memories

As seen in the preceding pages, two types of societies confront one another in the colonial experience, each with its own memory. The colonial system is coherent, seems monolithic, and is supported by its expansionist practices. It faces a multitude of African social formations with different, often particularist memories competing with each other. Thus, at the end of the nineteenth century, colonization cohesively binds the diverse, often antagonistic, collective memories of many African cultures. Offering and imposing the desirability of its own memory, colonization promises a vision of progressive enrichment to the colonized. How does this transformation of diverse African memories take place? What arguments can a colonial policy, manipulating desires, employ to emphasize convincingly the advantages of converting to a new memory which concurrently should inaugurate a radically new social order?

A Spatial Model: *Le Centre Extra-Coutumier d'Elisabethville*

F. Grevisse in *Le Centre Extra-Coutumier d'Elisabethville* (1950), speaks from the perspective of being both a colonial civil servant and a historian of the region of Katanga. In his book, Grevisse examines the Belgian policy which effectively introduced a body politics of delineation and domestication. This newly circumscribed social "body" was composed of Africans who were supposed to incarnate an absolute beginning of history, and the Centre Extra-Coutumier (C.E.C.) became the exclusive locus for bridging the gulf between traditional memory and a radically reconstructed one.

Under the direction of Governor Heenan and a few "enlightened" colonists, the C.E.C. became an experiment and was transformed into a "native community." Since its conception, the C.E.C. had been an experimental memory, or, more exactly, an intermingling of African and colonial elements. This newly emerging memory was, in fact, a dynamic force. Its transformation was oriented according to a series of demands associated with the purpose of the colonial school, a new strongly hierarchical administration, and the presence of a secret and permanent police surveillance, which served as a force of constraint. The school's mission was seen as providing education for the masses. The orientation of this education, directed according to the terms of the official programs of 1889 and 1930, was toward the promotion of a new system of values. The school, in practice, promoted a new *Weltanschauung* and an ideology marked by the Judeo-Christian tradition. The students were taught a morality based upon family values and civic responsibility. After completing their education, the students became minor officials of the colonial administration or tradespeople within the Center—thus forming a middle class needed by the Belgians.

The administrative structure of the C.E.C. drew upon elements of the indirect style of British colonial rule and the direct style of the French. A colonial administrator (who rose through the ranks from territorial agent to head of the C.E.C.) administered the interests of a variety of councils and exercised control over the police force, the budget, and the Africans employed by the C.E.C. These Africans served a double role. On the one hand, they were responsible for the transmission, as well as the execution, of policies regarding concrete means of social and cultural conversion. In this capacity, they conveyed information from high-ranking colonial officials to the population of the Center. On the other hand, they transmitted news about different activities and the possible problems arising therein that could affect the processes of conversion. Hence, behind the mass of the C.E.C.'s administrative paperwork and the boredom of the young African bureaucrats, well versed in the complex acronyms which began every letter and every report, there was an order, one of conversion. The head of the C.E.C. was responsible for the daily organization of this conversion process, but this was also under the watchful eye of the Comité Protecteur du Centre, which "a pour mission de veiller a l'amélioration des conditions morales et matérielles d'existence des habitants du ou des centres" ([the Committee's] mission is to check the amelioration of moral and material conditions of existence of inhabitants at the Center), and "a le droit d'inspecter le centre en tout temps afin d'être tenu informé de la gestion du patrimoine" ([the Committee] has the right to inspect the Center at any time in order to be informed on the state of the patrimony) (K. Mabanza 1979: 142).

This desire for transformation is remarkably evident in the system of justice and in the distribution of various professions among the inhabitants of the Center. A decree made on April 15, 1886, established a special jurisdiction for the Congolese inhabiting *centres extra-coutumiers*. This jurisdiction was both separate from traditional African ones, and on the very perimeter of the system of organized justice for the colonials. In 1932, A. Sohier, commenting on the decree, noted that the whole judicial complex system was simply controversial: it did not respect the African traditional systems and was not really submitted to the principles of colonial law (1949). As for the police, two separate branches, that of a general permanent police force and that of a more specialized detective force, were responsible for the maintenance of order and morality. The former was a visible presence in the daily life of C.E.C. inhabitants. Its double was soon created in the form of a specialized unit, the judicial police, which was commanded by the colonial judicial hierarchy, and the invisible detective force. The latter was responsible for surveillance of all individuals or social movements presenting a direct or indirect potential threat to the space and memory under construction. This police force concerned itself not only with criminals but also with any person who happened to stand out from the anonymous masses of C.E.C. inhabitants.

According to P. Minon, at the time of the Center's creation, in 1932, the population consisted of 9,000 inhabitants, a number which in the 1950s had grown to 440,000 (Minon 1957). When Grevisse published his study on Elisabethville in 1950, this population was composed of diverse ethnic origins: approximately 44 percent came from the province of Katanga, 39 percent from Kasai, and the rest were from neighboring countries such as Angola, Rhodesia, Nyassaland, Rwanda-Burundi, and a number from West Africa. This genetic diversity was itself a cultural problem. It was the ground upon which the colonial authorities could promote the development of a new memory, or upon which they could foster rifts within the human environment if their role or authority became threatened. In fact, this cultural diversity indicated the coexistence of a variety of customs in the same space. The physical space of the Center, divided among the ethnolinguistic subgroups, was the site of a sociological competition waged among the different languages, such as Bemba, Sanga, Swahili, and Luba, as well as the various systems of matrilineage and patrilineage descent. This diversity and its inherent conflicts would be accented in times of political crisis.

However, from the 1930s on, the colonial objective might be defined as the invention of a new cohesive culture. In the C.E.C., this culture was evident on three different levels. First, patrilineal succession was imposed *de facto* as the one model and project obedient to Christian norms. Christian marriages and patrilineal succession symbolized integration within the colonial order. Next, languages became arranged hierarchically. French, the language of the "master," was at the top of the pyramid. Although the colonized peoples were not forbidden to speak French, it was nevertheless the "property" of the elite, and knowledge of it was meted out with great cautiousness. The colonized peoples desirous of its social status came to view French as a means to social promotion and prestige. While African languages (Bemba, Sanga, Songye, Luba, etc.) were spoken in the Center—for example, at meetings of linguistic associations run by Father Coussement since 1925—French was the language adopted for discussion and communication in the Clerical Society—created by the same missionary—as well as in the medical associations. It was also the language employed in the meetings of the Cercle Saint Benoit, whose mission, according to Bishop Jean-Félix de Hemptinne, Apostolic Vicar of Katanga, was to "réunir les évolués régulièrement en une ambiance saine," and "leur donner un complément de formation humaine et intellectuelle" (to bring regulary together the évolués in a healthy atmosphere and give them a complement in human and intellectual formation). As a means of communication, French signified a culture transformed into an absolute index of civilization. Sociologically, it overcame all ethnic differences within the compounds of the Center and created a union of *évolués* (i.e., of blacks in the midst of a transition from ethnic customs to a new culture), under the watchful eye of the colonizer and the missionary. French was thus the domain wherein African traditions were actively eroded in order to permit the growth of a new memory.

The next language in order of distinction is Swahili. It was used for general education at the primary school level, and it was the quasi-official language of the Center. Used by the administration for communication with the inhabitants, Swahili became their "common" language and, as such, confirmed the Center's status as an autonomous body, distinct from the surrounding villages where other ethnic languages were spoken. It characterized a new colonial, urban culture, in that it was used throughout the school system, the churches, the administration, and everyday life. On the one hand, Swahili denied the existence of ethnic and social differences, reuniting and representing the entire population according to its own system of representation. On the other hand, the Center set apart. Its format and role distinguished sharply its space from that of the surrounding territories. In terms of prestige within the Center, Swahili was located between French at the top of the linguistic hierarchy and the other African languages at the bottom. These "other" languages were directly tied to a place of lowered prestige and power in the social system. Paradoxically, however, this perceived inferiority did not result in a total loss of power. Being closely tied to factors determining the general distribution of the Center's population in terms of genetic nomenclature (i.e., Bemba, Hemba, Luba, Sanga, etc.) and to the proportional representation of peoples from the various groups on a professional level, these divergent languages and cultures often vied for prominence, and this competition occasionally developed into a confrontation, or a sort of ethnic warfare. This competition could be used as a weapon by the colonial administration; the perpetual tension could be manipulated politically. But such policies can backfire: Moise Tshombe, a pure-bred product of the *évolué* culture, coldly used it during the dawn of independence in the Belgian Congo, in 1960.

The third level on which the invention of a new colonial memory was evident was that of the professionalization of the inhabitants. It illustrated the gradual construction of social classes. In his work, which described one of the principal turning points in the development of this process, Grevisse noted the existence of six major professional categories: (a) clerks, nurses, etc.; (b) qualified construction workers; (c) servants; (d) handymen; (e) merchants; (f) independent craftsmen. From this list of professions, we can distinguish the development of three principal social categories: (a) technicians working for the administration or for one of the new institutions, such as banks, hospitals, judicial services, factories, etc.; those who gradually maneuvered themselves into the lower echelons of the colonial power structure; (b) a *petite bourgeoisie* involved in business (merchants, craftsmen, etc.), which capitalized on the internal needs of the C.E.C. and on the latter's ideological power throughout the region; (c) a newborn working class attracted by the new system.

It should be noted that this system of organization indicated the existence of a cultural conversion "economy" in which market norms, such as competition, the individual's quality as a product of the new culture, his or her profit-earning capacity, etc., controlled and regulated the gradual integration of those deemed "apt" for domestication. Caught between two memories, the *évoluant* of the Center attempted to prove that in his thoughts, life, and work he had succeeded in repressing the traditional African memory and was thus open to assimilation into the new memory. His own history, as well as his individual consciousness, was supposed to begin with the colonial system. In concrete terms, a series of procedures and tests for selection was permanently in place, forcing the *évoluant* to submit to this transformation. The schools and churches constantly evaluated intellectual capacities, facilitating a careful screening of potential candidates from early childhood for integration into the new professional hierarchy. On the other hand, constant surveillance by the detective force exerted close control on the way in which the candidate reacted to the demands of new ethical, professional, and cultural codes on a daily basis.

These three levels—Christian marriages and patrilineal succession, the language hierarchy, and professionalization—which I separated for analytical reasons, are, in fact, complementary. All three are concerned with conversion to a new order, that is, the erasure of tradition and the production of the convert within "modernity." For example, for the Cercle Saint-Benoit, the objective of conversion ever since the 1930s had been, according to Father Coussement, to reduce ethnic constraints seen as negative, and to oppose both black racism and opposition to colonization and evangelization (Coussement 1932). The cover of a contemporary small magazine of the *évolués* of the Cercle Saint-Benoit serves as a possible symbol of the conversion project: a banner celebrates the hope for a communion between blacks and whites in the name of a cross that spells out conditions: charity, fraternity, mutual comprehension, reciprocal respect (Grevisse 1950: 362).

The Gap of Place: The Named Order

The metamorphosis of a memory, such as that found in an African colonial territory, is not simply a symbolic occurrence. It takes place during a process of neutralization, re-creation, and rearrangement of a site, of its geography, and of the values by which a tradition distinguished it. Such has been the meaning, since the fifteenth century, of the principle of *"terra nullius,"* which granted Christian princes the right to dispossess non-European peoples and to transform their histories. The principle of conversion, embedded within the system of values taught by the schools and fostered within European civilization as a whole, found concrete expression in the colonization of the "pagans." In this colonial gesture, the metamorphosis of memory was an inescapable moral duty. It was also most obviously a force of domination, and its counterpart, subjugation, marks the transformation of a memory whose reconstruction testifies to this very violence.

The place-name united all of these values in a spectacular way. A colonial policy of toponymy existed between 1885 and 1935, operating in the same manner as other models of colonization. New names transformed African locations into signs of monarchist allegiance. Albertville replaced Kalemie, Baudoinville replaced Moba, and Léopoldville replaced Kinshasa. Other names offered a recital of the living memory of the period of exploration, as was the case for Baningville (Bandundu), Coquilhatville (Mbandaka), and Stanleyville (Kisangani). Still others acted as duplicates or stand-ins of European localities. The post of Kwilu-Ngongo became Moerbeke. The criticism of this practice and "debaptism" which took place in Zaïre between 1965 and 1970, in the name of historical and spatial authenticity, never claimed, nor could it have, for that matter, to have rediscovered and brought the old memory back to a real, primary status by the reestablishment and recovery of the old names. After all, not only was colonial toponymy a radical reorganization of an ancient site and of its political makeup, but, more important, generally, it indicated the *invention* of a new site and body whose routes and movements reflected a new political economy. The Catholic missionaries provided a good example of this. Since 1875 they filled the geographic map with semantic tropisms. These encoded names indicated the progress of their activity, and served as evidence of the installation of a new order. Limiting ourselves to a few posts founded by the Scheut missionaries in Kasai, we find such examples as Hemptinne–Saint Benoit, Kabwe–Christ Roi, Katende–Saint Trudon, Mikalayi–Saint Joseph, etc. The African term or name succumbed directly to the grace and power of conversion. Joined to the name of a saint, it became an adjective and lost its status as a proper noun. In this way it permitted a distinction between, for example, Panda–Saint Joseph in the southwest of Katanga (at Likasi) and Mikalayi–Saint Joseph in Kasai.

As Michel de Certeau recently stated, the proper noun excavates the pockets of familiar or hidden values. The best way to describe this phenomenon is through the example of "the walk," which for de Certeau is paradoxically the result of external factors—I must go there, I need it for this or that, etc.,— which impose themselves upon the person advancing outside of himself/herself or his/her home. But walking also consists of spatializing and extending an internal space, in keeping with internal convictions which the act makes possible. This is *my* garden, *my* street, *my* village, *my* region, etc.

Take, for instance, the proper noun "Kapolowe." Kapolowe is a *locality* situated between Likasi and Lubumbashi. It is a small railway station on the route between Ndola and Port Franqui (Ilebo). On June 30, 1960, while the Belgian Congo was celebrating the end of an era, marking the erasure of its adjective, a Benedictine friend dropped me off at the southern gate of Jadotville. Instinctively, I decided *to walk* to Kapolowe. It was late afternoon, so I expected to arrive at the Kapolowe station around midnight. I walked slowly. I was *in situ* and continued forward, glad to be able to name the concrete links between, on the one hand, the order imposed by the conquest and the metamorphosis of the area I was crossing and, on the other hand, the marks and signs of a past *(un avant)* which ought to be able to repeat and to recite that night their otherness, which is that of violated experiences. In the name Belgian Congo the adjective which disappeared is a symbol. The empty space which it left behind will be inscribed in the history that was then just beginning. Nevertheless, it is clear that evidence of the rupture, if indeed there was one, is not to be found in the disappearance of the adjective nor in the new signs generated by its suppression. The body which lives or survives as the transcript of the metamorphosis is still that which testifies to the break.

Kapolowe brings to mind the images of other locations, such as Mpala, for example. This occurs not only because the two cities were made possible by Catholic missions and because, economically, both derive their living mainly from fishing, but also because the space of both cities is organized in a similar manner. At one end stands the mission with its various buildings (the priests' residence, the church, the sisters' house, the school, etc.). At the other end lies the village, which, in both cases, consists of a single central street, huts, and a few shops. Between the two areas, there is an empty space, a vaguely defined area of great interest. It is neither a garden nor a forest. It is not a collection of flowerbeds, nor is it a complete disorder. It is annoying because of what it reveals: separation. It is tactical. It repeats and illustrates in a concrete manner the classic division of a colonial city, as in the case of Elisabethville: Limits-Sud Avenue. The symbolism of this distance and this separation of black and white areas seems to evoke, paradoxically, a connection between the two extremities. In other words, the south might one day become the north, which is to say that it might one day, by modeling itself on the north, reflect the order and values contained therein. We know that this is geographically impossible. But the ideology of development lies in this ambiguous space, as a dream and a challenge. In this instance, racial separation as a geographic element finds meaning in the metaphor provided by the symbolic conjunction of two names, an African and a European, that of Kapolowe–Saint Gerard as a new locus.

Let us consider another example: the village of Mpala. It seems to represent a sort of absolute. Historically, Mpala is an "addition": it is alive due to the Emile Storms fortress, inherited by the White Fathers' mission in 1885. The mission buildings are massive. Upon first impression, they appear to be solid, immense, and closed in on themselves. The towers remind one of the regiments of guards once found there, and the gun-slots witness to the original purpose of the fort. The building is a *synecdoche:* it determines its own space, as well as the project which initially rendered it possible. Consider the following images: the enslavement practices carried out by the Arabicized peoples who exploited the region during the nineteenth century; the missionary project which followed as a stage in the construction of the Christian Kingdom dreamed of by Cardinal Lavigerie; and, finally, the Catholic mission, which fashioned itself after the model of a political fort, issuing its own money and organizing its own military protection. Indeed, it welcomed the protégés of both the Church and Belgium (symbolically referred to as the "mother country"); it resisted the attacks and cannon-fire of the German troops originating on the other side of the lake separating the Belgian Congo from Deutsch Ost-Afrika, during the First World War; and it celebrated a historical *Te Deum* in 1918, at the end of a European war with which the mission had identified itself literally with flesh and blood.

Thus the Mission of Mpala, as a political and religious sign, indicates a semantic expansion that is more than a simple annexation of a territory to the Catholic parish. A church and its dependents are fragments of a spatial project expressed as a locus of a new memory or, more precisely, as the memory resulting from processes of conversion. This new collective memory is tied to both a location and a tradition. It appears as the operation and the process of a double casuality, being both *ad extram* and *ad intram*. Regardless, therefore, of the wealth of or lack of historical associations, this memory serves as a common ground where antagonistic, competing, noncompatible influences and hence tensions converge. The external causes are the determining factors at Mpala: they account for ecclesiastical power and importance accorded to colonial ideology.

Paradoxically, the geographical setting of the Mpala mission calls to mind another image: that of the *asyndeton*. The latter bursts the bonds that hold together the diachronic continuity of events and erases that which brings together, in much the same way as conjunction, the coherence of the new memory. The ties which, before independence, served as a logical connection between, for example, the Lufuko River, the village, and the mission church will become disentangled after the 1960s. Indeed, the European missionaries abandoned a project and a Zaïrian catechist. They thereby ensured the realization of the direct opposite of the desires which founded the fortress, those of Lieutenant Storms, the White Fathers Moinet and Moncet, and Captain Jou-

Mpala, 1975. Photograph and Copyright by Allen Roberts and Christopher Davis.

bert. Thus, on the one hand, the various elements of the Empire and of the Conquest established themselves as signs of a civilization opposed to slavery and paganism, while, simultaneously, they developed into a fertile site for mythical expression. On the other hand, at the other end of the time span, an old catechist watches over the immense, deserted buildings. He seems to be completely preoccupied with the absurd hope for his own conversion to the

Mpala, the other order. Photograph and Copyright by Allen Roberts and Christopher Davis.

law of conquest and the memory which underlies this vision. They are imposed on him as being necessary for his integration into the kingdom of a new power structure.

Another illustration, perhaps more easily seen, of the *asyndeton* can easily be drawn from that which the setting itself suggests. Imagine that I am going from the "mission" to the "village" of Mpala. I am going from north to south. Behind me is the mission, Cape Tembwe, and the Lufuko delta. In front of me is the village and, far in the distance, Mount Nzawa, which dominates the southern horizon, growing up out of the forest that stretches to the west. The inhabitants of Mpala, being Christian converts, officially abandoned the spirit of the earth, which lives in Nzawa. After one century of gradual transformation, the north with its chimes, which organize life, work, and prayer, and with its stone walls becomes the veritable exemplary body. This north, with its new economic, cultural, and spiritual values, took the place of the old system of values that had previously coordinated activity in the south. This modification was, and is to this day, considered a rupture, illustrated by the arrogant attitudes regarding the perceived deficiency of the African cultures. Commentary on the transformation of the Mpala setting, whether it be in terms of modernization, development, or, since the 1970s, the condemnation of a regression, is always negatively conceived and presented in place of, or in silent reference to, a so-called traditional field or system represented by, for example, the Nzawa divinity.

Emil Nolde. *The Missionary.* 1912. Oil on canvas. Collection Berthold Glauerdt, Solingen.

The rupture or displacement represented by the opposition of north and south in Mpala (represented in the promises of the school in the northern sector and in its distance from the values and symbolic arguments taught to those who are instructed in the forest to the south) shows that, in reality, the *asyndeton* marks a positive rupture in a progressive plan. The fragmentation of time corresponds both in appearance and in reality to the separation in the Mpala setting, which, right up until the 1960s, places two sets of forms and symbols in opposition to one another: the north versus the south, the future versus the past, modernity versus tradition. If rigorously analyzed, this opposition might be considered as providing the context for an encounter between the *asyndeton* and the *synecdoche*. The "more" of the whole presented by the *synecdoche*, mobilizing ties, conjuctions, and expansion, corresponds to the "lesser" of the *asyndeton* and its games of separation and fragmentation.

The cultural assimilation between north and south promoted by this space provided very small compensation to the colonized people and their society. It becomes possible to imagine a mediation or even a power of subversion in the presence of the south, the old, or, more appropriately, that which was, there, the order of "civilization." To establish itself, the new power was obliged to construct a new society. As we have seen, at Mpala as elsewhere in the Congo, the setting's renewal is based upon three principal paradigms: religion and the Christian code of ethics (beliefs and practices); a strictly elementary education (reading, writing, and arithmetic), complemented upon rare occasions with the study of the French language; and the promotion of manual labor and its usefulness for the Congolese. This official program shows its worth during the 1930s. In *L'Enseignment des Indigènes au Congo Belge* (1931), E. De Jonghe complains of the black who has lost his roots and who imagines himself to be the equal and even superior to the white.

Thus, it is in the village, midway between the totalitarian signs of "the Mission" in the north and "the forest" in the south, that a possible union between modern and traditional symbols becomes thinkable (Roberts and Maurer 1985). For example, in the Mpala area the huts, made out of beaten earth or occasionally of cement blocks, are rectangular. This geometrical shape is a *recent text*. It integrates in its structure the ancient method of construction observed by Emile Storms and the first White Fathers, which is, of course, still visible in the straw used to build the roof and in the glaze and molded wood used to make the walls. But this rectangular form, which is very common nowadays, comes initially from the extension of an architectural Swahili model which the mission and the colonial authorities promoted at the turn of the century. It replaces the Tabwas' round hut covered by a conical roof (Roberts and Maurer 1985), which Léon Dardenne (1865–1912) seems to have reproduced quite accurately in his sketches made during Charles Lemaire's scientific mission to Katanga from 1889 to 1900.

A Conflict between Memories

Both the colonizer and the missionary believe, by their own admission, that the promotion of a model for dwellings that are ventilated in an alternative fashion and, above all, that are independent of the ancient village site is the price that must be paid to ensure that the conversion of the African collective memory survives. This is, in fact, true. Thus both Kapalowe and Mpala are models of a more general activity, which is well-illustrated by the significance and vocation of the Elisabethville Centre Extra-Coutumier. A rectangular form of habitation, open to the outside world and its forces, replaces the circular village. The concentration of the various traditional elements expresses the different functions of the interiorized interdependence, simultaneously eliciting both communal obligation (mutual aid, protection, solidarity, etc.) and specific social interactions within the locality of a common closed space.

With regard to the construction of a new collective memory, the mission reformulated spatial coherency, establishing a new type of organization in which each function must correspond to a specific place, each aspect of an activity to a special site in which a temporal ordering is rigorously maintained. Thus, the geography of the village is no longer the simple reflection of a method of conversion. Due to the force of circumstances and to necessity, the old order must renounce *its own movement* in order to master the process of self-transformation indicative of progress. Daily routines also change. From now on, these daily practices are obedient to the demands of modernity. Conversion to the Christian ethic, to the school's power, or to a new linguistic social hierarchy is part of this transformation of the collective memory. The *believable* and the *memorable* tend to be understood from now on as that which denies whatever is ancient or primitive. For example, it is not only the cement versus the glaze or the aluminum (or sometimes galvanized iron) versus the straw roof which suggests, for better or for worse, a new possible origin, but the tension presented by the space between the mission and the village. The promise of integration (having the goal of an improved level of living) corresponds to the scattering and the disintegration of the specifically African space. Indeed, the original village grows through the homogenization of the initial ethnic and linguistic diversity. New inhabitants appear, attracted by the promises held forth by the new Center. A new culture is invented within a space of non-customary cultural dimensions. It draws upon the contributions of both the mission and the village nucleus, without being either one or the other. As a result of its needs and customs, it must, sooner or later, both confront the mission's power and challenge the original village's authority.

In this topology, we analyze a conflict of memories. To clarify the problem, we should study, one after the other, the tension between the mission and the village, and the dilemmas of the *évoluant* situated between the two areas. First, the village, at one extremity, is almost always a sign of something else, of a tradition which, as we have already seen, is, in the language of conversion, in opposition to the memory presented by the mission. As J. L. Litt has analytically demonstrated (1970: 55–61), the village represents the site where numerous types of propositions become mixed up together. On the one hand, there are those statements which support the necessity of conversion and which, therefore, elaborate or comment on the stereotypes of the "savage" and "degeneracy." In the face of numerous pressures, the village sees itself as the site to be erased in the name of civilization. It does, in fact, come to incorporate the terms of abnegation of an "outcast" population or race. Such an "absence of civilization" needs to "be replaced" (Litt 1970: 55). On the other hand, between 1930 and 1932, a few rare authors began to speak of black civilization, recognizing its humanity and, as in the case of the Belgian Jesuit Swartenbroeks, wondering about the shortcomings of certain "civilizing" doctrines and the prejudice of white racial supremacy (see Litt 1970). These are, of course, the exception to the rule, and contradict neither the mission of civilization nor the benefits resulting through conversion. Even this new discourse on the village produces no more than a certain reactionary excessiveness which implicitly justifies the colonial effort and the missionary enterprise. The documents of the period seem unanimous on this point. The village dwells in "materialism," "debasement," "slow, moral progress," under the "demoralizing, if not pernicious influence of the family." In any case, it would seem to be "enslaved to the appetites and instincts of its life," a "poorly-tempered character," "impulsive and versatile." Religiously, its practices and beliefs all arise from "sorcery" and the "belief in magic," which "do not correspond to the divine plan of redemption." Intellectually, the village-dwelling black is considered to be incapable of distinguishing the relationships "between the phenomena he notices and the causes which produce them"; it is assumed that he has neither "reasoning faculties" nor "a very profound mind," and that he lives "in the shadows of ignorance" (Litt 1970).

This schema justifies the mission as being a necessary part of the task of human development, while it discreetly considers the project's economic advantages/worth. In 1930, Father J. J. Lambin S.J. clearly described the complementarity of these two aspects of the colonization process in respect to the Third Colonial Congress. His discourse draws upon two principles of Natural Law as perceived by Christian thinkers of the period: (1) the right to exploit the wealth granted by God for all humanity and (2) the natural law of charity amongst men. In everyday practice, both the colonizer and the missionary tend to place more emphasis upon the second principle, thus demonstrating the generosity of their actions which gave rise to the evolving village. In the same act, as a general rule, they minimized the violence of the first principle. In an adverse action, the *évoluants* from the Second World War onward, and the nationalists in the wake of the Bandoeng Conference, would tend to question and criticize the usage of the first principle, passing over the effective realization of the second. It was, in fact, the educational system which "enabled" them to speak.

One ought to point out that, between 1930 and 1945, the African *évoluant* almost always preferred the mission to the village. Given the tension between the "night" of the carnal depths of the village and the "day" of the mission, bathed in its salutary light, as described by colonial literature, it was not in effect much of a choice. The *évoluant* often internalized the directly visible and material signs of the new power: the new ethical and social life codes, the linguistic hierarchy (some natives being so well-versed in Latin that they would often speak it better than the French), and the capitalist choreography of profitability and competition.

The best example of this type of *évoluant* is the group known in the 1930s as the "native clergy." Baudoinville (Moba) witnessed their birth in 1917, at the sacerdotal ordination of Stefano Kaoze, who became the first Catholic priest in Central Africa. There were large numbers of native clergy in the eastern parts of the Belgian Congo, and both Mpala and Moba frequently saw them arrive and pass on to other sites. They had a decisive influence on the sense given to the mission and have remained, to this day, the embodiment of the mission. They signify, in both a literal and a figurative sense, the games and alliances between the mission and the old systems. They are the living signs of assimilation. This point is vividly illustrated by their integration into the communities of White Fathers and their task as missionaries among their own people. They outrank all white colonizers who are not their ecclesiastical superior in the structure of the Catholic Church. Taken alone, this fact is of capital importance, for it renders necessary the dissociation of colonial policies and those of the Catholic Church, despite the ill-defined areas which united the two.

In reality, however, the Catholic Church's policies did not contradict the colonial project. They simply drew upon the two principles of the right to colonization and the metaphorics of conversion at an early stage and chose assimilation as the symbol of a Christian identity and a new memory, from the 1920s onward. It is true that the White Fathers' activities in the eastern part of the Belgian Congo and in Rwanda-Burundi seem to go against the conservative spirit of a Monsignor de Hemptinne in Katanga. Nevertheless, to the west, in Kwango, Belgian Jesuits, such as J. J. Lambin in 1931 and H. Vanderyst from 1927 on, considered creating a type of higher education which would give the local inhabitants the initiative to ensure their own economic and spiritual conversion (Litt 1970). In a brief article published in *La Revue de l'Aucam* (2, 1935: 44–59) in Louvain in 1935, another Jesuit, N. Nimal, advocated a possibility totally unacceptable for colonial authorities: the right of sovereignty as consequent from that of exploitation and vice-versa. Is it possible that, had the voices of these liberal Jesuits been able, with the activities of the White Fathers in the east, to determine the colonial program from 1933–1935 onward, the future of the Belgian Congo would have been different? No one can be certain.

In any case, from the 1930s on, the Jesuits try, in keeping with colonial policies, to create a moral "elite" that would "elevate" native society. A good example would be the formation of the medical elite. From its creation in 1926, Formulac (the Medical Foundation of the Unversity of Louvain in the Congo) insisted upon certain principal objectives: first, the promotion of professional values; second, the inculcation of Catholic and moral values; third, the formation of an "esprit de corps"; and, finally, the creation of a feeling of responsibility toward the masses. Thus, on the one hand, this elite represented the formation of a group which would be called upon, sooner or later, to form a distinct social class, and, on the other hand, simply due to its existence, this group embodied the passage from the old memory to the promises of colonial history. Its main task was the radical transformation of Congolese society into a new dream.

Every memory pertains both to life and to a history that is constantly in motion. It is clear, therefore, that, far from opposing one another, the two "African" memories, the ancient one and the colonial one, complement one another. The *évoluants* found in the tension between the two poles a very ordinary paradigm that is, in itself, completely neutral. These two memories signify simply that there is neither social transformation nor the corresponding social relations without a certain discontinuity indicated by the appearance of a new type of conscience. Absolutely nothing prevents us from imagining that a transfer from one memory to another, such as that illustrated by the C.E.C., could have taken place without the intervention of colonization. However, the fact remains that it did occur under the colonization in Central Africa. Paradoxically, it is due to this context, which both rendered it possible and serves as an explanation of it, that this transformation appears suspicious because it seems to imply a rejection of the old memory. One can thus understand how ideologies as different and even as contradictory as Pan-Africanism, negritude, and "consciencism" could simultaneously, in an identical impetus, oppose colonialism and plead for modernization and cross-breeding. One also comprehends why any initiative such as the Zaïrian project of the 1970s, which promotes authenticity as the only alternative to a postcolonial, critical, exacting modernity, can only be rejected as an extreme oversimplification. It is readily agreed that modernity is neither ideally symbolized in the Mpala "forts" nor even conceived of in the conversion policies which governed the Elisabethville C.E.C. On the other hand, the tension between "the Mission" at Kapolowe and the new town born out of the nightmare of independence is not necessarily any more indicative of modernity. Due to economic necessity and a reorganization of political power, the two memories had to fuse in order to project a promise of being modern and African. We should concentrate our efforts on the production of this *"plus être,"* which represents our evolution better than consciences and liberties ever could.

The Economy of Conflicting Memories

The conflict of memories can be seen concretely in the everyday life of real peoples. Let me illustrate this by focusing on two of its "reflections," on what is given back as both an image and an interpretation of reality: first, by analyzing the tension between the real and the imaginary in Zaïre's political discourse; second, by critically reading two exegeses of Kimbanguism, a Central African syncretic church. I propose a hypothesis about the relationships between political discourse and praxis in Zaïre on the basis of a widely accepted criterion that distinguishes three major moments in Zaïrean history: the colonial period, the First Republic (1960–1965), and its contrary, Mobutu's regime, which, since its inception in 1965, has been called the Second Republic. Can one confirm these distinctions by clearly disclosing three discursive periods from a perspective which would differentiate the play of conflicting themes and metaphors and thus characterize and legitimize the particularity of three types of political discourse reflecting three different forms of political programs? One might ask, are you not forcing opened doors? Is your project useful, and what purpose could it serve? Should one not accept the historical evidence and the fully transparent messages which marked the closing of one period and the opening of another? The discourse of the period of independence clearly situated itself as a negation of the colonial *logos,* and Mobutu's idiom has always played in the boundaries of the "new" and "original."

It is not my intention to debate the sociohistorical significance of these discontinuities, but, rather, on the basis of what they mean and imply, I would like to circumscribe and define their site, to situate their images in the field of both their possibility and their motivation, and, finally to suggest an interpretation regarding their internal rationality.

My real focus will be upon Mobutu's discourse, which, beyond its apparent disorder, changing themes, and contradictory ideological appropriations, individualizes its locus quite well, indicates its paradoxical determinations, and reveals its structural madness. To put it in a different way, in response to Crawford Young's question, "Zaïre: Is There a State?" (1984), I answer yes. The State is isomorphic with a sociolinguistic machine, "Mobutuism," within which, for more than twenty-five years, a fellowship of discourse has been reproducing itself whose most apparent traits are (a) a language claiming an absolute newness even though it is fundamentally a mixture of images that repeat, in an incantatory way, desires and projects already formulated under colonial rule and during the First Republic; what is original and new in this language is its style, which is direct, simple, and passionate, telescoping time and historical periods while confusing political dreams with socioeconomic diagnoses and objective demands of development; (b) a language describing itself as an explanatory idiom of socioeconomic projects and contingencies, and also as the revelatory image of an autonomous, new African culture; however, it is, in its intention and expression, an explicit, conscious, systematic elision of reality; (c) a language defining itself through the curious paradigm of military clarity, directness, and continuity of purpose; this claim has foundations, yet one could also note the confusing succession and transformations of rhetorical figures directly linked to an amazingly regular centering and decentering of the most productive myths of nationalism and the most controversial themes of colonial policies.

Mobutuism appears to be an organized system operating and articulating itself through representation. It turns and returns figures and images, analogies and resemblances in figurative constructions that simulate reality rather than signifying or representing it. Its legitimacy derives from a real but ambiguous political rupture: the 1965 coup. Its aims toward societal transformation and development have remained pure metaphor, animating parabolic narratives in which the very notions of continuity and discontinuity, colonialism and anticolonialism, development and recession, and others, do not seem to have any other sense than that given by an orthodoxy addressing itself to itself, modifying its own normative references, in order to maintain its credibility both as mediation and as formulation of what is really going on in the country. In terms of political science, Mobutuism, a totalitarian fellowship of discourse, appears as a complete absurdity (Young 1978; 1984). But, from a different viewpoint, K. Ilunga (1984) describes the organic form of Mobutuism psychologically as a value-filled experience having operational, structuring deployments. If he is correct, it has brought about a sociological complex that could last longer than we might believe. Concretely, this fellowship of discourse would mirror its own consequences: a theater-space in which one can read a simple usage of an ordering relation opposing the stronger to the weaker in the most colonialist tradition that reproduced the dialectic of the master and the slave. The manipulation of the order is such that it also creates, to refer to Michel Serres commenting on a classical paradigm: the stronger is always right: "la raison du plus fort est toujours la meilleure," a confusion between meaning-effect and meaning-affect in political discourse. Here is Serres's schema (1979):

Absolute limit	Ordering relation	Model
the strongest	stronger-weaker	biological
the best	better-worse	ethical
source	upstream-downstream	spatial
	cause-effect	rational
	purity-mixture	physical
king	dominator-subject	political
birth-death	before-after	temporal
	ancestor-descendant	genealogical
	protector-protected	social
maximum	greater-lesser	ordered structure

In this game-space, to use Serres's categories, a *majorant* and a *minorant* face each other. Before 1960, the first is white, and a conqueror; the second is black and conquered. The *majorant* idiom institutionalizes these basic oppositions into opposed biological and political models. An order founded on the absolute limits of the conqueror organizes the colonial space so that everything is classified according to a global binary balance. The balance is polarized according to extreme and regulatory points/metaphors: on the one hand, savagery identified with the conquered, and on the other, civilization incarnated in both the conqueror and his project. The latter thus has total right and control not only of the new organization of the space that he reduced to his historicity but also of enunciative fields, which account for the "why" of his historical responsibility and also illuminate, from his own memory, the process of colonization, that is, a process of rearrangement of a foreign human space and its inhabitants. Therefore, it is safe to say that, in the colonizing period, a discursive field superimposes itself upon an empirical *saga,* validates the enterprise through powerful figures (light vs. obscurity, health vs. disease, vitality vs. degeneration, etc.), and endlessly formulates the rights of the strongest and the procedures for implementing his mission and objectives. Strictly speaking, one might refer to the paradigm of the fable: "The reason of the strongest is always the best." But let us note that if the paradigm maximizes de facto the power of the strongest through his models, it also links them, in the colonial experience, to procedures of systematizing and transferring into the colony the achievements of "the source." *Dominer pour Servir* and other founding binary themes of the colonial model are completely autonomous figures, but stand in reciprocal obedience with the empirical schemata of transforming the African space. As a consequence, if one can question the recurrent logic of statements and their pertinence, it might be said that, despite their possible internal weaknesses in terms of logical inferences, they enunciate the absolute norms and limits for a specific distribution and division of roles within a *story* and a *history* in the making.

The mode of being of this kind of *story/history* is, in essence, paradoxical. Its coherence is relative to the "ordering relation:" *quo nihil majus cogitari potest,* as Serres put it about the fable.

> The fable is a perfect operational definition—perfect in that it is free of all psychologism—of hypocrisy. In fact, the term *hypocrisy* comes from the verb to judge, to choose, to decide, and from the prefix underneath. In other words, if you want to win, play the role of the minorant. I imagine that all *Fables,* by the metamorphosis that they represent, function in a similar fashion. (Serres 1979: 266–67)

In this sense, the political discourse of independence is an apt illustration of the fable. It shows that the colonial space is a game-space, and the dichotomy of ordering relations does not close the *story/history.* Thus, during the First Republic a new discourse pretends to take into account the field of liberties and potentialities which were negated through the privileges of the colonial project. I would like to insist on the particularity of this questioning, which, in its explicit and sustained economy, defines itself as a reinterpretation of the game. The weaker claims that the dichotomy is absurd and challenges the sequence of models, particularly the biological and the ethical. Concretely, a rereading of both the reciprocal relationships between political and discursive policies and the correlations between figures and formulas relativizes the axiomatic meaning of the models. A new horizon opens with its founding acts and images (Matumele 1976). Independence as myth reorganizes the colonial story with its own statements and criteria, as in Lumumba's comment: "le soleil rejaillit dans ce pays pour faire face à l'obscurantisme séculaire du régime colonial" (Van Lierde 1963: 193) (the sun is rising in this country, taking the place of the century-old obscurantism of colonialism). Therefore, there is the possibility of a reordering of the space-game in terms of both "a guaranteed winning strategy" (Serres 1979: 275) and the transfer of historical responsibility within the positive aspects of the colonial legacy.

From 1965 to the 1980s, Mobutu's discourse took the form of a radical reversal by defining itself as doctrinal and cultural lessons regulated by two major principles: a principle of discontinuity and a principle of interiority. The first emphasizes differences existing between the preceding political practices (colonial and First Republic) and Mobutu's schemata; the second designates a series of new ideological articulations (*Rétroussons Manchisme* or self-reliance, *nationalisme authentique,* and *Mobutuisme*), which, supposedly, outline new founding myths for, at last, a genuine liberation from all dependencies. Though this new discourse represented an attempt to promote a theory of political and economic succession depending on new conditions of cultural nationalism *(l'idéologie de l'authenticité),* it constituted, from its inception, a double peril. It was inadequate in facing the real socioeconomic problems and characterized itself not so much by its programs as by its *verbal style.* On the other hand, it was incompatible with the most obvious implications of its own narrative.

For example: (a) The "colonial legacy vs. independence" paradigm laid down the importance of the fathers of independence, particularly Lumumba *(héros national),* while on the other hand, this new political normativity (the new avenues to health and development) established itself as a complete rejection of the sickness represented by the political objectives of the First Republic. (b) The strategy for the new national autonomy is described in terms of religious inspiration: a Guide-Messiah inaugurates a project of social transformations *(Moto na moto abongisa)* within a fundamentally capitalistic space, on the (theoretical) assumption that they are not inherent rules of the game, nor specific enunciative fields for expressing the organizing principles of power and production: "ni à gauche, ni à droite, ni même au centre," neither to the left, nor the right, not even in the center. And this fabulous dream prescribes arguments for conformity to African authenticity and, through the "Manifeste de la Nsele," the promotion of almost socialist presuppositions for the emergence of a new society.

Within such a framework, governing statements can have no more than religious value. They cannot account for a social reality from which they are divorced by the very fact of their internal contradiction. On the other hand, they make sense only in terms of what permits them to exist: a radical exclusion of discursive diversity, which, defining the configuration of a fellowship of discourse (MPR: Mobutu's party-state, the Mouvement Populaire de la Révolution, the Popular Movement of Revolution), identifies the movement with its religious source and origin, the Guide-Messiah: "le Mobutisme est constitué par l'ensemble des paroles et des actes du Guide Mobutu!" ("Mobutuism is constituted by the ensemble of speeches and acts of Mobutu the Guide!")

One could, therefore, debate whether Mobutuism is a doctrine offering well-circumscribed objectives and presenting, over time, an identity of purposes and governing rationality. At any rate, it seems to me that one thing is unquestionable: Mobutuist discourse insists on the sovereignty of its being without revealing either the reasons for its existence, or its connections with the realities it claims to account for. For the First Republic's questioning of colonial absolute limits, it substitutes the articulation of these very limits in a dramatization of their colonial forms. A whole set of images, coming from the most controversial African tradition, unfolds the majesty of the king and recites his virtues through three types of exegesis:

(a) a temporal model comments on the opposition "before vs. after," and reveals the magnificence of the MPR centralization of power as the designation and arrangement of a salvation;
(b) a genealogical exegesis of the "ancestor vs. descendant" relation makes explicit the isomorphism between this theoretical model and a mythical African configuration;
(c) a social exegesis shows to what extent the paternalistic model "protector vs. protected" organizes the MPR pyramid as a "community" of interest.

In sum, a discursive drama claims to be the sign of a social reality. However, it does not voice this reality, but, rather, muzzles its paradoxes and contradictions. Thus concrete mistakes are erased, errors are transformed into victories, and failures are covered. For example, the official spoliation of foreigners' goods and enterprises is "a process of Zaïreanization" and is validated as a "nationalist policy" for the local promotion of medium scale private enterprises. Its failure, which humiliates the party-state and forces the regime to call back foreigners, is given a wonderful name, "retrocession," as a regulated political decision based on the MPR pragmatic ideology. In the same vein, the unpredictable shifts of major figures—from *"nationalisme"* to *"nationalisme authentique,"* from this to "authenticity," its "radicalization," and, finally, to "Mobutuism"—show that everything takes place as though an arrangement of images and words in the order of a discourse constitutes the only and final objective of the party-state.

I would like to think that my hypothesis fixes an original way of looking at the precarious boundaries of classical distinctions from the colonial era to Mobutuism. Mobutu replaced the critique of colonial models made by the fathers of independence by implementing a fellowship of discourse which has its reasons and its objectives in its own being rather than in the uncovering of social tensions and the formulation of policies for mastering the processes of production and social relations of production and their effects on the organization of power for a necessary transformation. This discourse has maintained itself by playing various memories, in their mythological forms, against each other: for example, the ancient, supposedly traditional, against that inherited from colonialism; the First Republic's dreams against Mobutu's presuppositions; the lessons of capitalism against a mythic African order of things. Reality seems muted. A discourse acquires a formidable function: one of producing a reflection of a reality that is not out there in the name of a memory that it invents by positing it as reflected by an absolute origin and the pragmaticality of contemporary circumstances.

A second illustration of the conflict of memories can be apprehended from two books: Susan Asch's *L'Eglise du Prophète Kimbangu* (1983) and Wyatt MacGaffey's *Modern Kongo Prophets* (1983). The authors are both American scholars, the first a junior and the second a senior student of Kimbanguism. What they spell out are exegeses of a first-level performance which itself is an interpretation of both a native and well-localized religious revelation and its successive appropriations by the followers of Kimbangu, the Kongo prophet. Their exegeses thus claim to translate and simultaneously to explain in a scientific manner things that happened and what was put in motion after the initial moment. One could say that the two authors actualize two projects: the first is a description (in fact, a translation of the *being-there*) of Kimbanguism and its local memory; the second makes explicit a different type of memory, that of a discipline, anthropology, and of its operations and its epistemological contexts. The dialogue back and forth puts in contact an everyday practice and language with technical procedures of spatializing knowledges. In this specific case, knowledges seem marked by highly conflicting memories: of African religious experiences, of Christianity and its history, of the meeting and the proceedings of these two currents, and, indeed, of their contradictory passions and politics.

It is with interest that one opens Susan Asch's book, whose objective is to describe the sixty years (1921–1981) of the Kimbanguist Church in Zaïre: its genesis, development, organization, and ambition. Asch's method is, as she states it, primarily interdisciplinary and uses history, demography, sociology, anthropology, political science, economics, and theology (1983: 285). Indeed, Asch attempts both too much and too little. She attempts a diachronic approach to Kimbanguism within the framework of the history of Zaïre and, at the same time, her study is a kind of socio-anthropological understanding of this African independent church. That is much, and probably too much, for someone who, evidently, despite a good academic knowledge of the topic, does not seem to know any Zaïrean language and, moreover, apart from brief sojourns, has never really lived in the country and does not seem to know very much about the cultural background which sustains Kimbanguism. The research is not rooted in a thorough and credible anthropological context.

Asch's book attempts too little because its project is very modest: to describe the history of Simon Kimbangu from the colonization period to the eve of independence and the constitution of the Kimbanguist Church: l'Eglise de Jésus-Christ sur Terre par le Prophète Simon Kimbangu (E.J.C.S.K.) (1983). The first portion is a narrative of the political history of Kimbanguism, already well-described by J. Chomé (1959), D. Feci (1972), A. Gills (1960); M. Sinda (1972), and others. If the account Asch presents is sound, it is only because it reaches the 1980s and gives a sense of Kimbanguism as a new orthodoxy.

The second part of the book is more original and quite intriguing. Asch analyzes the two faces of the Kimbanguist religion. She distinguishes an "official Kimbanguism" from the "Kimbanguism of Kimbanguists," the first being an expression of a Protestant-oriented organization promoted by the officials of the church, and the second a popular religion largely influenced by traditional beliefs that are often in contradiction with the normative teachings of the church. The third part is a critical evaluation of Kimbanguism's socioeconomic programs in Zaïre. According to Asch, this program has been conceived in terms of competition with the material achievements of the Roman Catholic and the United Protestant (ECZ) churches. In sum, the major themes of Asch's research are church and state relationships during the colonial era, Kimbanguism in the colonial period, and its transformation and socioeconomic ambition after independence.

There is much that can be said in favor of Asch's treatment of her subject. She has based her book on an extensive use of good documentation from certain archives and, mainly, on brief visits to Zaïre. She convincingly sets Kimbanguism in the wider colonial and postcolonial context. Finally, the book is well organized and attractively printed.

Unfortunately, the value of her analysis, from the viewpoint of memories she faces, is diminished by serious weaknesses. Although she makes a remarkable effort to comprehend Kimbanguism from African Kimbanguist contexts, one comes away from her work wondering whether the author ever really understood what religion and this particular "religion" meant (and means) to BaKongo in particular and to the inhabitants of the Belgian Congo in general. For example, the discrepancy that she has observed between the official and the popular religion might be a sign of something else than what she perceives. In the same vein, the difference in beliefs, practices, and policies that she does not understand in the cases of Bandundu, Equateur, Shaba-Katanga, and the two Kasais, can be explained more simply by cultural factors rather than by the sociological criteria used in the book. Secondly, insofar as Kimbanguism is a religion, one looks for a well-documented chapter on its theology. One cannot consider the rapid analysis of the ambiguity of the concepts of the Holy Spirit and the Prophet (1983: 113–115) as an acceptable presentation of Kimbanguist theology. The point she makes about the identification of Simon Kimbangu with the Holy Spirit (1983: 176) is important but should have been carefully studied and tested. One can also question the author's silence on very useful and recent contributions which could have helped her research. She writes that, according to A. Geuns, there are more than six hundred books and articles on Kimbanguism (1983: 43). This is not a reason to ignore contributions which, if she had consulted them, would have modified certain gross and vague generalizations (see 1983: 45–51). It is a pity that Asch has failed to use J. M. Janzen's work on *The Tradition of Renewal in Kongo Religion* (in N. S. Booth, ed., *African Religions*, 1977) and, more important, Janzen's and W. MacGaffey's book *An Anthology of Kongo Religion* (University of Kansas Publications in Anthropology, 1974). They could have guided her discussion concerning whether, in terms of memory, Kinbanguism is a purely religious movement, a political institution, or both. Finally, a careful reader will be puzzled by Asch's ways of proving her points. For example, she presents her sources (1983: 274) when she speaks about the beauty of the Kivu region (how important!), but forgets to cite them for such exceptional information as the competition in Lubambashi in 1974 between the Zaïrean state, the Roman Catholic Church, and the E.J.C.S.K. (the Kimbanguist Church) to buy the prison in which Kimbangu was detained (1983: 171), and how the E.J.C.S.K. succeeded in acquiring the estate.

Asch's book is well-intentioned. Unfortunately, it brings nothing new to serious students of Kimbanguism. On the other hand, in its confusion, it illustrates magnificently the conflicting memories of Kimbanguism.

Wyatt MacGaffey's *Modern Kongo Prophets,* a book in the series "African Systems of Thought," addresses Africanists as well as students of comparative religion. Specifically, the book attempts an "adequate presentation of Kimbanguism," which, according to the author, requires "revising much of the existing literature regarding it and rebuilding some of the tools of the anthropology of religion" (1983: xi). Vigorous, perhaps too ambitious, methodological paradigms set the theoretical framework:

> this study attempts to distinguish between representations of events in the categories of social science and the same events as understood by BaKongo [. . .]. The distinction is worth attempting, although in practice no radical segregation can be maintained. No matter how sympathetic the anthropologist, his project is his own and not that of the people on whose behalf he undertakes to speak. Secondly, the potential incompatibility of the two perspectives should not be exaggerated; they are often congruent. (1983: xii)

The book is divided into three parts. In the first, MacGaffey sets out to take a fresh look at the ethnography of conversion in Kongo. He examines Kongolese prophetism within the context of "the modern conversion of Ba-Kongo to Christianity and especially to Protestant (Baptist) Christianity." The account explains a sociohistorical process of acculturation and, at the same time, offers a vivid synthesis of the emergence of prophetisms as both political and religious heresies that ultimately become new orthodoxies. MacGaffey then goes on to describe churches in modern Kongo, emphasizing their relative strength and some sociological factors which determine them, such as employment, education, and ethnic and political factors. In the second part of the book, the reader is given a meticulous analysis of Kongo as a plural society, a society in which are incorporated two different models, the *kimundele* (European system) and the *kindombe* (African system). MacGaffey's command of the literature and the "Congolese-Zaïrean" context is impeccable, and his account of prophetism as a product of conflicting systems and ideologies is well done. Even so, one comes away from this analysis with some questions. On the one hand it is clear that, from the *kimundele* and its memory, as well as from the *kindombe* background, what MacGaffey studies is a disorder, which implies the production of social disequilibrium and, thus, of potential and dangerous changes. On the other hand, one of the basic postulates of the

book states that because BaKongo lack "an ideology of progress or modernization, they are aware of the simultaneity of the conjoined structures which
organize their lives, although their own ideology imposes an idea of it at least
as misleading as 'modernization'" (1983: 16). These two facts mean that one
is dealing with a society which, to use Claude Lévi-Strauss's vocabulary, would
fall between the strictly "cold" type and the firmly "hot" type. As a consequence, MacGaffey's findings seem somewhat less satisfying insofar as they
hide rather than illuminate the social meaning of Kongo prophetism and its
memories as "entropy," as disorder. Finally, in the third part, MacGaffey
discusses some Kongo perspectives, focusing on cosmology, healing, and socioreligious frameworks of prophetism. Candid autobiographical sketches provide very stimulating insights about the involvement of the author in his
research and one begins to understand in which sense this book really "breaks
new ground." The subjective but well-documented analysis of the relationships between *Mputu* (the West), slave trade, and Catholicism (1983: 130–40)
is a work of art on the dialectical tension existing between methods and
categories of social sciences and, on the other hand, Kongo interpretations
of history.

I admire MacGaffey's firsthand glimpses of Kongo culture and subcultures,
and the brilliance with which he writes about Kongo prophetism. He has
chosen in this book on the practice of Kongo memories to dismiss the concept
of social aberration, to emphasize prophetism as event, and to promote an
integration of psychology and sociology in order to interpret prophets' person-
alities. That is an anthropologist's *grandeur*. I wonder if a great part of what
MacGaffey considers as prophetic behavior and vision—for example, Ndo
Mvuzi (1983: 236–43)—should not have been treated from a simply psycho-
pathological viewpoint.

V.

REPRENDRE

O weaving reeds, may you never be poverty-
stricken
May you never be taken for sale in the
market
May none be ignorant of your maker
May no unworthy man ever tread on you.

—Anonymous women's work song.
Somalia (Loughran et al. 1986: 59)

Enunciations and Strategies in Contemporary African Arts

The word *reprendre*—strangely difficult to translate—I intend as an image of the contemporary activity of African art. I mean it first in the sense of taking up an interrupted tradition, not out of a desire for purity, which would testify only to the imaginations of dead ancestors, but in a way that reflects the conditions of today. Second, *reprendre,* suggests a methodical assessment, the artist's labor beginning, in effect, with an evaluation of the tools, means, and projects of art within a social context transformed by colonialism and by later currents, influences, and fashions from abroad. Finally, *reprendre* implies a pause, a meditation, a query on the meaning of the two preceding exercises.

If, however, an African artist does go through these critical phases, consciously or unconsciously, in the creation of art, viewers of the finished work, even some of the most attentive ones, may find themselves looking for traces, for strata and symbols, that might qualify the piece as part of such-and-such a trend in the vague domain of "primitive art." Naive, uninformed, sometimes prejudiced, this kind of looking often involves two *a priori* assumptions, the first concerning the Western notion of art itself and its ambiguous extension to non-Western oeuvres, the second supposing the immobility, the stasis, of non-Western arts (see Price 1989). Yet, against these assumptions there is a history, or more exactly there are histories, of African arts. In his *Art History in Africa* (1984), Jan Vansina convincingly analyzes the variety of the continent's artistic processes, the readjustments and transformations of methods and techniques there, the dynamics of acculturation and diffusion and their impact on creativity. Furthermore, there is no such thing today as "an" Afri-

Head of a king. c.1750. Ashanti. Ghana.

can art. Senegalese trends are different from Nigerian, Tanzanian, or Mozambican, and each is immersed in its own sociohistorical context. Even in traditional masterpieces (see, e.g., Vogel and N'Diaye 1985) the evidence of regional styles and the variety of their histories is clear.

I do not address these historical movements in this study, but I try to indicate broad rhythms, tendencies, and discontinuities extending from a recent period of rupture that brought about new types of artistic imaginations. On the whole, I am interested not in causal successions but in new artistic thresholds, displacements of inspiration, and what we may call an "architectonic" system—an underlying order that would account for some basic similarities in the amazingly diverse, complex, and conflicting regional styles. This order has led some analysts to suppose a unifying, very ancient "creative complex" in Africa. I have chosen a more sociological approach, which pays attention to history but is principally concerned with incidences of conversion, patterns of discontinuity, and conflicting or complementary influences.

I move from the radical reconversion of African arts in the colonial settings to their subsequent development. A general overview, this description is intended to avoid mystifying technicalities in the discussion of both broad artistic tendencies and particular pieces. It may seem to focus on sculpture and paintings, but does so only for purposes of illustration; the analysis can be extended to batiks, ceramics, engravings, paintings on glass, and so on. Finally, I would like to point out that my approach has a theoretical *a priori* concerning the status of a work of art: I suggest that we consider African artworks as we do literary texts, that is as linguistic (narrative) phenomena as well as discursive circuits (see Kristeva 1980). I hope my analysis will demonstrate the usefulness of such a position.

The Issue of a "Nilotic" Imagination

"It is," wrote Pierre Romain-Desfossés, "precisely an Asiatic complex that we find in our Katangais painters and which allows us to use the etiquette of Nilotic" (Cornet et al. 1989: 68–69). In this amazing statement, which links geography, race, and art, the founder of the Atelier d'Art "Le Hangar" in Elisabethville (now Lubumbashi, Zaïre) seeks to explain the originality of his African pupils' artistic imagination. A Frenchman, Romain-Desfossés arrived in the Congo after the last European war. Seduced by what he considered extraordinary artistic potential, he decided to stay, and was soon organizing an atelier for a few carefully chosen students. His program is summarized in his remark, "We must strongly oppose every method tending toward the abolition of the [African] personality to the advantage of a uniformizing aesthetics of White masters" (Cornet et al. 1989: 66).

Romain-Desfossés's project, its missionary zeal giving rise also to a remarkable generosity, united the political and the artistic to constitute a new aesthetic. But he traced this aesthetic, and the creativity of his students in general, back to an "Asiatic complex," a "Nilotic etiquette." His task as he conceived it was to awaken in his students this ancient, unchanging aesthetic memory.

Independently of its technical implications, this concept seems important as a reference to a lost configuration interrupted or, at least, blurred by history. It suggests a kind of aesthetic unconscious, common to sub-Saharan Africans, that a patient, sensitive, disciplined search could awaken. In 1957, Frank McEwen, founder of a national gallery at Salisbury, Rhodesia (now Harare, Zimbabwe), suggested something similar, by way of a metaphor: "One of the strangest, inexplicable features occurs in the early stages of development through which many of the artists pass, when they appear to reflect conceptually, and even symbolically, but not stylistically, the art of ancient civilization, mainly pre-Colombian. We refer to it as their 'Mexican period' which evolves finally into a high individualistic style" (McEwen 1970: 16). Whether we refer to a "Nilotic etiquette" or to a "Mexican period," the phrase seems to describe something Carl Jung might have called an "archetypal image," "essentially an unconscious content that is altered by becoming conscious and by being perceived, and [that] takes its colour from the individual consciousness in which it happens to appear." Jung continues, "The term 'archetype' [. . .] applies, only indirectly to the *'représentations collectives'*, since it designates only those psychic contents which have not yet been submitted to conscious elaboration and are therefore an immediate datum of psychic experience" (Jung 1980: 5).

Romain-Desfossés, however, in his "Nilotic etiquette," was probably thinking of something else—a very ancient datum, something like a lost web, completely forgotten, but still alive, well buried in the unconscious. And, he was convinced that the works of his best disciples—Bela, Kalela, Mwenze Kibwanga, Pilipili—testified to its existence. But the concept of a primitive "Nilotic" or other complex is very questionable. It might be more prudent to suppose that these young artists invented an *original* texture and a style, situated as they were at the intersection of local traditions and the artistic modernity of Romain-Desfossés. On one side of them was the luminous, inescapable influence of village life; on the other, the not-so-neutral gaze and speech of their teacher. Romain-Desfossés played father (he called his students "my children," and attended to both their physical and their emotional well-being), master (he saw his mission as one of teaching them how "to see"), guide in a new discipline: "painting . . . is in itself a new art that we bring to the black African." As Wim Toebosch writes, Romain-Desfossés dreamed of re-creating a new artistic universe: "Rather than giving instructions or imposing criteria or principles, he simply asks his disciples, his children as he calls them, to explore with their eyes, to study the world around them and to try to grasp its totality, but also its essence, without referring to this or that notion of faith—or of superstition" (Toebosch, in Cornet et al. 1989: 66).

Moreover, Romain-Desfossés also had very definite opinions on art history. He was a romantic, celebrating his pupils' creativity as springing from "pure and fresh sources," as opposed to what he called "Western degeneracy," "snobism," and "folly"—labels escaped only by a few European artists, such as Picasso, Braque, and the like. A black-and-white photograph of Romain-Desfossés's "family" is the best illustration of the way he imagined the new artistic world that he was trying to create: the Africans are posed in a subtle arrangement, a kind of square, with Romain-Desfossés, the only white in the picture, at its center. The overly well-organized balance between left and right and front and back, the sitters' geometric positioning, the exploitation of nature—everything is calculated to produce a sense of communion, friendship, and love uniting the white "father" and his black "children." The dark forest around the group, and the two cultivated banana trees right next to them, seem meant to establish both a gradual progression from nature to culture

Pierre Romain-Desfossés with his disciples. Photo courtesy Jeune Afrique.
The Museum for African Art, New York.

and the inverse—a regression of sensibilities from the master and guide,
through the young artists almost religiously surrounding him, toward the
night of the symbolic unconquered forest. Following Freud, one might refer
here to a will to master a psychic topography and the cathexis or investment
of energy in that pursuit. Finally there is the calm confrontation of looks: the
respectful deference in the students' gazes on the master, as if awaiting an
oracle; and Romain-Desfossés's own eyes, which seem unfocused, as if semi-
closed in meditation. Or is he looking at the three students to the left of the
group, or at his own, slightly raised right hand? In any case, the most striking
feature in his white visage is his enigmatic smile, the father, master, guide
holding a secret he will reveal only when he thinks the time is right.

Whoever plotted the photograph succeeded well in picturing the spiritual
frame of the Atelier d'Art "Le Hangar" d'Elisabethville, and of its offspring,
"L'Ecole de Lubumbashi." The photograph is a remarkable representation
of the workshop's symbolic intersections between sociocultural conceptions
bequeathed to it by colonialism and the new politics of acculturation. Romain-
Desfossés appears here as a paradigm. The artistic constellation he represents
crosses the frontiers of at least two traditions, two orders of difference. And
the aim of the art he inspired was to bring to light the desire of a new subject,
emerging out of a fragile connection between radically different psychic
topographies.

Romain-Desfossés was not alone in incarnating such an ambition. The Belgian frère Marc Stanislas (Victor Wallenda), for example, founded the School Saint Luc in Gombe-Matadi (Lower Zaïre) in 1943. The school moved to Léopoldville (now Kinshasa, Zaïre) in 1949, and, in 1957, became the Académie des Beaux Arts. A strong believer in the theory of an "innate African aesthetic imagination," Wallenda, during his long tenure as director of the institution, obliged his students to inspire themselves only from "traditional oeuvres." He ensured that they would not be exposed to European art and still less to books on the history of art. Another such figure was Frank McEwen, the founder of a workshop at the Museum of Harare (an offshoot of the Rhodesian National Gallery, opened in 1957). His educational principles were based on a refusal to "corrupt" African artists by exposing them to "the influence of Western art schools" (Mount 1973: 119). Sharing the same philosophy were Margaret Trowell, director of the Makerere School of Art in Uganda, and Pierre Lods and Rolf Italiander, at the Poto-Poto School in Brazzaville. One could add the names of Tome Blomfield, who organized a workshop on his farm at Tengenenge (Zimbabwe) for unemployed workers; Cecil Todd, a resolute modernist who, in the 1960s, compulsorily exposed his students at Makerere (Uganda) and later at the University of Benin (Nigeria) to modern European art; and, between the conservatism of Romain-Desfossés and Wallenda and the more recent modernism of Todd, fathers Kevin Carrol and Sean O'Mahoney of the African Mission Society, who, since 1947, have worked among Yoruba craftsmen to promote an art combining "European ideas and African forms" (Mount 1973: 32). And all of Romain-Desfossés's white colleagues had a number of things in common: they consciously assumed the role and the functions of the father figure; they believed in an innate African artistic imagination, one radically different from that of Europe; and they invited the local artists they considered capable of growth into a discipline that, by digging into blurred or forgotten memories, could bring forth new arguments and ideas, a new, acculturated ground of creativity.

Between Two Traditions

Marshall W. Mount has distinguished four main categories of contemporary African art (Mount 1989). First are survivals of traditional styles, exemplified by such practices as brass-casting in Benin, Nigeria, Ashanti wood-carving in Ghana, and cloth work in Abomey in the Republic of Benin. Second is the art inspired by the Christian missions. On the west coast and particularly in Central Africa, this kind of work goes back to the first contacts with the Portuguese, in the late fifteenth and the early sixteenth centuries; a religious art, it received a boost in the 1950s when Christian parishes began to sponsor artists' workshops. This art, then, is apologetic, in the sense that it is concerned with the defense and illustration of Christianity, which adapts to the African context. And the works—crucifixes, sculptures, canvases depicting biblical themes, carved doors, and so on—are generally used to decorate

churches, parish buildings, and schools. Third is the souvenir-art category—
"tourist art" or "airport art" (see Jules-Rosette 1984). This work is made to
please Europeans; as an East African carver put it, "We find out what the
[Westerners] like. We make what they like when we are hungry" (Mount
1989: 39). And last is an emerging new art requiring "techniques that were
unknown or rare in traditional African art." Mount writes, "The representation of this new subject matter is varied in style. There are works that are
conservatively and academically rendered as well as abstract paintings that
are reminiscent of Abstract Expressionist work. Most of this new African art,
however, falls between these two stylistic poles, and as a consequence it avoids
a close following of either" (Mount 1989: 62–63).

Mount's pedagogical classifications seem useful for a first approach to African arts. Not surprisingly, however, their clarity and apparent coherence cannot account for the complexity of genres, schools of thought, and artistic
traditions in Africa. One may wonder, for example, whether to situate the
work of Mwenze Kibwanga, Pilipili (disciples of Romain-Desfossés), and
Thomas Mukarobgwa (a student of McEwen) in the first or the fourth category of Mount's classification. And what about East African batik, or the
Senegalese Souwer or glass-painting tradition? There is also a second problem,
and a serious one: in which category should one include "popular art"? This
work testifies to emerging trends, yet few of its producers have attended art
school, and still fewer have been "recipients of government scholarships in
art schools abroad" (Mount 1989: 62), like many of the artists in Mount's
fourth category. Furthermore, though a number of its creators work with
Christian themes, popular art is not, strictly speaking, inspired by the Christian missions. And no one will deny this art's modernity, which places it, in
principle, in Mount's fourth category. Yet the motifs of an impressive list of
popular artworks are explicitly inspired by traditional objects. What to do?

Mount's classification may be revised according to a simpler notion: the
complementarity of the traditions in all the categories he separates. The Aus-
trian born teacher Ulli Beier considered this complementarity one of the most
significant signs of the "Afro-European culture contact":

> It is no longer possible to look at African art and see nothing but a continuous
> and rapid process of disintegration. We can now see that African art has re-
> sponded to the social and political upheavals that have taken place all over the
> continent. The African artist has refused to be fossilized. New types of artists
> give expression to new ideas, work for different clients, fulfill new functions.
> Accepting the challenge of Europe, the African artist does not hesitate to adopt
> new materials, be inspired by foreign art, look for a different role in society.
> New forms, new styles and new personalities are emerging everywhere and this
> contemporary African art is rapidly becoming as rich and as varied as were the
> more rigid artistic conventions of several generations ago. (Beier 1968: 14)

We see, then, an aesthetic acculturation between, on the one hand, the
complex of African representations and inspirations, its various discursive

circuits displaying their depths and tracing their trajectories, and, on the other hand, the European, familiar yet strange to the African artist, and, at the same time, signifying a new starting point. The former belongs to the stubborn local cultural fabric, and reproduces regional *Weltanschauungs* in demonstrative or decorative, naive or sophisticated fashion. The latter should be posited as a more intellectual and sociological frame.

For the artist trained in colonial-era workshops and art schools, the curriculum there has prescribed powerful reflexes and responses. Even in the most conservative institutions, education meant a conversion, or at least an opening, to another cultural tradition. For all these artists, the organic reality of a modernity was embodied by the discourses, values, aesthetics, and exchange economy of colonialism. One might, in consequence, be tempted by Edmund Leach's general system of oppositions between the two traditions, and might hypothesize a discreet competition between them: the more traditional the inspiration for a work of art, the less its general configuration and style could allow a clear assessment of the qualities of its forms, its content, and the maker's technical skills; conversely, the more Westernized an oeuvre, the more easily an observer can make distinctions among these constituent elements. Leach's suggestion is brilliant, but unfortunately it does not address the difficult issue of styles, of "the formal properties of a work of art," which constitute the core specificity of an artistic tradition (see Focillon 1934 and Vansina 1984).

Two sets of criteria—internal (the artwork's style, motifs, theme, and content) and external (the context of its creation, that context's cultural history, the sociological milieu, and the artist's purpose)—should permit the distinction of three main currents (not categories) in contemporary African arts. There is a tradition-inspired trend, a modernist trend, and a popular art. Such orientations as Christian religious art, tourist art, and so on should be situated between the tradition-inspired and the modernist trends.

These two trends aim, on the one hand, to revitalize the styles, motifs, and themes of yesterday, to bring the past among us, as in the case of the schools founded by Romain-Desfossés, McEwen, and Victor Wallenda; on the other hand, these two trends search for a new, modern aesthetic, a conscious inscription of a modern cultural setting (as in the case, for example, of the Nigerian Lamidi Fakeye). The two ambitions may seem dissimilar but are actually quite compatible. The third trend, recent popular art, made in the years of independence, tends to run parallel to the art of the trend toward modernity. But the art of the modernist trend is more intellectual; it is usually made by educated artists, and their work explores an academic language acquired in art school. Besides its artistic achievement, such work is also monetarily significant, for it is made primarily to be sold. Indeed, both the modernist and the tradition-inspired work function in African countries as "export goods" for the international market.

The third current, the popular art, is perceived as the antithesis of these culminations of aesthetic acculturation. Its artists are generally self-trained,

use inexpensive materials, and paint not for export but for ordinary people
on the fringes of the local bourgeoisie (like many of the artists themselves).
The styles, motifs, and themes of popular art allegorize commonsense perceptions; in naive formal style, they comment vividly on historical events, social
issues, and the cultural struggles of working-class and rural peoples (see, e.g.,
Fabian and Szombati-Fabian 1980). In contrast to a "high" culture sanctioned
by international authority and by the respectability of the European art genres, popular art is structured as a number of regional discursive formations
whose meanings, codings, status, distribution, and consumption are quite specific to the different places in which they emerge. In short, where modernist
and tradition-inspired art reflect the highest cultural values as defined and,
supposedly, lived out in the inner circles of acculturated African society, popular art, made at the periphery of the same society, scans, interprets, and occasionally defies such values by confusing their explicitness, challenging their
discursivity, and bringing into circulation new readings of founding events,
mythologies, and social injustices, as well as popular representations of a
history of alienation (see, e.g., Beier 1968 and Jewsiewicki 1989b).

Regrouping

I still remember the 1983 exhibition of Senegalese tapestries at the Wally
Findlay Galleries, New York, and the more recent show "Contemporary African Artists" at New York's Studio Museum in Harlem in 1990. What was
striking in both exhibitions was the modernist styles of these collections of
works. Introducing the Senegalese pieces, James R. Borynack, president of the
Wally Findlay Galleries, observed that "the totality of [works] is immersed in
a sort of mythological retrospection which seems to issue from the collective
unconscious" (Borynack 1983: 4; Catal. CARS); and the introduction to the
catalogue salutes the tapestries as validating "a true African aesthetic" (Borynack 1983: 6; Catal. CARS). The tapestry technique comes from the French
Ecole Nationale d'Aubusson, and the execution of the pieces, at least from
1964 to the 1970s, faithfully followed the Aubusson canons. Yet there was a
discreet change in the motifs of these works, and it coincided with the introduction, around 1960, of the themes of "negritude." The personal influence of
Léopold Sédar Senghor, then president of Senegal, patron of the Manufactures
Sénégalaises, and the best-known theorist of negritude, was visible in many
of the pieces' celebration of ancient styles. Color, line, and movement fused
and broke as if worked by a vibrant rhythm. The work was a grand illustration, in fact, of Senghor's idea of the whole School of Dakar: "an African
cultural heritage," an "aesthetics of feeling," "images impregnated with
rhythm" (Axt and Babacar Sy 1989: 19). A critic might ask whether such
pieces, which claim to expose the virtues of an ancient bubbling aesthetic
source, qualify as variants of traditional art. The success of the Senegalese
tapestries in this regard, and of School of Dakar art in general, is indubitable,
responds the artist and writer Issa Samb (Axt and Babacar Sy 1989: 129–30).

Yet Samb, though reluctant to stem criticism of any kind, fears that the usual critique, emphasizing the work's African heritage rather than the individuality of the artist, "unmasks and misleads simultaneously the system on which the *'Ecole de Dakar'* rests." "The critique confuses denotation in the sense that the exhibits which have been around the world actually denote Negritude but connote something quite different. And this 'quite different' is principally undefinable, it is the painters' psyche" (Axt and Babacar Sy 1989: 130).

The "Contemporary African Artists" exhibition was touched by the same issue: how truly "African is modern African art?" (Catal. CAA 1990: 36). Apart from the self-trained Nicholas Mukomberanwa of Zimbabwe, all the artists in the show—El Anatsui (Ghana), Youssouf Bath (Ivory Coast), Ablade Glover (Ghana), Tapfuma Gutsa (Zimbabwe), Rosemary Karuga (Kenya), Souleymane Keita (Senegal), Nicholas Mukomberanwa, Henry Munyaradzi (Zimbabwe), and Bruce Onobrakpeya (Nigeria)—were educated at specialized institutions in Africa and overseas; most of them belong to a second generation in the field, and if they consciously relate to earlier African art they know how to distort it, how to submit it to their own creative process. In fact, they discover in the African past simply art that has preceded them, art both beautiful and ugly. If the past inspires them, it does not bind them. Gutsa, for example, quite consciously distances himself from his Shona culture and conventions by exploring foreign themes (in, for example, *The Guitar,* 1988, in wood, newsprint, and serpentine, and in *The Mask, the Dancer,* 1989, in serpentine, steel, and wood). And Mukomberanwa's *Chembere Mukadzi* (1988–1989; serpentine) expresses a contemporary political agenda of women's rights.

The ideological position of the Senegalese artist Iba N'Diaye suggests the attitude of a number of contemporary artists:

> I have no desire to be fashionable. Certain Europeans, seeking exotic thrills, expect me to serve them folklore. I refuse to do it—otherwise, I would exist only as a function of their segregationist ideas of the African artist. (Catal. IN 1 and IN 2)

N'Diaye invokes a right to a personal subjectivity and individual practice. Why should an artist by condemned to the simple reproduction of other narratives?

N'Diaye's forceful statement, of course, brings to mind the well-known lament of William Fagg: "we are in at the death of all that is best in African art" (Catal. IN 1 and IN 2). And the era of independence in Africa indeed brought about radical sociocultural transformations and mutations. But why should one *a priori* decide that the ancient art was best? Ulli Beier writes that Fagg's statement "describes the well-known tragic phenomenon in Africa. All over Africa the carvers down their tools. The rituals that inspired the artist are dying out. The kings who were his patrons have lost their power" (Beier 1968: 3). So what? This discontinuity, despite its violence, doesn't necessarily mean the end of African art; it seems, rather, that the ancient models are being richly readapted. Beier himself still finds admirable pieces, evolving "between two worlds," by artists such as the traditional Yoruba brass-caster Yemi Bisiri, the Benin wood-carver Ovia Idah, and the Muslim carver Lamidi Fakeye. And elsewhere he praises the 1960s work of Twins Seven-Seven, Muraina Oyelami, Adebisi Fabunmi, Jacob Afolabi, Rufus Ogundele, and others of the Oshogbo school whose art—and this was new at the time—was aimed not at the Western market alone. This work reflected a drive to say and illustrate something new, to transcend the crisis of tribal societies and art disorganized by the impact of European culture, and to express the emerging new consciousness. As N'Diaye asserts,

> For me painting is an internal necessity, a need to express myself while trying to be clear about my intentions concerning subjects that have affected me—to commit myself concerning vital problems, the problems of our existence. (Catal. IN 1 and IN 2)

The real explodes on N'Diaye's canvases. Sometimes the paintings enunciate an intense narrative of violence—a ritual sacrifice in the series *Tabaski, sacrifice du mouton* (Tabaski, sacrifice of the sheep, 1970–1987), or a frightening surprise in *Juan de Pareja agressé par les chiens* (Juan de Pareja menaced by dogs, 1985–1986). Of the artists of the younger generation of painters, Sokari Douglas Camp, of Nigeria, seems fascinated by the everyday life of her people, the Kalabari of the Niger Delta, whose traditions her thrilling compositions show. Fodé Camara, of Senegal, creates complex dances of colors that reflect another game of colors in his native Gorée: the blue of the sea, of Gorée, of voyages, opposed to the red of fear, of violence (Catal. RFT: 35–39). Gorée, that outpost of the slave trade on the Atlantic ocean! Finally the cosmic conjunctions of Ouattara, from Côte d'Ivoire, reiterate old Senufo and Dogon mythologies in symbolic lines, blocks, and hollows (Catal. O). They also make me think of the more peaceful, more domesticated mysticism of another young painter, the Senegalese Ery Camara.

This ongoing work and the many masterpieces it has already produced really began in the colonial-era ateliers. New generations have learned from the successes and failures of those workshops-cum-laboratories, at the same time that they have interrogated their own traditional arts. The artists of the present generation are the children of two traditions, two worlds, both of which they challenge, merging mechanics and masks, machines and the memories of gods.

Popular Art

The term "popular art" has at least three different meanings. First, popular art may simply be the art regarded with favor, sympathy, and approval by a given community; in this sense, the traditional masks of the Dogon of Mali, Pilipili's abstract paintings, and Twins Seven-Seven's figural sculptures are all popular. The phrase may also refer to art that represents the common people:

as the Mozambican artist Malangatana put it, "Art for me is a collective expression that comes from the uses and customs of the people and leads to their social, mental, cultural and political evolution" (Alpers 1988: 85). Finally, there is a popular art suited to and intended for an ordinary intelligence and a common taste. The description might seem pejorative, yet such art can be highly sophisticated, as in the advertising art designed for the manipulation of the masses.

The term "African popular art" is generally used to refer to this last kind of work. The artists who make it include Anthony Akoto and Ofori Danso of Ghana and Cheri Samba and Kalume of Zaïre. Their art is neither a residue of traditional art nor an offshoot of the tradition-inspired and modernist trends in contemporary art. Those trends, as the importance of nonfigurative painting in both of them attests, are less mimetic or representational than symbolic. The meaning of a Tanzanian Makonde mask, for example, or of a canvas by the Nigerian artist Bruce Onobrakpeya or the Zambian Henry Tayali, or of a sculpture by Bernhard Matemera of Zimbabwe, comes from its structuring of signs, signs that combine both with each other and with signs outside the work to suggest coincidences of values and ideas. Such works are polysemous and symbolic. The art of Akoto, Danso, and Samba, on the other hand, popular by virtue of its media, the texture of its canvases, the narrative sequences it displays, and its populist messages, is fundamentally mimetic and may seem, prima facie, almost monosemous. Works of this kind carry a message, manipulating, arranging, and combining signs so as to make an unambiguous pronouncement. The use of written language—frequent in Samba's paintings—is part of this ambition for a militant clarity, a negation of the polysemous, associative, open principles of most works of art. In this sense, popular art seems fundamentally antivisionary and anti-imaginative. To what extent, then, does this work really qualify as visual art?

This is the challenge of popular art, which often takes the form of a visual narrative relaying events, phenomena, and issues that the local spectator already knows (see Fabian and Szombati-Fabian 1980). *La Mort historique de Lumumba* (The historic death of Lumumba, 1970s) and *Héro National Lumumba* (1970s) by Tshibumba Kanda-Matulu, or Samba's *Lutte contre les moustiques* (Battle with the mosquitoes, 1989), are simply new versions of events and issues familiar from other means—even from other art. Yet there is something new in these canvases: themes are ritualized, objectified, their complex textures transformed into a neat, transparent, limpid frame. Each of them stands, then, as a closed discourse. This ritualization is of considerable significance insofar as it works out a transmigration of symbols: from the complexity of history, of a real cultural experience, the artist chooses what can speak out the most clearly. The artist essentializes the event, or, perhaps better, symbolizes it—in which case it may have been premature to speak of the monosemy of popular art. Indeed, the message of Patrice Lumumba's walk to death in *Héro National Lumumba* is ambiguous. The painting's surface clarity does not prevent the viewer from gleaning a variety of meanings from

Tshibumba Kanda-Matulu, *Patrice Lumumba*, in *Héro National Lumumba*.
1970s. Collection Bogumil Jewsiewicki, with permission.

Cheri Samba. *Battle with the Mosquitoes*. 1989. Paint on canvas. Zaïre.
Collection Raymond J. Learsy. With permission, E. Kujawski, curator.

it: the dignity of the nationalist hero, the symbolic link between the Western-built helicopter and the three Katangan officials, the morality of the soldiers serving a state capable of such a crime, the physical presence of the Belgians themselves, and so on. Meanings, suggestions, images emerge from the frame, and history meets symbols in the mind of a "popular" viewer with an efficiency impossible in even the best book.

Popular art is both narrative and art. The grammar of its content, its chromatic logic, and the economy of its compositions escape most of the constraints of academic art. It witnesses something specific: a practice of everyday life. And it does so in an original style—that is, it has "the meaning of recreating the world according to the values of the man who discovers it" (Merleau-Ponty 1973: 59).

An Open Space

> Il faudra, avant de revêtir le bleu de chauffe du mécanicien, que nous mettions notre âme en lieu sûr (Before changing back into the mechanic's overalls, we need to put our soul in certainty).
>
> CHEIKH HAMIDOU KANE, 1961

A traveler, Dorcas MacClintock, a curatorial affiliate at the Peabody Museum of Natural History, Yale University, has a chance meeting with Ugo Mochi, an Italian artist who specializes in the silhouette. An ordinary incident. But then MacClintock discovers Africa, and, eventually, publishes *African Images* (1984), with pictures by Mochi. The book's creators would like it to be a window on African scenery. They introduce it as "a look at animals in Africa"; and the animals are indeed seen fully the way the dictionary defines them, as living, other than human, beings.

Both MacClintock and Mochi seem concerned not with the actuality of African animals but with the impact on the eye of these "beings" in the landscapes that frame them. MacClintock notes,

> Nowhere on earth is beauty of animal form, modeled through time by physical function and environment, so apparent. Hoofed mammals, always watchful for *predators*, reveal tension in the brightness of an eye, the alert stance, the poise of a head or the curve of neck, the stamp of a forefoot, or the whisk of a tail. Predators, too, are tense as they stalk, wait in ambush, or sprint after their prey. At other times they loll about in the heat of the day. There is beauty of color as well as of form. Patterns have evolved on some animals—stripes, splotches, and spots—that break up body outlines or provide camouflage. Other animals have conspicuous markings on face, ears, or legs that function for recognition among their own kind, emphasize mood or intent or are flaunted in displays of dominance between rivals. (MacClintock 1984: xii)

In the vision of this observer, the beauty of a landscape is rearranged according to the criteria of a "natural" art. Yes, MacClintock claims to tell the truth about an order she sees clearly. But what she says nevertheless arises out of a grid of feeling (which is not to say—need I add?—that it is fictitious). In theory, anyone could verify what she has to say. Yet the poetic ensemble she offers is a translation of what she has perceived. Through aesthetic desire, the eye stylizes the perceived, then returns to the observer her or his own investment.

Natural sceneries might seem to spring from nature but do not: it is in the gaze of the observer that African animals in their spaces are transmuted into aesthetic objects and take on semiotic status, becoming narratives of the natural. In the forest, for example, the appearance and habits of bongo antelopes seem to constitute a discourse: their "body stripes merge with narrow patterns of sunlight to make their antelope outlines almost invisible. [. . .] Once a bongo scents danger, it freezes. Then breaking cover, it vanishes as though by magic" (MacClintock 1984: 2–3). Duikers, okapis, drills, porcupines, hogs, and other animals have discourses of their own. Along rivers, lakeshores, and rift-valley walls, MacClintock finds variations on the discursive circuits she has found in the forests: dignified baboons socialize in families or walk alone, and small armies of bush pigs raid village crops under the moon; light, elegant, colorful bands of flamingos and pelicans fly or feed. In swamps and marshes one may "read" the activities of sitatungas, colobus monkeys, waterbucks, crocodiles, and hippopotamuses. Is not theirs a *scriptural* activity, asserting a type of existence and beauty of narrative? Other discursive texts can be observed in the bush and in the savannas: the movements and social lives of elephants, black rhinoceroses, and warthogs, or of sable and roan antelopes and elands; the grace and majesty of giraffes, the handsomeness of nyalas; and, of course, the jubilation of a remarkable variety of birds.

Can "natural" African landscapes be thought of as texts, as paintings? Do they present themselves to the observer as linguistic and pictorial phenomena, to be read, understood, enjoyed? Do they constitute an incredible number of delightful discursive styles? One must remember that the style of a narrative always grows out of a context—that, as Maurice Merleau-Ponty writes, "style cannot be taken as an object since it is still nothing and will become visible only in the work" (1973: 59). The "style" of animals living in their natural milieu, then, is obviously not "a means of representation" (how could it be?), but emerges in the exchange between the African landscapes and animals and the eyes of the observer. In her epilogue, MacClintock daydreams:

> Africa, with its vast skies and far-off horizons, evokes a sense of wildness, freedom, and wonder. It is a land that echoes the past, where natural order prevails and days are without time. [. . .]
>
> In the delicate springlike shade of an acacia, a gerenuk browses, its tail switching, ears batting, and front hoofs propped among the branches. A tiny dik-dik with enormous mouse-like eyes ringed in white stares shyly from a thicket. A

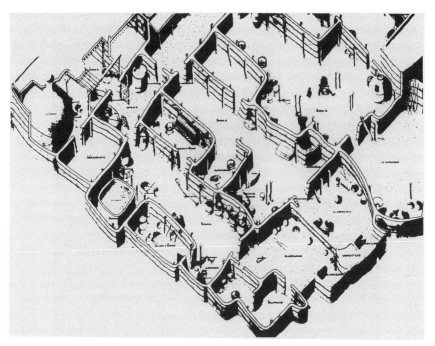

A design for living. J. P. Bourdier and Trinh T. Minh-ha, *African Spaces*. New York: African Publishing Company, Holmes and Meier, 1985.

bull elephant threatens, flaring huge veined ears, brandishing tusks, testing with trunk, and swinging his pendulumlike foreleg sideways. (1984: 140)

The first paragraph reconstructs (unconsciously?) an old image of Africa; the second consolidates it. The question of the truth of this image seems unimportant, however, since the image credibly represents a possible "natural" African painting or narrative. It is exotic, true, and might then be a fake—an imitation of an ancient figure from some other, extraneous narrative. Even so, however, what it signifies remains pertinent, since it sustains the mimesis of a perception imitating itself in what it stylizes and succumbing to the beauty it has thus invented.

If, as we have known since Husserl, no forming can transcend its space, its context, its language (Husserl 1970: 370–71), we must posit a relation between African styles and their natural context. MacClintock's language shows one such relation—a Franciscan impulse that transmutes every picture into a narrative celebrating the beauty and joy in nature. Another step might be to try to reconstruct the complex interactions between physical and human milieus, and the passage of these interactions into art. Ulli Beier has wonderfully described such an interaction in his discussion of the Mbari Mbayo Club at Oshogbo (1968: 101–11). In quite a different vein, Jean-Paul Bourdier and Trinh T. Minh-ha (1985), focusing on vernacular architecture in the Sahel area of Burkina Faso, have shown how the Gurunsi culture has aesthetically

Trigo Puila, *Materna*. 1984. Oil on canvas. Congo. The Museum for African Art, New York.

domesticated a natural milieu, coherently integrating into it a spatial organization of compounds and the human activities of daily life.

Images of everyday life also appear in the wall paintings of the Ndebele women of Pretoria, where, as Margaret Courtney-Clarke writes, "the traditional abstract designs have merged with representational forms to create a unique, highly stylized art that combines the elements of the past with the realities of the present" (1986: 23). If acculturation smacks of necessity in artistic activity such as the Ndebele's, it also sustains the continuity of ancient rituals, techniques, and customs. Furthermore, this art not only inserts itself in a tradition, it also espouses the clear light of the Kwandebele region. Thus

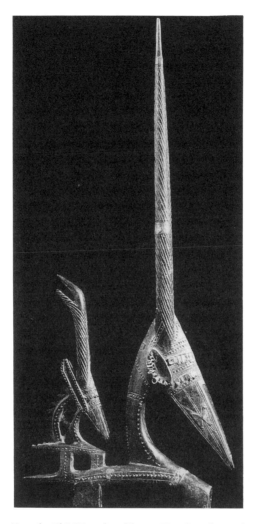

Female Chi Wara headdress. Wood and metal.
Bamana artist, Mali. Musée de l'Homme,
Palais Chaillot, Paris.

a conjunction: space, time, and human tradition interrelate. MacClintock's beautifully stylized animals have their counterparts, their stylistic variations, in, say, such narratives as Pilipili's paintings of fish or crocodiles; the sculptures of elephants, leopards, and birds sold in tourist shops; and even—why not?— in such Malian masterpieces as the Bamana antelope headdress or the Dogon antelope mask (see Vogel and N'Diaye 1985). The Gurunsi compounds illustrate an aesthetic coherence between human and natural milieus; the Ndebele women's murals demonstrate an evolving tradition. We see, then, that the work of art "is not fashioned far from things and in some intimate laboratory to which [the artist] alone possesses the key. This also means that [. . .] the work is not an arbitrary decree and that it always relates to its world as if the principle of equivalences through which it manifests the world had always been buried in it" (Merleau-Ponty 1973: 61). As Michel Leiris has written, one should "conceive of the overall approach to African arts less as primarily 'a history of arts and styles' and more as the search for, and the according of spatio-temporal form to, the 'visible products of a certain society's history'" (in Perrois 1989: 526).

Conjugating

The Ndebele mural paintings have a sociohistory of their own, but somewhere they become part of the changing permanence of African artistic imaginations, canons, and traditional skills, as witnessed, for example, in pieces from different regions of Central and West Africa which were made between the late seventeenth and the early twentieth centuries and which specialists class in the category of "extinct" art. Of various styles and morphologies, they yet retain loose common features: like most traditional artworks, they were made by anonymous authors, the creator's consciousness being fused, then, with his or her social group; and they can be linked to a number of general cultural canons, trends, and sets of symbols. As an African, I relate to them through a double articulation. On the one hand I find in them a common signifying structure that makes them seem part of a single cultural economy. On the other, I also see regional characteristics in each of them, the Grebo masks from Côte d'Ivoire, say, obeying formal customs foreign to those of the Benin plaques. The first articulation is highly subjective, and reflects the ideological climate of Africa since the 1960s, a period when the notion of African cultural unity has been promoted in such books as Willy Abraham's *The Mind of Africa* (1966), Cheikh Anta Diop's *L'Unité culturelle de l'Afrique noire* (1960), and in many other places. The second response depends on the findings of anthropologists and art historians, and allows for the exploration of each artist's individuality: the morphological forms, geometric features, chromatic techniques, and symbolisms particular to his or her vocabulary.

In the dialectic between the two articulations, the extinction of the artistic trends of the past ceases to be a closure. In effect, I can credit the ancient styles with inspirational power, and can examine the more recent pieces for their idiosyncratic patterns and styles. A creative continuity appears, and transcends the objective ruptures described by laboratory specialists. Mid-twentieth-century Dogon masks from Mali and early-twentieth-century Makonde masks from Tanzania appear to me part of the same cultural order (in Vogel and N'Diaye 1985). They can be seen and admired not only in their difference, but also as variations mirroring transformations of the archetypes in a basic imagination. And why shouldn't we relate the style of the early-twentieth-century Dogon antelope mask to what appears in the African land-

Mukishi wa pwo. Idealized woman symbolizing the primordial mythic mother. Wood, fiber. Tshokwe, Zaïre.

scape, which amazed countless African artists before Dorcas MacClintock got to it? This suggestion puts the various forms and styles of African art over time in touch with equivalents in nature.

The practices of traditional artists are of interest, say the specialists, because their works are not realistic yet participate in establishing the meaning of reality. They provide metonyms and metaphors for real beings, things, events, and natural forces in the world at the same time that they abstract the world. Their perfect insertion in African peoples' ordinary lives has led students of African art to conclude, a bit lazily, that this art is essentially functional.

This conclusion erases the complexity of the art's symbolic and allegorical meanings. The mask, for example, a clear objectification of a signifier, refers also to other orders of meanings without which it is useless.

Unlike traditional art, contemporary popular art assumes some of the virtues of realism, advancing its pictures as reflections of a modern culture and its history. Concerned with the politics of the signified, it reinforces its realism with ethical points (as Samba does) or, more generally, with various sociological functions, thus distancing itself from the symbolic and decorative activity typifying atelier and art-school trends since the 1940s.

In Sum

The three trends in current African art—tradition-inspired, modernist, and popular—are recent: the oldest examples date from the first quarter of this century. One might be tempted, then, to relate their genesis to the impact of the colonial era; yet a number of their themes and motifs—reproductions of crucifixes and Madonnas, biblical references, and so on, all along the western coast of the continent—are part of a history of acculturation that goes back to the fifteenth and sixteenth centuries. Viewed in the light of history, the distinction between the tradition-inspired and the modernist trends in contemporary African arts, though useful for the sake of analysis, indicates in the end a kind of enthrallment to traditional art. For these two trends in fact constitute a single current. First, both oeuvres are created mostly in ateliers and art schools, and even when they are made by self-trained artists they illustrate the colonial acculturation of African societies; second, unlike traditional artworks, both reveal the consciousness, the artistic identity, of their makers; and third, both have as their raison d'être not the imitation of reality but the creation of beauty.

The first of these three shared traits describes the sociocultural context of the new artistic imagination. The second is philosophical, indicating a far-reaching spiritual and intellectual revolution and its new legitimacy in an acculturated social milieu. The third is aesthetic, and brings these two trends into focus: both involve interpretative, symbolic processes of coding what is out there rather than mimetic renderings of reality. And both the tradition-inspired and the modernist impulses often fuse in the work of one artist, for example Malangatana, N'Diaye, or Twins Seven-Seven.

Popular artworks situate themselves somehow between these two trends. They often relate to a particular region and its history. As narratives, they deconstruct the memory of this history from the perspective of a single individual. In many respects, popular arts, mostly paintings, are structured as *histoire immédiate*, in Benoît Verhaegen's expression; they are literally a capturing of ordinary, banal stories and events (a market, a drinking party, a political event), of violence and tragedy (a civil war, an assassination), or of mythological motifs, for example Mami Wata. In their extreme manifestations, popular arts come close to publicity and advertisement.

Mami Wata. Collection Bogumil Jewsiewicki, with permission.

To academic rules of representation and techniques of arriving at "the beautiful," popular artists propose an opposing vision. They want to transmit a clear message; they claim the virtue of sociological and historical truth; and they try to name and unveil even the unnameable and the taboo. Here technical flaws become marks of originality. The artist appears as the "undisciplinable" hero, challenging social institutions, including art practices, particularly academic ones. Yet this "deviant," who sometimes attacks both a tradition and its modern currents, incarnates clearly the locus of their confrontation. In popular art, the politics of mimesis inserts in the "maternal" territory of the tradition a practice that questions both art and history in the name of the subject. This is work that aims to bring together art, the past, and the community's dreams for a better tomorrow.

African Literature: Myth or Reality?

Numerous books and articles have been written about African literature. They describe what is now commonly accepted as a "young" literature in African or European languages and the traditional oral experience of black Africans despite the fact that these literatures are very old: the oral or *orature* goes back to the very foundation of human communities; as for the written, putting aside the complex issues concerning African graphs, let us note briefly that one may find in Donald Herdeck's dictionary (1973) a presentation of

African authors (*African Authors: A Companion to Black African Writing*). The earliest African authors mentioned there lived in the sixth and eighth centuries A.D.: Antar (ca. 550–615) from Arabia, and Abu Dulama Ibn al-Djaun (ca. 720–777). I can, as a matter of curiosity, go further back and refer to numerous North Africans who, in the Greek or Roman *oikumene,* wrote in Greek and Latin. The Christian literature for several centuries, from the first to the end of the third century, is almost completely dominated by thinkers of African origin. To be more specific and focus only on the Latin tradition, for more than two centuries, precisely from the period of the first version of the Latin Bible, which specialists date around 160 A.D., during the reign of Marcus Aurelius, to the end of the third century, African writers are the most important contributors to the constitution of Christian thought. Tertullianus, Minucius, Felix, Cyprianus, Commodianus, Arnobius, Lactantius, and other minor thinkers are from Africa. What would have been the Christian tradition without them? They were before, and prepared the possibility of, an Augustine of Hippo, an African, one of the most powerful thinkers in the history of Christianity.

It is possible to go back even further. In 1979 I published, in a specialized book, *Africa et Roma* (Acta Omnium Gentium ac Nationum Conventus Latinis Litteris Linguaeque Fovendis, Rome: L'Erma di Bretschneider), a brief article on a little-known writer, Florus. He lived under the reigns of the Roman emperors Domitianus and Hadrianus, at the end of the first century and the beginning of the second. After what he considered to be a major literary failure, he left Rome and decided to settle in Tarragone. There he met a traveler who recognized him. The address of the foreigner is in itself a remarkable statement. "So," he said to the writer, "You are Florus the African whom unanimously we wanted to coronate [in Rome as the best poet]! Unfortunately, the Emperor rejected our decision. He had nothing against your young age; but, simply, did not want Jupiter's crown to go to Africa." Is not the story beautiful?

In any case, let me say this: Herdeck's classification of authors by chronological order gives us a sense of the richness and variety of African contributions. We can mention four black writers before the eighteenth century: from Guinea, Juan Latino, who lived in Spain and wrote verses in Latin; from Mali, Mahmud Kati, Ahmad Baba, and Abdulrahman as-Sadi, who wrote short stories in Arabic. To my knowledge, the first text of poetry in Somali was published by Ugaas Raage in about 1730; and we have also verses in Swahili, published by Abdallah Saiyid from East Africa in the middle of the eighteenth century.

This digression is a sign. One should be careful in manipulating the concept of African literature. Such early literature has historical implications and refers back to the very concept of Africa. We should also keep in mind that some African writers have been writing in African languages since the eighteenth century. Generally, specialists of African literature, when they talk about this literature, focus on the beginning of this century and link the promotion of

African literature in African languages and in foreign languages to the colonial experience, which divided the continent and imposed upon us new languages, specifically, French, English, Portuguese, Spanish, and so on. There is a history of literature in African languages which should be done. We have some books on the subject, but they depend mainly upon the colonial epistemology and its political activity of converting Africans. Thus when one speaks of African literature one is referring both to a body of texts whose authors are known and to anonymous discourses which carry on successive deposits of supposedly unknown imaginations. This is already a problem, and it has, so far, not been addressed in a convincing way by specialists of African studies. It is the view of these existing bodies of written texts and oral discourses that accounts for much of the intellectual generosity of those who believe in Africa as well as for the purely aesthetic activity of those who use these texts as objects for exotic curiosity or literary and ideological demands. One could think that African literary criticism grew up not so much as a necessity, nor as an original project within the framework of a scholarly tradition that interrogates the massiveness of discourses, but rather as a consequence of a process of inventing and organizing something else.

Can we face here a hypothesis and a wish? I would like, on the one hand, to indicate under which conditions African literature is, today, thinkable and, on the other, to formulate, in terms of possible undertakings, the perspectives from which commentaries on and analysis of African discourses could become a means of understanding African experiences from a more useful viewpoint. Can we arrive at any explicative norms as to the real nature of African literature that will put it into some sort of relation with other literatures and not give us this uncomfortable feeling that it is somehow an indigenized imitation of something else, or an adapted reproduction of genres and their confusions imported from the West? New perspectives might answer this question. So far, traditional literary criticism and even ideological interpretation of discourses from an Afrocentric perspective have not, I believe, brought about the contributions that their premises imply. Yet it is precisely in this impotence that we may find the signs of new possible interpretations about African literature and discourses (see Chinweizu et al. 1983).

African literature as a commodity is a recent invention, and authors as well as critics and specialists in the field tend to resist this fact. They seem more interested in this literature not for what it is as discourse and what, in the variety of its events and signification, it could mean in a larger context of other local and regional discourses, but rather for its significance as a mirror of something else, say, for instance, of Africa's political struggle, of processes of acculturation, or of human rights objectives. This orientation is accounted for by the fact that the world of literature is sustained by and reflects the real universe, particularly the social relationships of production and the silent impact of ideological signals. Thus, the literary world could well be a mythical space; yet, it seems to unveil the concrete experience of human communities. For example, Lilyan Kesteloot's book on the genesis of Négritude literature

(1965) and Jean Wagner's study on black literature in the United States (1962) are both valid as sociohistorical and literary criticisms. In the same vein, Janheinz Jahn's considerations on neo-African literature (1961, 1968) witness to the symbolic currrency as well as the intellectual and sociological rationality of black cultures.

Yet, what these monuments provide most clearly are, on the one hand, processes of promoting constructs and, on the other, procedures of limiting the meaning and the multiplicity of discourses. Thanks to these books, the art and significance of African discourses are commented upon, celebrated, and bought on the basis of their value as indications of functional rules of creativity. But these rules are not the efficient references that are the basis of the scholarly validity of Kesteloot's or Jahn's enterprises. They are signs of the possibility of a recent concept of African literature, an "invention" that Jahn, Kesteloot, Wagner, and most of us—literary critics and authors—can work on and live upon.

Doubtless Michel Foucault's students have already understood where I am heading. In his *The Discourse on Language,* the then Professor of the History of Systems of Thought at the College de France distinguished three major types of rules of exclusion (Foucault 1982: 215–27): (1) External procedures such as *prohibition* ("covering objects, ritual with its surrounding circumstances, the privileged or exclusive right to speak of a particular subject": 216), the *division of reason and madness,* and the *will to truth* (which integrates the preceding and orders them in a project). (2) Internal procedures of controlling discourses, procedures that are directly concerned with "principles of classification, ordering and distribution": that is, the *commentary* which signifies philology in terms of reconstruction and reading primary texts, but also literary criticism as an intellectual exercise on given documents; secondly, the *author* as a center of coherence, locus of reference, and theme of unity of his/her works; finally, the *organization of disciplines,* whose prescription is, as Foucault put it, that "what is supposed at the point of departure is not some meaning which must be rediscovered, nor an identity to be reiterated; it is that which is required for the constructions of new statements" (223). (3) The third type of procedure of exclusion includes systems of rarefaction of discourses such as *ritual,* which "[define] the qualifications required of the speaker" (225); the *fellowships of discourse*—about which, in order to get an illuminating illustration, one could think of journals of African Studies and their policies in terms of promoting articles, researches, and names; and finally, *the social appropriation of discourse,* about which Foucault exemplifies education as "the instrument whereby every individual, in a society like our own, can gain access to any kind of discourse" (227).

It is clear that this table of systems of exclusion can serve as an order for new intellectual initiatives which would simultaneously test Foucault's insights and interrogate the standardization and uniformity of so-called African literature vis-à-vis the supposed disorder of African discourses in general. A few examples will illustrate what I mean. (a) Aimé Césaire's work might be understood as a creation against the procedures of prohibition(s) and division of reason. The terror and violence in Césaire's work witness more to these procedures than to the vitalistic and genitalistic dimensions noted by Sartre in *Black Orpheus*. Thus, rather than being symbols of a "Black Orpheus," this work could signify a way of questioning a will to truth. (b) It has been suggested that there are two main sociological explanations for the genesis of African literature in European languages: first, that this literature is a direct consequence of colonization; second, that it has been made possible by the Western system of schooling. In other words, these explanations imply that African literary works as well as commentaries on them depend on, and at the same time can be accounted for by, the European norms of social appropriations of discourse. Thus this literature, if it makes sense, would do so only insofar as these external conditions of possibility determine it as literature. (c) One could say that the mere existence of this new African literature proceeds from the extension to Africa of Western fellowships of discourse. Therefore, despite all the invitations for an Afrocentric perspective that have been made these last years, the language of our agreements and disagreements might fundamentally be marked by a surprising and obvious coherence: an epistemological space.

What is interesting about interrogating such hypotheses? In terms of theoretical perspectives, it is obvious that such hypotheses, in principle, would confirm or invalidate Foucault's proposition: "I am supposing that in every society the production of discourse is at once controlled, selected, organized and redistributed according to a certain number of procedures, whose role is to avert its powers and its dangers, to cope with chance events, to evade its ponderous, awesome materiality" (Foucault 1982: 216). On the other side, it might be useful, using this hypothesis, to find out whether or not similar processes of taming discourses function in Africa, and under which conditions.

My own hypothesis is that two major rules of exclusion have, in a radical manner, provided the steps for the "invention" and organization of African literature: the notions of commentary and author as used by the myths of Africanism since the eighteenth century. Tylor and Lévy-Bruhl limit their inquiries to the question of evolution. As a consequence, they resolve their intellectual and scientific interests in the reading of non-Western experiences as fragmentary discourses and strange anonymous bodies. Anthropological texts arose in the nineteenth century as commentaries on silent and irrational organizations, emphasizing two main issues: the background of the theorists and the relative anonymity of the objects of the studies. In the first case, the commentary describes the history of humankind from the exteriority of a silent and exotic African history. As examples, let us rapidly look at two paradoxical cases of *Einfühlung*. Frobenius, at the beginning of this century, could wander throughout Black Africa reading Pigafetta and Portuguese travelers' reports instead of seriously listening to Africans. And, in the 1920s and the 1930s, Wilhelm Schmidt, in Austria, after his numerous Germanophone predecessors, contributed to anthropology on the assumption of an absolute inexistence of clear signed writings in African societies.

Nevertheless, it is within the violence of these commentaries on exoticism that, by means of what was ideologically signified by the dialectical ratio on civilization and primitiveness, the new reality of an "African author" in the Western sense appeared. In the 1940s, for example, whereas Marcel Griaule (1948), in a kind of revelation, recognized Ogotommêli as subject of a knowledge that he had received and was obviously interpreting in his own discourse, Placide Tempels (1949) was still favoring the classical opposition and exploiting the so-called break existing between the anonymous wisdom of traditional Bantus and the moral corruption of évolués, those bad copies of European individualism.

The break indicates the foundation of what, after Jack Goody (1977), may be called the "grand dichotomy," for it determines, in present-day scholarship, types of economic structures and social situations as well as our familiar field of African literature. In binary oppositions, we would note the following gaps or tensions: at the economic level, the agrarian society dominated by economic structures of subsistence versus the highly sophisticated processes of production and social relations of urban civilization and international markets; at the sociocultural level, the oral and customary setting qualified as monocultural, versus the complex pluricultural contexts of big cities; at the level of religious superstructures, societies characterized by an integration of the sacred and the profane versus societies functioning on the principle of a distinction between the sacred and the profane. I do not exaggerate if I affirm that, rather than analyzing the complexity of African discourses, most of our textbooks and monographs are still essentially preoccupied with this dichotomy and its signs. Let us look at the best of them and we will find the basic assumptions of the dichotomy. First: the forms and the content of the oral literature are supposed to witness to and translate a monocultural experience which, up to now, is still called a "primitive" civilization in anthropology. Second: with the Westernization and Christianization processes under colonial rule, two new types of expression—written literature in African and in European languages—appeared, which describe the contradictions and the problems implied by the metamorphosis signified by colonization. Third, this conversion has promoted authored texts, which, although fundamentally different from those of the past, do not constitute a hiatus in terms of vital African experiences. Fourth, the notion of neo-African literature marks an internal historical and sociological dimension but it does not and cannot mean that its possibility could be elsewhere than on the exteriority of this very literature.

We have learned how to live with these contradictory assumptions. In fact, they are norms and systems, since they are simultaneously the paradoxical references of our professional activities and the events which make thinkable our literary praxes. Moreover, depending on our state of mind, these norms allow us all the liberties we wish. From them we can today decide that Chinua

Achebe's and E. Mphahlele's works are internal parts of English literature, Senghor's, Rabemananjara's, or Camara Laye's of the French. And, tomorrow, with the same conviction we could demonstrate exactly the contrary and celebrate our authors as mirrors of African authenticity. Pessimistically, I remember that Northrop Frye once wrote: "literature, like other subjects, has a theory and a practice: poems and plays and novels form the practical side, and the centre of criticism is the theory of literature" (1975: 206). What serious theory could support the fantastic liberties of our investigations in African literature, if, at least, on the one hand, we do agree on the urgency of analyzing the conditions of existence of this literature, and, on the other, we do not accept the hypothesis that African criticism might not be an African practice at all? Christopher Miller and Bernadette Cailler face this challenge in two controversial books that I would like to question from a psychoanalytic viewpoint.

Letters of Reference

> We are seeing, though, that the wounds which we are inflicting on the body of our civilization are wounds which we must address, but address more deeply than we do address them.
>
> —MARC GLASSMAN (*Border/Lines* [Toronto, Canada] 15 [1989]: 25)

> Le sujet n'est sujet que d'être assujettissement synchronique dans le champ de l'Autre.
>
> —JACQUES LACAN (Séminaire, May 20, 1964)

A well-known story might introduce us to some essential problems concerning the idea of Africa as "difference" in today's academic studies of African literature.

It's an ordinary day at the office of a highly regarded French psychoanalyst. Each hour one patient leaves and another comes in. What we have is a ritual. The great man knows his role: comfortably seated in a corner armchair, condescending but sincere, he generously listens to his successive patients. This particular day, he seems a bit tired. As usual, though, the women attendants do a remarkable job, managing the comings and goings of the patients. The hours go by. Around 5 P.M., the last patient, an obsessive, is still on the couch: talkative, proud of his fluency of expression, he is commenting at length on some of his verbal flights. As the time is up, very satisfied with himself and with his performance, he gets up, and, looking at the psychoanalyst peacefully at ease in his armchair, he concludes: "It was a wonderful session, wasn't it?" Silence. Hesitant, the patient collects himself and repeats the ritual concluding words favored by the psychoanalyst himself: "Very good; we shall stop here for today." Silence. Something is not right. The psychoanalyst seems unusually distant, aloof. Is he sleeping? No, but he is very pale, very cold. The women attendants come in and take charge of the situation. A doctor is summoned, arrives, checks the body. The diagnosis is straightforward: the psychoanalyst has been dead for more than three hours.

The story, as I've told it, is summarized from Serge Leclaire's account in *Démasquer le Réel* (1971), a collection of essays on the object of psychoanalysis, and it is significant, as Leclaire shows, in that it narrates a particular kind of death wish. The patient wants the death of the psychoanalyst as most of us, consciously or unconsciously, want that of people in power. Such a wish has nothing to do, at least in principle, with love or hatred; or, more exactly, it takes place beside or beyond what these sentiments might mean. The story illustrates a fantasy entertained by many patients confined within an "analytical relation" and who, all around the world, play symbolically upon it.

To make his argument clearer, Leclaire adds another case, one that actually happened, and in which one can observe the boomerang effects of the first story. Another renowned Parisian psychoanalyst is receiving a patient. This time the context is different: the analysand is undergoing "training" analysis en route to becoming an analyst himself. So we have, on the one side, a "guide" and, on the other, a "disciple" who has to go through his own nightmares in order to gain access to the profession. One day, in the last session of the day, our disciple-patient begins to comment on the very story that I have just summarized. The "master-guide" reacts moodily: "So you like this story, don't you?" The disciple shrugs: "Why not?"

This addendum makes it easier to draw lessons from the story. Two main themes come to mind. First, by imagining the death of the powerful in a relationship, what one wants really is to kill him. Thus someone who can decode the story may well ask, "So do you really want to kill your 'master'?" Or, in a more dramatic fashion: "Have you really been wishing the death of your father?" But the story illustrates something else as well, namely that the psychoanalyst incarnates silence. He is the one who is paid to listen, and, occasionally, to guide, but not to speak. He is the exact reverse of a professor. The psychoanalyst is therefore a specialist in a "deathly silence," which, as Leclaire would remind us, simply symbolizes death in most of our own dreams. On the other hand, one could ask: what about the patient? Lying down on the couch he or she is often silent, like a dead thing, as if waiting for someone who could put "it" elsewhere, in its place. Isn't it the patient who most obviously signifies death?

The Practice of the Word

It is interesting to note that when the notion of death, whether actual or symbolic, surfaces in a psychoanalytic relation, the analyst will, in principle, always refer to three main keys: desire or fear of death, identification with death, symbolic representation of death.

I want to begin my meditation on "African theories" with two of Leclaire's statements, which will sum up what I have presented. (The translations are my own.)

> Assuredly, if the analyst is silent, there are, indeed, also patients who play at being dead [. . .] and they tell you so. That could last a long time. (1971: 124)
>
> Briefly, it seems to me that the analysts' interest, Freud being an exception, has been mainly, from the viewpoint of the subject we are discussing, on the theme of death as if, by thematizing it, one could better veil it. On the contrary, what we are proposing is [. . .] to reintroduce the question of death, as it is lived, for example, by obsessed patients. (1971: 127)

Christopher Miller's *Theories of Africans* (1990) illustrates what could be described as obsessive nightmares about a possibly real or symbolic death. That such an obsession, after the slave trade and the colonial exploitation and in the present-day neocolonial postindependence era, might be well founded is not, however, the topic of the project. Miller's research is well delimited and focused on "Francophone Literature and Anthropology." And yet it suggests images that could be decoded by the three keys used by the psychoanalyst when he faces an obsessed patient.

First, there is the fear of death (symbolic or real), expressing itself in a wish for the disappearance of the "father": after all, what does he really know of my problems? What is he still doing around? The father's discourse does not address my real experience, seems completely nonsensical, and I cannot submit to it. From this point of view, the rejection of Western criticism, so bitterly exemplified by the Nigerians Chinweizu, Jemie, and Madubuike in their *Toward the Decolonization of African Literature* (1983), becomes a transparent sign: it wishes—and how!—the death of symbolic fathers. Second, there is an identification with death at the very basis of the most significant African ideologies: *"Négritude,"* "African personality," "Pan-Africanism." I refer to the identification—for good, sacred, and highly respectable reasons—with the millions of victims of the slave trade and the identification with those who resisted the process of colonization and were killed. This identification is accompanied by forms of introjection and incorporation, which present explicit and conflicting signs of both a wish and a refusal to die. But these African ideologies of self-affirmation are also haunted by the specter of *cultural* death, which they associate, for example, with the French policies of *assimilation*. So we have finally to consider the symbolic representation of death, the silence of the conquered, who, on the psychoanalyst's couch, represent another silence, the massive and shameful silence of men who discover themselves incapable of explaining to their children what happened. Those who have *submitted* now confront doubts about themselves, want to know what is wrong with them, and face an awful question: could it be that the other, the "conquistador" or the "colonizer," has a response to their predicament? Indeed, he has one. But let's note something else. Another silence, a frightening one, lingers within the general economy of new African words, languages, theories commenting upon the catastrophe and articulating in new ways other objects of desire: African women do not seem to speak. In any case, their presence in the Francophone field of literature has been, until very recently, marked by silence.

I first want to give an overview of Miller's book, and then come back to these problems that he raises. The book is divided into six sections. The first, the introduction, "Reading through Western Eyes," deals with the main theoretical issues that dominate Miller's larger intellectual exploration. Among these, two seem central, the usefulness of anthropology and of dialogism.

> Thinking programmatically about Western approaches to African literature leads me to one major hypothesis, around which the rest of this book will turn: that a fair Western reading of African literatures demands engagement with, and even dependence on, anthropology. The demonstration of this point begins from the premise that good reading does not result from ignorance and that Westerners simply do not know enough about Africa. (Miller 1990: 4)

> If anthropology becomes dialogical, infused with the complexities and contradictions of interacting systems of thought, it seems that everyone will gain. The demise of false transparency may make it more difficult to "look up" the meaning of a "symbol," but the meanings we do construct will consequently be more valuable. But if description and representation themselves are renounced, if the focus of ethnography shifts completely from observed to observer, then its use value as an interlocutor from the criticism of African literatures will have been lost. (Miller 1990: 27)

The idea of bringing together anthropology and African literature *en bloc* seems original. So far, specialists have conceived this collaboration only between anthropology and oral literature. Miller goes beyond that. His expressed aim of placing literature and anthropology in dialogue represents an advance on those who would exalt anthropology as a mirror of African contexts and realities.

The second section, "Ethnicity and Ethics," begins with a conceptual analysis of "ethnicity" and its relation to "ethics" and "ethos." Miller argues that "ethnicity and ethics in fact constitute the central topos in the criticism of African literature" and suggests a distinction "between enthnographies that are 'ethical' and those that are in need of ethical critique." He then applies this lesson to the Marxist critique of ethnicity, as principally illustrated in a collective book edited by Georg M. Gugelberger, *Marxism and African Literature* (1985). This collection of essays, Miller argues, tends to contain and discount ethnicity.

The point is a major one, since Miller explicitly links Amilcar Cabral's and Frantz Fanon's theories to matters of life and death. He uses as an example what he calls "The Prison-House of Guinea," and comments on the execution of the writer and artist Kéita Fodeba, who "was not accused of partisan ethnicity that we know of, except in the etymological sense, in that Sékou Touré made him into a heathen, a pagan, an exile from a kingdom in which one discourse reigned" (61–62). Indeed, Miller distinguishes the "'pragmatic,' local use of Marxist ideology in the cynical sense" by Sékou Touré from, say, Gugelberger's book, Fanon's invocation of violence as means for political liberation, and Sékou Touré's political madness. Let me note that Miller is critical of such a possible interpretation of his argument:

> The sequence of events I have described remains open to a variety of interpreta-
> tions, and I do not offer Kéita Fodeba's fate as a necessary outgrowth of either
> Marxism or Fanon's theories, or as a tale whose moral is that nothing can ever
> change [. . .]. Does the fact that Sékou Touré wrapped himself in Marxist and
> Fanonian discourse make Fanon responsible for the reign of terror in Guinea?
> The question is reminiscent of debates on the relation of Nietzsche to Nazism:
> to what extent is an author responsible for readings and misreadings of his or
> her texts? A full and sensitive reading of Fanon's texts might reveal an "open"
> system that has been wrongly "closed" by critics; but the problem that concerns
> me is precisely how the textual paradoxes in Fanon's writing were translated
> into unambiguous political oppression by a "misreader" like Sékou Touré.
> (Miller 1990: 62)

The question is important: if we allow that Fanon is culpably implicated by the putative (and really quite mystifying) relation between his work and Sékou Touré's practice, then where should one stop in shifting responsibilities and indicting people? Whom to condemn—Aristotle, or his European disciples who concocted, in his name, elaborate theories justifying the slave trade? Whom to charge—Saint Paul and Thomas Aquinas on the one hand, or, on the other, Christian churches' centuries-long anti-women ideologies and practices? Whom to vilify—the nineteenth- and twentieth-century cultural anthropologists who invented African tribes and models, or, on the other hand, their African disciples who exploited these contrivances for their crimi-nal policies of "authenticity"?

I have addressed elsewhere the intellectual and political ambiguities, and generosity, of French-educated Marxists. They do not, generally speaking, correspond to the caricature described by Miller. Unlike most colonists, non-Marxist Africanists, and other God-sent missionaries, Marxists have had the courage to draw publicly the lessons of their African commitment in all its naïveté.

In any case, the complexity and ugliness of the whole issue bring us back to where we began. We know that the son wishes for the death of the father, the slave wishes for the death of the master, the colonized wishes for the death of the colonizer, the patient wishes for the death of the psychoanalyst, an idea well exemplified in Fanon's work. Yet, how to act out such a wish? Sartre, for instance, set forth such an alternative in a little-known and controversial text, *Between Existentialism and Marxism* (1974: 189–223). And what to think and to do when, in the name of an irresponsible will to truth, this wish transforms itself into acts of sheer madness? Prudently, Miller focuses on fundamentals. Against Fanon's discourse on the right to violence and its "un-ethical" application by Sékou Touré, Miller remarks that "what *is* ethical would be a dialectical relationship between a transcendental truth and respect for the other, for difference. A self relating to itself has few ethical problems. In this sense, *there is no real ethics without ethnicity*, without the disquieting, untidy presence of the other" (Miller 1990: 63).

Chapter 3 is on "Orality through Literacy," focusing on "Mande Verbal Art"; chapter 4 analyzes the anthropological context and the content of Camara Laye's well-known *L'Enfant noir;* chapter 5 uses *Les Soleils des Indé-pendances* by Ahmadou Kourouma for a critique of the "Francophone" ideology, and, analytically, examines the internal politics of the book itself; finally, the last chapter of Miller's book is devoted to "Senegalese Women Writers." These case studies, he writes, constitute his "response to the bind of relativism" and are "a reflection of my milieu, but equally a reflection of the discursive field that exists in African studies." Significantly, Miller adds that he will "not pretend to transcend or abandon the American academic scene but from within it [. . .] attempt a dialogue with another scene, whose issues and language are partially, *problematically,* different: francophone Africa" (1990: 67). On the whole, the studies elegantly handle "the ethics of projection," and, with a brilliant theoretical awareness, comment on what Miller himself calls the "difference between projecting for someone else or another people" (1990: 296).

Three important problems inform Miller's project, a project which proceeds under the rubric "Theories of Africans" but which finds its coherence in a particular reading of those theories as they spring from their context. The first of these problems is an idea of Africa as circumscribed by a series of "ethnicities" or differences. At least in the contemporary scholarly literature, the concept of "ethnicity" represents a recent current that (as against the 1960s concept of a culturally unified Africa) emphasizes the alterity of some basic cultural entities defined by a language and a particular history. The second problem follows from this: that anthropology—or, more precisely, an anthropological library—seems to be a necessary recourse in order to decode "ethnicities" as well as "the complexity of cultural questions in Africa and their translation into Western understanding" (1990: 5). Finally, there is a most delicate problem: the politics of symbolic and, unfortunately, real death that insistently mirrors itself in Miller's discussion on ethical ethnographies and projections.

"To think anthropologically is to validate *ethnicity* as category, and this has become a problematic idea," Miller writes (1990: 31). Perhaps it is worth noting that by "anthropology," here and elsewhere, Miller means cultural anthropology, a tradition that embraces evolutionist, diffusionist, and func-tionalist schools. The origins of cultural anthropology, as I've argued else-where, lie in the Western desire to discover its own past, and it constructed an imaginary trajectory that begins with the so-called primitive and culminates in the attainments of European civilization. And this hidden telos can continue to tinge even those schools of anthropology that ostensibly disclaim such notions. I want to insist, however, that these concerns do not tell against the Kantian tradition of philosophical anthropology—as in, for example, the validation of difference in Emmanuel Levinas's philosophy of otherness. (Surprising as it may seem, moreover, I would argue that it is to this Kantian tradition that the structuralist anthropology associated with Claude Lévi-Strauss properly belongs.)

Miller correlates "ethnicity" and "otherness"; and, referring to Jean-Loup Amselle's deconstruction of the concept of "African ethnicity," Miller accepts that African *"ethnies"* were "constructed by the colonizers in order to divide and conquer." He then poses a question: "Does this mean that ethnicity itself is an illusion, a useless category of interpretation?" His own preference is to keep this notion "for an inquiry into notions of identity and difference," and he defines it as "a sense of identity and difference among peoples, founded on a fiction of origin and descent and subject to forces of politics, commerce, language and religious culture" (1990: 34–35). Still, the fragility of the notion becomes obvious in Miller's own reading of the Mande cultural "space," and his acknowledgment that "the ethnographic sources on the Mande—from the late nineteenth century through the late 1980s—are full of terminological squabbles and substantive disagreements" (1990: 75). Why, then, does Miller choose to retain a concept whose value he has called into question?

The answer lies in his faith in anthropology—or, should one call it a "vigilantly skeptical resignation"? "Taken at face value," he writes, "my hypothesis means simply that any non-African reader (or even an African reader from a different cultural area) seeking to cross the information gap between himself or herself and an African text will very probably be obliged to look in books that are classified as anthropology" (1990: 4). Miller is well aware of the dangers of this approach. First of all, the representations found in the anthropological library are neither the best nor the most reliable introduction to African images of otherness. As Miller concedes, the "access to non-Western systems" it seems to offer is "mediated through a discipline that has been invented and controlled by the West." Second, though, the methodological and ideological tensions and shifts from evolutionist to functionalist and structuralist models in anthropology are such that they have, over time, completely transformed the field and its representations. And Miller knows this. He submits to anthropology, yet he is very critical of its authority. He notes that in the politics of the early pre-Independence era, anthropology was "the most powerful mode of colonial discourse." If his reliance on anthropology entails (as he writes) a "surrender to that paradox," I would only insist that it does not entail the surrender of our critical awareness that his anthropological sources and readings may not always be reliable. As Miller recognizes, "to make use of anthropology is to borrow trouble."

There are other questions that arise from the privilege Miller gives to cultural anthropology and not, say, to history. I still wonder what would have happened if Miller had taken the risk of bringing to his analyses, explicitly and systematically, the perspective of philosophical anthropology rather than cultural anthropology. At any rate, the chronological succession of the subjects chosen—Mande verbal art, Laye's *L'Enfant noir,* Kourouma's *Les Soleils des Indépendances,* and Senegalese women writers—fits magnificently into a historical frame of Francophone literature. Moreover, rather than merely reflecting those mute values and sociocultural confrontations that are the preserve of static anthropologies, his topics advance, describe, unveil a particular African history in the making.

But let me put aside these difficult issues and turn to the four anthropologico-literary chapters. The author explores a number of delicate questions about the origin of texts and Senegalese women's *prise de parole.* At the same time, he theorizes about the characters and sociocultural complexity of chosen texts. Here, then, we can bring back the analytical preoccupation with which we began. Leclaire writes:

> Someone, in front of someone else, speaks. He is interrogating what he is. He asks himself, in his very singular manner, how he who feels, with an unequal happiness (or unhappiness), to be one who is more or less distinguished, situates himself in connection to others, everybody dead or living; in turn, what kind of void might his disappearance create, or what place does his presence occupy? (Leclaire 1968: 175)

This *quelqu'un* (someone) is multiple. Indeed, it provides an account of Christopher Miller's dialogue with the African Francophone writers he comments upon. The *quelqu'un* may also serve as a figure for the way Miller's readers can situate themselves in a conversation with the author and establish a discourse on Miller's discourse, as I do in this essay. Readers can also bring into the conversation their own understanding of the basic texts and contexts that Miller employs. At any rate, by the end of *Theories of Africans,* readers will know what they have been subjected to. They can, variously, reject or integrate totally or partially, an interpretation that is about a primary play, the "zero complex" that Camara Laye and Ahmadou Kourouma claim to narrate. In any case, they will have to face anthropology and, if they are patient, apropos of *L'Enfant Noir,* intellectual scenarios concerning the evolution of humans.

Using Miller's analyses, I'd like now to focus on three related motifs about power and symbolic death, and, in so doing, show the strength of Miller's contribution to the field of African literature. The motifs are African childhood as metaphor, the French language as a sign of male power, and the refused voice of African women as the other side of an intellectual and social canon.

The African child, in *L'Enfant noir,* enunciates signs and rules of a cultural order telling us how good it is to live in communion within what seems like an exceptional affinity between culture and nature. Is he lying? That's probable, as many critics have said. Is he playing on a "political" myth? That's not impossible. The vision of childhood frames itself in Laye's text as a romantic setting whose secret movements and balance form an amazing picture. Should we imagine a trap, since the real volume that the story seems to confront is not named explicitly? Doesn't Camara Laye's narrative celebrate a mythical space, an idealized environment? There are contrary signs, such as some Western technologies. On the whole, however, the narrative only decorates an imagined zero, primitive, immediate experience in which a bright boy uses his childhood as a play for power and conjugates, in his *"stretto"* field, the complicated games of the grown-ups with his own. But is it the child or the writer who is manipulating the reader? Christopher Miller credits the writer as responsible for "a shrewd metaphor, a tactic used to gain influence, and ultimately an ironic comment on the politics of knowledge" (1990: 128).

Dedicated to the mother, the book makes a startling revelation about the relationship existing between the father and the son: "I left my father too soon." Miller's commentary catches this: the narrator "states a very simple, very significant reason: he left his father too soon. The father is knowledge; in the pages that follow, he will begin to reveal some of his secret knowledge to his son" (1990: 134). As we can already guess, from the son's viewpoint, the supreme secret is in the very name of the father. In this trace of his origin and, thus, of a possible identification with what made him possible, the son can become someone like his father. Miller specifies the complexity of the desire:

> The identity of the father figure, le nom du père, is the condition to which the narrator aspires and to which he cannot seem to gain access. In the passage of *Le Maître de la parole* pertaining to Fran Camara, Camara Laye was working on the same problem of origin, identity, and status. To be a "father-child" (faden) is to have or to seek a certain relation with the father's totem. So when we read about the ancestor's relation to a snake in *Le Maître de la parole*, explaining genealogically the totemic relation, we will be in a better position to continue reading *L'Enfant noir*. (1990: 142)

In this way, the child's game with a serpent in the story becomes a metaphor. Should he kill it, so he can, finally, know the father's secrets or (to defer to Freud and put it theoretically) so he can transcend the Oedipus complex? Miller correctly insists that, in this specific case, "the identification is *total* within what Freud calls physical reality, and his explanation of the 'return of totemism in childhood' as an atavistic manifestation of the Oedipus complex might be applied to a reading of *L'Enfant noir*." There are immense problems here. From Freud's *Totem and Taboo,* one could follow Miller's analysis of hypotheses—those of Malinowski, Lévi-Strauss, the Ortigues, etc.—concerning Oedipus and the evolution of humans. At the end, one faces Miller's statement:

> Within the Mande, the totem would indeed appear to be "that which remains of a diminished totality," the totality being the orderly systems of relations, customs, and beliefs that hark back to the glory days of the empire. The Sunjata

epic is the principal reminder of the last plenitude; the griots' verbal art seeks
to revive the totality but is suspected of diminishing it. Totemism is another
reminder. (1990: 154)

There is then the case of Ahmadou Kourouma's *Les Soleils des Indépendances*. It is an "anthropological novel," as Miller describes it, in which "at the
moments when the personified narrator emerges and reminds the reader of
his superior knowledge, an authoritarian structure has been exposed and subjected to irony; irony because the authority of this narrator-character is limited by the dialogical exchange in which he participates with the reader"
(1990: 224). One may consider another possibility: *Les Soleils des Indé-
pendances* as a sociological novel about a past facing a present and inscribing
its political agenda according to new determinations of inequality and differences. The French language, in this case, becomes a symbol of power. To face
it down, to destructure it in the name of an "Africanity"—what a temptation!
For his part, Miller, after a careful analysis of the "Francophonie ideology,"
comments on Kourouma's modes of Africanizing the French and dialectizing
it in the name of what I have proposed to call the "zero complex." That such
a book should then be celebrated by the "Francophonie" may seem a mystery.
Yet such are the vagaries of history. Miller cites Senghor's expressed hope that
his "participation as one of the 'immortals' of the French Academy will allow
him to 'work on [. . .] the crossbreeding of the French language [. . .]. I hope
to introduce into the French Academy's dictionary words like 'négritude'"
(1990: 199). Kourouma acted out this sentiment, dialectizing French and inscribing it as the crossing juncture of the old Mande traditional politics and
the new, shattered dreams for modernity.

The pleasure of speaking, the mastery of the word, unveils the game of
multiple voices, representing shattered symbols, ironizing about languages—
and thus about the limit, the origin; in sum, this speech relates the mourning
of a lost object, an identification with a dead yet signifying figure. Miller
glosses the ending of Kourouma's novel: "a Mande utopia has been lost on
earth, but the implication is that it survives in the mind. Politics will belong
to the new structures, but culture will remain unchanged" (1990: 239).

Finally, Miller addresses the issue of women's absence in Francophone literature: "The glaring absence of women novelists before 1976—the deafening
silence—commands any approach to this topic and demands explanation"
(1990: 247). There are reasons for this absence. Among the most visible would
be the patterns of control in precolonial and colonial Africa, the colonial
politics of literacy, and "the ambiguous adventure of education." I would like
to insist, briefly, on a correlation. Miller remarks, several times, that Camara
Laye's book is dedicated to the mother. In fact, the dedication goes beyond
the mother, Dâman, and includes all black women, all African mothers:
"Femme noire, femme africaine, ô toi ma mère je pense à toi." "Black woman,
African woman, oh you, my mother, I think of you." Now, let us note that

in the culture, *speech* is presented as female. Synthesizing Sory Camara's *Gens de la parole* and *Paroles très anciennes,* Miller observes:

> His depiction of the sexes as at odds with each other in Mande culture, and of women as subordinated and muted ('a citizen who is an eternal minor') is confirmed and expanded in his subsequent work, *Paroles très anciennes.* In this ethnopsychoanalytic study of Mande culture, Camara interprets circumcision, hunting, agriculture, and polygamy as symbolic strategies by which the Mande male hero (acting under the flag of fadenya, father-childness) seeks to bypass the female and engender himself. (1990: 263)

Symbolically, therefore, if speech is female, culture is male and its origins are in the hands of asexual, neutral specialists, the *griots.* In this framework, the father incarnates the law that the hero of *L'Enfant noir* would have liked, as we've seen, to have confronted sooner. Sensitive to the privileges of the mother, yet subjected to the determining exigencies of the culture, the hero assembles the two conflicting poles: he is the beloved "object" of a mother, and the "child" of a culture, that is, the "son" of his father. Could we then, as a hypothesis, imagine the author, in novelizing himself, and in dedicating the book to the mother, formulating very decisively what Jacques Lacan called the mother's relation to the father's speech? One step more, and the father will cease to be the "refused reference" or, strictly, the "refused" and the "referred to" who, in the mind of the hero (and the author), stands at the opposed side of the central, loving, and balancing figure of the mother-*génitrix.*

There is a remarkable absence in this conflictual space that may well explain the women's "deafening silence," which Miller describes: the absence of the *génitrix* of the mother and her order. I would like to use this absence as a key to my reading of Bernadette Cailler's book *Conquérants de la nuit nue: Edouard Glissant et l'H(h)istoire antillaise* (1988).

The Death of False Fathers

In the conclusion of her study of Glissant, Bernadette Cailler observes that the Caribbean writer "wants to work out the crisis of the psychic space in which lies the Caribbean adventure of the text" (1988: 172). At issue is the experience of history for someone who is excluded from the very archives of history. What does it mean to be an intellectual and reflect upon the meaning of history for someone like Glissant, someone who has no choice but to think within the French tradition yet who cannot forget that his ancestors came to the Caribbean as slaves? This crisis, Cailler thinks, "buries its roots deeply in the death of fathers (false fathers), producers of discourses that have been coded in advance; a crisis in which the discourses of love are eroded by holes on every side, and in which the myths of filiation grow indistinct; a crisis in which, each day, the connection requires suffering, an opening out onto make-believe" (1988: 172). The thesis is fascinating.

I want first to clarify the concept of the false father, then to approach Cailler's book in a critical fashion and to measure its interest and relevance by broadening some of the issues that it raises within the psychoanalytic register she has adopted.

Consider some of the complexities of the child's relation to his father. It is our father who, in the name of privileges of the blood, seniority, tradition, summons us in our fantasies and establishes us within an order of duties and ambitions conceived by an ancient memory that he represents. The father is tradition. He is what came before, and he incarnates the law of survival and the sign of the future. He thus enjoins: Fear not, son, this is the past of our people.

The father's autobiography here becomes a kind of history. His word is accorded a permanence that follows us from place to place and across the years. It becomes the memory of the world. Hence the burden of generations that is conveyed in the phrase "I am your father." The child, crushed by such authority, withdraws into a position of weakness while, at the same time, the child would like to affirm a new authority and the voice of new ways to come. But a sovereign discourse, that of the father, clearly signifies a mortal refusal to the child's desire for power. "I am going to look elsewhere," the child thinks, and thus arouses suspicions that dictate a rereading of the familial memory. "And what if my father was wrong?"

What if the father to which you have subjected yourrself is an imposter: a false father who wrongly usurped the position of authority? What happens then to the son? What about the status of memory: if I'm confronting a false father who has imposed a false word on me, what sort of memory am I rejecting? This has long been the case in colonized Black Africa: Having been drilled from textbooks that speak of "our ancestors, the Gauls," what happens when you wake up and discover that your ancestors were not the Gauls? Do you remain silent—or shout yourself hoarse? What are the implications here for a practice and politics of patrimony and tradition?

Using a psychoanalytic model for the historical dislocation of the colonial subject, Cailler offers a compelling figure for paternity, power, and memory. Who really is my father? Much more lies behind this question than the mirage of trying to identify, say, the inventor of the ballpoint pen or the cigarette filter. It is, indeed, a question of inserting oneself in a genealogy of the blood and of defining oneself as a descendant of a memory that is part of a particular history; and for someone like Glissant, it means the task of trying to articulate a continuity, a history, a future. Cailler's book indicates persistently what is at stake: Where is the father? How do we name him and his power? Should the child's memory correspond with his father's, and should his discourse conform to his father's?

Cailler begins with an image of dejection, the figure of the maroon—that is, the fugitive slave—as an entry into Glissant's work. For it is her aim to map the historical experience of the maroon upon the unique course Glissant has traveled. As for the historical experience, Bernadette Cailler elaborates on it at great length through a rereading of a chapter by David Patrick Geggus (in his *Slavery, War and Revolution,* 1982) and two books by Richard Price (*Maroon Societies,* 1973, and *First-Time: The Historical Vision of an Afro-American People,* 1983), in addition to the testimonies of earlier writers such as Moreau de Saint-Méry, César de Rochefort, Jean-Baptiste Dutertre, and Jean-Baptiste Labat. In brief, the epic of the fugitive slave is made to represent the negation of slavery, and will be considered in that light. Is the slave's flight a simple escape toward a new fortune or, as it has been celebrated, a political act that rejects servitude in absolute terms: liberty or death? Cailler tells us that "serious researchers today agree on establishing love of liberty as the first priority among the causes of the flight of slaves." Thus, she can reveal the emotion of their remarkable sacrifices: "Rooted in strong first négritudes (the suicidal slave who swallows his tongue, the slave who jumps into the sea, the smothering of one's children . . .), the stories of the maroons had to be, should be written some day" (1988: 66).

As a reflection of this historical level of slave runaways, the author details a symbolic and political course traveled by Edouard Glissant, as a new sign of the maroon. Born to a respectable family at Bezaudin, educated at Lamentin and then at the Lycée Schoelcher in Fort-de-France, Glissant departed for France in 1946, where he studied philosophy and ethnology. Cailler emphasizes certain encounters that Glissant had along the way. For example, Glissant had Aimé Césaire as a teacher at the Lycée Schoelcher. In the early 1940s, "it would seem that Glissant very much wanted to keep his distance from the Négritude of Césaire [. . .]" (1988: 40); and, once in France, "it seems that he lived rather isolatedly [. . .]; certain pages of *Soleil de la Conscience,* a poetic essay published in 1955, evoke this difficult adjustment to the French landscape; they are introspective pages in which are already obvious all the ambiguity of the relation to the Other, but also the strength of the 'poetic intention' that resists deadlock, aimless roaming, as well as segregation" (1988: 41).

The question is presented in simple terms: to what extent does the outline of Glissant's biography reproduce the passion of the historical maroons and the risks they ran? Now, among Glissant's friends or acquaintances were black intellectuals such as René Depestre, Frantz Fanon, and the Algerian writer Kateb Yacine. But Glissant was also a French intellectual, whose dissertation for the *Diplôme d'études supérieures* dealt with French poets: Césaire, Reverdy, Char, and Claudel. And yet Césaire is among them: doesn't his presence validate the order of the entourage?

To establish a correspondence between the road traveled by Glissant and that of the runaway slave, Cailler actually invites us to make a leap from the author's life to his texts as they are transformed from the 1950s on. And we needn't stop with Glissant. Frantz Fanon, for example, would be a maroon of the first order. Or we could point to even more evocative figures, such as the Cuban Esteban Montejo, a more than hundred-year-old maroon who, in Miguel Barnet's book (1968), says that for him the escape was a spirit, a vocation. The parallel Cailler develops between the itinerary of the Caribbean intellectual and that of the runaway slave is meant to celebrate the former by reference to the martyrdom of the latter. We should observe, however, that, if Glissant's words issue forth from the flight of the slaves it is because they resist the silent turning of the pages of a story. Metaphorically, Fanon has reenacted Montejo's gesture. Glissant, in a different move, chooses to maintain the *textual* meaning of an *oral* discourse on liberty.

But Cailler suggests that the maroon be understood as a "negator," that is to say, as a "metonymy" (1988: 59n.30). This time, the split between the two stories could be bridged. The first genre establishes the memory of the past in the written history of the historians. Thus, Glissant's own tests of history can be superimposed upon historical time and the version of history represented by the speech of the "father." It is thus not an accident if the major sign of the second negator reflects the shadow of Hegel. Glissant writes,

> Truly, every history (and consequently, every Reason of History conceived projected therein) has decidedly been to the exclusion of the others: which is what consoles me for having been excluded by Hegel from the historical movement.
>
> 'What we understand under the name Africa, is an ahistoric, underdeveloped world, entirely prisoner to natural spirit, whose place is still at the threshold of universal history.' Wherein totalizing Reason was less poetic, shrewd, than the tolerant relativism of Montaigne. The Hegelian investigation of the world, so beautifully systematic and so advantageous to the Western methodologies, often stumbles against the details in which Montaigne's very vigorous interest is practiced. (in Cailler 1988: 54)

Faced with this confrontation, Cailler elaborates on four principal responses. In the first place, Glissant's reflection on the subject of history originates from "the interior of the intercontinental triangle; what is added to the European and African visions on Africa, for one who meditates on this, are the European, American, African, indeed planetary visions on the Caribbean; all of this overshadowing the vision of the Caribbean on his past in which the Ancestor remains to be defined, in which the importance—or the absurd—of the 'other side of the waters' has not yet found its true measure" (1988: 55).

Secondly, it should be noted that Glissant's quest for his roots unfolds as a search for a history denied or, at least, not well known: "in what way did the Africans of the past live their perception of History?" But, in the face of such historiography, in the face of the legacy of Hegelian philosophy, we find a profound anxiety:

> In Glissant's work, there is a constant tension between the feeling of powerlessness, sadness, before historical "deficiency," and the conviction that the ultimate need is not a knowledge of "facts," but the acquisition of a feeling of duration, starting with "a new surge of funds," or, as he says again, with a "record": as if the documentary paucity nevertheless would serve as a springboard for meditation, fruitful to all, on what constitutes collective conscience. (Cailler 1988: 56)

And this is what explains the importance that Glissant appears to lend to the *us,* the first-person plural, as a "concrete reality or abstract notion," both upstream and downstream of a real feeling of helplessness.

I would like to stop there for a moment and raise a few questions. First, note that Hegel crushes Marx in this reading of Glissant. There's a certain despair that seems to be occasioned by Hegel's statement. We cannot name a silent history, since it cannot be thought of except in relation to a Hegelian scheme in which Africa is a void. How, then, to limn the incursion of Hegel into Africanist thought? One could call upon Marx. Or, if one is frightened off by him, at least invoke Bergson, who has taught us that creativity is comparable to a game of patience.

Perhaps the sense of helplessness that drifts through Glissant's discourse originates not so much in the history that he craves but which cannot give satisfaction, as in the very fact of the quest for the denied history itself. "False fathers," masters of a sovereign and efficacious speech—efficacious in the sense that the speech of the biblical patriarchs is—would, in fact, have condemned such a quest in advance. In any case, the project seems to define itself as a function of lack, that is to say (to quote Serge Leclaire), as what pretends to be and affirms itself "in the place of," the empty space that exists between "what is never achieved" and "what is constituted since all eternity" (Leclaire 1968: 144).

Let me suggest an alternative approach. Perhaps we might interrogate the claims of such history to be a repository of truths. We might follow Husserl, say, and accept that the affirmation of a truth is merely the assertation of a subjective proposition that only reflects our individual experiences—and, consequently, that its normative force is only a mirage. What credibility would Caribbean or African history still enjoy in the Hegelian schema, and vice versa? But of course we don't need such severe skepticism and "truth" in order to have doubts about Hegel's intellectual "geography" and its implications. On the other hand, we should not let that more thoroughgoing skepticism invalidate, at the naive level where I find myself, the pertinence of the game that I'm sketching out by opposing the Hegelian scene to the radical doubt of Husserl.

I have here pushed to the extreme the tensions that Bernadette Cailler has read in the work of Glissant. One might reproach me for denying the possibility of some historical coherence. And, all in all, I would lean toward conceiving of history, all history, as an invention of the present. Whatever the historian discerns in the past as forms of behavior, systems, or institutions—we know this better and better today thanks to the works of Paul Veyne in particular (e.g., 1984)—it is with respect to the present that the historian gives them significance and understands them. From this perspective, Glissant's nightmare could be dissipated. Not only does he incarnate history, but he writes it in such a way as to create for himself a distinctive vision and thus an object of knowledge.

Between night and light, then, memory rises up as a sign—or, to pick up on Cailler's word, as a negator. Cailler names and analyzes other negators: the character, the land, the text. Yet memory reunites them, to the extent that it is the beach and the language that can provide an inventory of a consciousness.

> In the Caribbean, the consciousness of the past necessarily passes through a contemplation of the 'reference' *(acte imageant)* imposed by a foreign writing of History; thus, consequently, passes not only through the absence of documents but through the presence of certain documents that must, nevertheless, be made to function in order to put the driving power of a history back on track (and the driving powers of other histories, in connection with this, at the threshold of 'new' civilizations of which, one can imagine, in the future all will undoubtedly be recipients). (1988, 133)

From this background a question arises: how do we narrate horror and for what reason? Bitter, Glissant remarks superlatively: "He who will gather up the strength and who will have the patience to do an autopsy on himself, will leave immortal pages on the subject. Slavery does not leave documents behind, it leaves not a single coherent image of itself for posterity" (in Cailler 1988, 134).

But memory remains, master, sovereign, working the material of the past, naming subjects and objects of desire. In the writing that can reflect it, it becomes a proposition of a will for truth and a history yet to come. "Not the oeuvre," thinks Cailler, "but a chapter of a driving, moving account, the text will, little by little, between 'night' and 'light', 'history' and 'fiction', 'referent' and 'reference', make the reader glimpse the narrative identity of a people in action. It is the construction of this identity, within its very limits, between dreamed land and real land" that she intends to describe (1988, 142).

What Bernadette Cailler demonstrates successfully in this remarkable book is that place of ambiguity where Caribbeanity intersects with negritude. The refusal to be reduced to the history of the Other is established as a paradox: it questions its own creativity in the space of the Other, and simultaneously finds its reasons in the alterity of a memory and an experience that are thinkable only in reference to the Other. It is this trap that has discredited negritude. But Cailler assures us that the ideological shock represented by the work of Glissant is of another dimension. It would indicate not only a rejection of all mimetic stammerings, but also a confrontation with a (false) father. The latter, to borrow a felicitous expression of Jacques Derrida, occupies "the place of form, of formal language. This place is untenable and he (the father) can, thus, only attempt to occupy it for form, speaking to this sole extent the language of the father" (Derrida 1983: 285).

> It seems to me [writes Cailler] "that the oeuvre [of Glissant] wants to work out the crisis of the psychic space, in which lies the Caribbean adventure of the text in this way: in a process of self-organization inscribed in a game of open systems. This crisis buries its roots deeply in the death of fathers (false fathers), producers

of discourses that have been coded in advance; a crisis in which the discourses of love are eroded by holes on every side, and in which the myths of the filiation grow indistinct; a crisis in which, each day, the connection requires suffering, an opening out onto the imaginary. (1988, 172)

Nevertheless, daily experience of the Caribbean or the African speech, the opening out onto make-believe, establishes another reign and a unique regime: those of the power and the love of the grandparents, and particularly of the grandmother, often perceived and defined as depository and matrix of the memory of the family, the social group, and the community. She would transcend, furthermore, the archetype of the mother, according to Jung, since she is of the universe of goddesses and gods (Jung 1980: 81). She is, in fact, the mother of the mother and, based on that, the grandest, that is to say the *grand* mother who can within herself reunite positive knowledge (wisdom) and negative knowledge (sorcery). She would incarnate all the formulas of power and their fabulous and mysterious virtues (Jung 1980: 102). On the other hand, through the "joking relationship," attested to in the Caribbean as well as in Africa, which links her to her grandchildren, she signifies, under the sign of play, the materialization of a smooth continuity. Based on this, the speech of the grandmother is a re-actualization of what was and what will be again, at one and the same time as testimony and as game of history. Cailler has gathered this (e.g., 112), but, unfortunately, does not explicitly deduce the conclusion to be drawn: the reign of the grandmother is the other side of the presence of the father (false or true, it matters little), whose power is questioned in the smile and the memory of the grandmother. It is known, in the psychoanalytic context, that shedding light on the lack of literal order (signifier), as Serge Leclaire suggests in his *Démasquer le Réel* (1971), constitutes the essence of the cure. By the signifier Leclaire understands "the phenomenon of the structure, the combinative game of the letters (signifiers), which is the armature of all representational constructions (or significants)." And, as he reminds us in the same book, "the work of the psychoanalyst would not be to allow himself to be taken into the literal game (signifier), but rather to bring the lack that is its driving force and, in some way, its 'absolute cause' into the open" (Leclaire 1971: 23).

Miller and Cailler have performed superbly the therapeutic task of bringing to light the fear of death and history that torments "black" literature. Their analyses are exemplary, and match the breadth of the authors' texts to the point of identifying with them. They command attention as models for rereading many Caribbean and African writers.

Did You Say "African" Philosophy?

Kwasi Wiredu's argument in his ongoing research on Akan philosophy (see in Mudimbe 1992) evolves through three positions. He begins by looking at what he thinks to be a subtle conceptual common ground between naturalists and their opponents in the Western philosophic tradition, precisely by focusing on a grid of contrasts (material versus nonmaterial, natural versus nonnatural, nature versus supernature). Second, applying this grid to his field, he states that none of these contrasts is intelligible within Akan thought. He then goes on to analyze Akan cosmology and concludes that Akan thought is empirical and Akan people believe that order runs through creation (see Mudimbe 1992). Does this conclusion confirm Placide Tempels's general hypothesis (1949) on the ontology of "primitive peoples," or Kagame's major theses on Banyarwanda, from his *La Philosophie bantu-rwandaise de l'être* (1956) to *La Philosophie bantu comparée* (1976)? On some specific issues it diverges from R. Horton's paradigms (1981) on "African Traditional Thought and Western Science."

It is not my objective to interrogate the credibility of these theses and hypotheses which cross Wiredu's analysis of the Akan worldview. I would like to insist simply on three questions of method to clarify the intellectual procedures which allow Wiredu's conclusion and his philosophical project.

First, in which sense can one say that Wiredu's project renders the Akan worldview in a *proper* interpretation? Let us, provisionally, bracket two problems: that of the philosophical *instrumentarium* which permits both his analysis and my critique, and Wiredu's notion of conceptual decolonization.

The distinction between proper and what is not proper is useful from a philosophical viewpoint. From a moral philosophical perspective, for example, a good reading means the squeezing of a positive ethical understanding out of a set of symbols, statements, or rules of behavior. In other words, the philosopher may investigate a cultural system and its positivities in order to face the following issues: Why are we here? What are the true reasons behind Akan motivations and actions? Is the Akan person such and such? The reading of symbolic or real meaning would then be not only descriptive but normative. In other words, the values that the Ghanaian or the English philosopher projects into the data and the conclusion therefore, in some way, reflect a number of discrete initial presuppositions. On the other hand, in science, and even in philosophy, a different connotation arises from the expression "proper interpretation." Before quantum mechanics, scientists used to accept Newtonian laws. The attainment of ultimate truth then did depend upon instrumental precision, and it was believed that once the tools of the experiments were perfected, the scientist could, in principle and in fact, achieve simultaneity between virtual and actual images. In a metaphysical sense, the symbols which mediated between the scientist and the supposed transcendentals would disappear, and the scientist would see a naked, unencumbered reality. Compared to the philosopher, the Newtonian scientist might assume a nonnormative stance.

There is one final notion of "a proper interpretation" which falls somewhere between the social scientist and the philosopher. It is wonderfully exemplified in the work of Claude Lévi-Strauss, a philosopher by education and an anthropologist by profession. Given enough time to analyze and understand a foreign culture, an anthropologist could, in principle, translate the content of every-thing that is a set of symbols or a set of rituals and myths into the system of symbolic and cultural grids. At any rate, Lévi-Strauss, in the case of American Indians, and Luc de Heusch, about Bantu Africans, maintain that the play of subjective biases that necessarily complicate the anthropologist's translation should be accepted as another reflection of the mind's activity, of its universal-ity, and, therefore, just as deserving of attention.

It should thus be obvious that one could evaluate a proper or improper reading from the Cartesian split between what is subjective and what is objec-tive. It seems that it is in the circulation of a post-Cartesian philosophic *instru-mentarium,* and the representation it supposes, that one should understand Wiredu's propositions. A metaphor on table manners may clarify the issue. A Franco-American fellow, perfectly well educated, recently told me the follow-ing story. He was participating in a meal in his French family. He reached for a loaf of bread, gently tore off a piece, and replaced the loaf on the table, not noticing that he had put it upside down, which, in some French milieus, is a sign of displeasure with the meal and an insult for the host.

The host in Wiredu's reading on Akan worldview is the ordinary Akan, who I would say would look at himself as reflected by Wiredu's subjective reading of his own *Weltanschauung.* It strikes me that throughout his project, Wiredu does not distinguish explicitly *Akan knowledge* from *thought.* In ef-fect, it should be possible, about Akan worldview, to separate *knowledge* as *"Verstand,"* that is, as a set of verifiable principles and norms for the mastery of what is what, from *thought* as *"Vernunft,"* or the drive to understanding. This Kantian distinction, which is clear yet implicit in Wiredu's discussion of the Akan concepts of *okra* and *sunsum,* could have explicated whose worldview we can get from Wiredu's analysis.

To refer to another example, one can compare Wiredu's project of iden-tifying his subjectivity with a culture to the prudent enterprise of Henri Maur-ier, who recently titled his book *Philosophy of Black Africa* (1976) and not Black African Philosophy. The distinction allowed him to describe critically the space of a philosophical exercise vis-à-vis African practices of everyday life.

I personally call *invention* Wiredu's process of appropriating meanings that establish a present relative to a time and a place. It is an *invention* in the two senses of the latin word: in + venire as meeting with, but also as a discovering and appropriating of what Michel de Certeau has nicely called a contract with another being. Let us focus on a marvelous "sin" of Wiredu and look at what he says about a given being, the Supreme Being. He gently mocks J. J. Maquet's inconsistent invention of a transcendent Ruandese god who is supposedly nonmaterial. He opposed him to the god of the Akan cosmological thought, who is an ancestor idealized *ad indefinitum.* Well, I happen to have met, in books, other nonmaterial gods: that of Mongo people as described by Hul-staert (1980), or that of Luba people as described by Van Canaeghem (1956). The problem here is not, and, I am afraid, cannot simply be, solved by the use of the opposition between physical and quasi-physical beings and phenomena. I would guess, from a shoemaker position, that one could really wonder why careful anthropologists such as Hulstaert (1980), Van Canaeghem (1956), and others invented nonmaterial gods whereas African students of philosophy—as in the case of Tshiamalenga (1977 a, b, and 1980) and Wiredu—tend to discover only an anthropocentric model of African gods. Yes, I know, one might invoke the demand of epistemological rigor and awareness. Yet I wish I could understand the methodological inconsistency of Alexis Kagame (1956, 1976), who chose the risk of building his philosophy on a linguistic corpus and who remarkably seems to agree with anthropologists. More important, on this question, why should one not tend to follow and trust anthropologists? Kagame was probably more a sort of anthropologist than a metaphysician.

To put it plainly, for the honor of Akan peoples, I would, following Foucault, and this is my second question of method, bring the philosophical discourse into its own margins and force it to face unphilosophical discursive practices. As a possible illustration one might invoke, for instance, Clifford Geertz's manipulation of Gilbert Ryle's notion of thick description. Here is the motif:

> A wink is simply the mechanical twitching of one eye. Yet twitching an eye may have no significance while a wink, mechanically the same, implies that some sort of conspiracy is being initiated. Another possibility is that one person, observing his or her friend attempting to wink discreetly, will wink in an exaggerated fashion to burlesque his friend. As a consequence, the mechanical action of twitching one eye takes on another meaning. Thick description requires that the ethnographer be able to interpret the distinction between all of the different twitches based on the role they play in a particular context. (Geertz 1973)

This celebration of anthropology made, let us be clear, I am not an empiricist. I highly suspect empiricism for being a kind of simplification of the phenomenon it comments upon. Concretely, we may say, using an apparently ambivalent expression, Akan cosmology is what it is not. In effect, I personally think of it as a discourse produced by a multiplicity of beings for themselves. And, strictly speaking, to use Sartre's vocabulary, these beings cannot be only what they are. There is no way of reducing them to the status of a vague in-itself as do ordinary ethnophilosophers. In other words, I wish very much Wiredu could speak more explicitly from his own existential locality as subject. More abstractly, I would say that the *Cogito* represents a radical and self-conscious mode of thought which can be elaborated into a discourse where self-invention and its derivations may become social science schemas.

It is thus on a paradox that I may insist, and it is my last question of method and concerns the issue of linguistic mediation: Wiredu is speaking a "British language." I am reading it in "French." What does this imply for both the Akan worldview in particular and "African" philosophy in general? The concept of alienation to which he refers in his invitation for a conceptual decolonization could be used a propos of our difficult dialogue. Yet it is perhaps a wonderful trap. What is at stake here seems more a question of method. It is, I would suspect, a question about our respective subjective choices for thinking the philosophical practice in Africa. As such, our disagreement witnesses to what we both believe in: philosophy as a critical thinking, even about Akans, cannot be but antidogmatic, for, as a colleague once put it, it is always an ongoing struggle for meaning, necessarily insecure, tentative, and thus resistant to all results and axioms, even its own.

And I serve now as an editor-in-chief of an encyclopedia of African religions and philosophy in which Wiredu is a main actor. This is linked to the very concept of "African" philosophy. Let me reformulate this ambition of practicing philosophy in Africa; or, more specifically, the ambition of philosophers who, accidently, happen to be blacks. Indeed, I cannot but refer to my own experience, and thus my own subjectivity.

For some years, an African colleague at the Ecole Pratique des Hautes Etudes en Sciences Sociales in Paris has been working as editor on the project of an encyclopedia of African cultures. By its scope and ambition, the enterprise brings to mind the successful ventures of two monumental historical series: the multivolume *Cambridge History of Africa* (1975) and the UNESCO series. In the field of literature, Ambroise Kom, from Cameroon, has recently edited an encyclopedic dictionary of African literature. Now, in the United States, Ruth Stone, at Indiana University, is editing an encyclopedia of African music, which will be in competition with another one on the same subject sponsored by UNESCO; and John Johnson, also from Indiana University, is editing an encyclopedia of African folklore. When the Garland Publishing Company invited me four years ago to be the editor-in-chief of an encyclopedia of African religions and philosophy, I thought of securing the collaboration of respected scholars in the fields of African humanities, social sciences, and theology. Among those I wrote to was John Middleton, Emeritus Professor of Anthropology at Yale University, whom I invited to serve on the editorial board. He responded, agreed to be part of the project, and let me know that we might be competing, since he was serving as editor-in-chief of a Simon and Schuster encyclopedia of Sub-Saharan Africa.

Obviously something was happening, something which seemed to me both paradoxical and interesting. All these encyclopedias signified something in terms both of reevaluating our knowledge about Africa and of producing new, up-to-date knowledge. What was happening was surprising when one takes into account a number of factors: the recession; the limited number of Africanists compared, say, to the army of specialists of European civilization; and the crisis and limited budgets of centers and programs of African and African-American Studies. The paradox seems thus a question—or, more exactly, it raises a series of questions: (a) How can one explain that such financial and intellectual investments are taking place now? (b) What kind of urgency would demand such an effort? (c) Could one suggest that some publishers have mi-

raculously become industrious servants of knowledge to the point of promoting or, more precisely, of trying to make visible a new will to truth that
some of us could relate back to trends that have been reorganizing our fields
since the late 1940s and early 1950s? To point out just a few names in African
Studies, I am thinking of anthropologists and sociologists such as Marcel
Griaule, Georges Balandier, Luc de Heusch, and Victor Turner; of historians
such as Catherine Coquery-Vidrovitch, Joseph Ki-Zerbo, Jean Suret-Canale,
and Jan Vansina; of philologists such as Alain Bourgeois, Engelbert Mveng,
and Frank Snowden; of theologians such as Henri Gravrand, John Mbiti, and
Vincent Mulago; of philosophers such as Placide Tempels, Alexis Kagame,
Frantz Crahay, Paulin Hountondji; and, indeed, of ideologues such as Cheikh
Anta Diop, Jomo Kenyatta, Kwame Nkrumah, Julius Nyerere, Jean-Paul
Sartre, and Léopold Sédar Senghor.

Should we believe in a miracle? How is one to explain the interest, commitment, and generosity of the publishers? Because by training and vocation we
do not accept miracles *(Timeo Danaos et dona ferentes),* in the United States
most of us editors-in-chief of African encyclopedias chose, against the capitalistic rule of competition, the principle of collaboration: we consult each other
about our projects, we exchange information, and we even serve on our respective advisory or consultative boards.

Questions of Method, Questions of Philosophy

As editor-in-chief of the encyclopedia of African religions and philosophy, here are my three principal nightmares. (a) Problems intellectual and
ideological. How should one organize this new knowledge on African
religions and philosophy? And, in this corpus, how do we demarcate African
savoirs (knowledge in general) from *connaissances* (disciplined and well-
particularized knowledge—e.g., mathematics, geography, or philosophy)? (b)
Problems of history and epistemology, in the specific sense described and
illustrated by Louis Althusser apropos of Marx. To use an example, how do
we move from a generality one, that is the extasis of a confusion in which
science and ideology mingle, to a generality three, or a new science and knowledge, thanks to a generality two, or a working and critical science? Let me
illustrate this. The "ethnophilosophical" practice in African philosophy (that
is, the belief that there is "out there" in everyday life an implicit philosophy
that can be brought to light by a careful observer using a rigorous philosophical *instrumentarium*), as actualized by Placide Tempels and his disciples, witnesses to a lazy but sincere cult of difference. I would tend to think that,
having accepted that, we might, in the encyclopedia, inscribe this moment and
its naïveté in the history of African philosophy, exactly in the same way as we
consider the pre-Socratics to be ancestors of Greek philosophy. (c) Problems of
philosophy, finally. And I have already referred to them.

Should I note that philosophy, in the Greek sense of its genesis and in the
very exact meaning of its tradition as well as in its contemporary practices,

defines itself as knowledge and discipline exactly as we understand history, economics, astronomy, or botany as knowledges? Yet it is also much more than that designated specific type of knowledge. One could, for example, think of Descartes's metaphoric definition of philosophy as a tree. Can we not think the possibility of considering philosophy as that discourse that can transcend dialogically, to refer to Paul Ricoeur's work, three complementary levels: (a) the level of discourses and interpretations of the founding events of a culture; (b) the level of experts' discourses which actualize disciplinary practices or, put simply, what one might consider to be scientific discourses; (c) finally, a third level, namely that of philosophy. Let me be clear: by philosophy I do understand an explicit, critical, autocritical, systematic discourse bearing on the language and experience of the first and the second levels without fusing with them, yet without being completely autonomous from them, since they have made philosophy possible and thinkable in the first place.

One could, indeed, inquire about the basic methodological principles that would organize not only African religions and philosophy in their general economy but also the table of the entries, their number, the variations of their length, as well as their complementarity. I had opted for two main principles: the first, classical, inspired by the one-century-old *French Vocabulaire technique et critique de la philosophie,* commonly known in Francophone circles as the *Lalande* (from the name of its first editor). The principle can read as follows: to present semantic descriptions that clarify a concept, and absolutely to avoid confusion, error, and sophism. The definitions should be historically and culturally grounded. In effect, to quote Lalande again, echoing Schopenhauer, a philosophy that claims to be without *a prioris* is a philosophical charlatanism. In my case, I have to admit two *a prioris:* ethnographic and technical.

African philosophy in its two meanings (as a critical, autocritical, and systematic discipline and as *Weltanschauung*) cannot but refer to ethnographic contexts, and, as already noted, to an epistemological context that distinguishes *savoir* from *connaissance*. In a note to his English translation of *l'Archéologie du Savoir* by the late Michel Foucault, M. Sheridan Smith notes that "the English 'knowledge' translates the French 'connaissance' and 'savoir'. *Connaissance* refers [. . .] to a particular corpus of knowledge, a particular discipline—biology or economics, for example. *Savoir,* which is usually defined as knowledge in general, the totality of *connaissances,* is used by Foucault in an underlying, rather than an overall, way." To complicate the matter of this distinction, Foucault specifies himself that "by *connaissance* I mean the relation of the subject to the object and the formal rules that govern it. *Savoir* refers to the conditions that are necessary in a particular period for this or that type of object to be given to *connaissance* and for this or that enunciation to be formulated" (1982: 15). Basically, the distinction in French stems from a separation between two conceptual areas well-defined in most Romance languages. The French *savoir,* for example, is the equivalent of the Spanish *saber* and the Italian *sapere.* They mean 'to know how, to be able, to be aware.' On the other hand, *connaissance,* a substantive related to the verb *connaître,* has, for equivalents, in Spanish *conocimiento* and *conocer,* and in Italian *conoscenza* and *conoscere,* whose basic meanings are 'to know, to be familiar with, to be acquainted with.'

The second *a priori,* a technical one, was inspired by André Jacob's guidelines in his recently published *Encyclopédie philosophique.* It is strictly organizational: (a) to present a maximum of conceptual entries within a minimal space and, in doing so, to respect the demands of intelligibility and intellectual efficiency; (b) to achieve a rational distribution between the classical and the contemporary, the known and the unknown from the philosophical tradition. Here I think of Michel Foucault's wish in *The Discourse on Language:* "if philosophy really must begin as an absolute discourse, then what of history, and what is this beginning which starts out with a singular individual, within a society and a social class, and in the midst of a struggle?" In themselves, these two principles are already programmatic. They express some of the most difficult issues I had to face: (a) the universality of certain concepts (finitude vs. infinitude, good vs. evil, etc.); (b) the pertinence of comparisons based on translated texts; (c) the concept of 'ethnocentrism' as a sign of the incommensurability between texts and cultures, and also as a question mark. To stress the last point: we, all of us, speak and analyze situations from somewhere, and to question this very fact is in itself already an important issue. An easy way out would be to look at the concrete practice of ethnography.

Philosophy and the Practice of Ethnography

Here is an exemplary and perturbing illustration: *The Missionary and the Diviner* by Michael C. Kirwen (1987). The book, in the words of Laurenti Magesa, who introduces it, "tackles what is perhaps one of the most central concerns for African theology today. What, from a Christian perspective, is the worth of the pre-Christian divine self-manifestation in Africa?" (Kirwen 1987: vii). This book clearly inscribes itself in the problematics of the African theology of enculturation. Michael C. Kirwen, a Maryknoll missionary in Tanzania since 1963, relates a personal experience. Kirwen writes:

> Over the more than twenty years that I have lived in Africa as a missionary, I have been deeply affected and changed by my African friends. I have not been 'converted' from my Christianity, but I have come to understand and live my religion differently and better through what I learned from them. Many of my African friends actually converted to Christianity; I would be ashamed if this had not also meant that they appreciated more fully their own African beliefs, so that they became better persons. (1987: xiv)

This book is a pedagogical tool: an introduction to a present-day practice of missionizing in Africa. Kirwen converses with a diviner–witch doctor on subjects such as the idea of God, the source of evil, divination, remembrance or resurrection, etc. The dialogues are contextualized and favor an explicitly pluralist epistemology. They claim to follow "the conversational style [. . . of] a Luo diviner from Nyambogo Village in North Mara, Tanzania" (Kirwen 1987: xxv). But the whole thing is a *montage:* "the diviner featured in the book is a composite figure," but "the settings and scenes in the book are descriptions of actual places and events." "Moreover, the conversations reported [. . .] are based on actual discussions; they are not contrived" (Kirwen 1987: xxiv). On the other hand, let us note that the author insists on the peculiarity of his dialogical method:

> [The] words, judgements, and observations [of the diviner] were drawn from live research sessions, which I—together with my students and African informants—conducted with a variety of African religious leaders over a ten-year period from 1974 to 1984.
>
> The commentaries that I have appended to each chapter seek to delineate the important issues and dilemmas arising out of the conversations that are relevant to the Christians of the Western world. This kind of reflection represents a type of reverse mission in which traditional African theology challenges, judges, and enriches Western Christian theology. (Kirwen 1987: xxiv–xxv)

This book has been praised in Tanzania. "Well-researched [. . .] recommended reading to any serious-minded pastoral agent, and to transcultural theologians," states Joseph T. Agbasiere from the Gaba Pastoral Institute. "Kirwen has skillfully combined a deep knowledge of Christian theology, his many years of productive pastoral work in Tanzania, and a systematic and tireless search for empirical explanations to the complex co-existence between Christianity and African indigenous religions," adds B. A. Rwezaura from the University of Dar es Salaam.

One would tend to trust these specialists despite the fact that the method used by Kirwen draws its strength from concordist techniques that seem to confuse the *documents* of revelation, the *vouloir dire,* or the message of gods, given to two radically different traditions, and the *vouloir entendre,* or the perceived meaning, which founds the beliefs of Kirwen and his African partners. The *montage,* at any rate, has produced an essay that is, in reality, fiction. It could have been molded as well into a novel, and its credibility and force would not have been transformed. In effect, both the essay and the potential novel would be situated at the point where social and religious African beliefs and practices intersect with the poetic imagination and theological techniques of Michael Kirwen. In principle, we can, I believe, from a strictly ethnographical viewpoint, perceive and describe in any society the linkages and the forms of articulation existing between the *thought (le pensé)* and *the formulatable,* between what has been thought and what has been or can be formulated, and its relation to what has been *acted out* and should be observable in sociohistorical traces. Such an analysis cannot but sort out and explain the intelligibility of behaviors vis-à-vis localized cultural representations and, thus, in the pure tradition of cultural anthropology, describe indigenous networks of local *savoirs* and *connaissances*. Recent and intelligent monographs have, brilliantly, illustrated this point: I cite, for example, three such publications: Louis Brenner's *West African Sufi: The Religious Heritage and Spiritual Search of Cerno Bokar Saalif Taal* (1984), which is an exploration of "Cerno Bokar's spiritual quest" and is, as Brenner himself writes, "a study of the interaction between, on the one hand, the influence of his social and religious environment and, on the other, his own personal yearning to find the 'Truth'"; Sally Falk Moore's book on *Social Facts and Fabrications: 'Customary' Law on Kilimanjaro 1888–1980* (1986), which is, fundamentally, about gaps, discontinuities between "law in the life of a people (the Chagga) and law in the courts"; and T. O. Beidelman's *Moral Imagination in Kaguru Modes of Thought* (1986), which brings together the Kaguru practice of everyday life, representations, and procedures for constituting moral concepts.

Although the English language distinguishes, as do the Romance languages, the concept of "thought" from that of "knowledge," it does not, with respect to the latter, separate the specialized values of two complementary sets of concepts: on the one hand, *savoir, saber, sapere,* and on the other hand, *connaître, conocer,* and *conoscere*. One may guess my predicament. The issue is a major one for the encyclopedia. In fact, two conceptual orders oppose each other, whether explicitly or implicitly. The first, probably the most visible order refers to and articulates historical and anthropological analyses on the transformations that, mainly since the contact with the West, gave rise to a new continental geography and promoted new systems of both *savoirs* and *connaissance* in Africa. These new sequences faced, broke, or simply disarticulated ancient forms and practices of knowledge. That these so-called "traditional" forms have not dissappeared should be obvious when one pays attention to present-day contradictions, which exist throughout the continent, particularly between the processes of production and the social relations of production, between the organization of power and of production and, on the other hand, the political discourses. Indeed, African cultures had and have their own *savoirs* and *connaissances* inscribed in, and dependent upon, traditions. Nonetheless, I believe that it would be illusory to look for pure originary and definitively fixed African traditions, even in the precolonial period. Nkrumah used to think, apropos of the African heritage (*Consciencism,* 1970), that the colonial experience and its powerful heritage exemplified something that, in terms of knowledge and experience, has been going on for centuries, namely, what the French calls *métissage* in the sense expounded recently by Jean-Loup Amselle in his *La Raison Métisse* (1990). The reality of *métissages* challenges the idea of tradition as a pure essence witnessing to its own originary being. Jan Vansina has recently demonstrated convincingly in his *Paths in the Rainforests: Toward a History of Political Tradition in Equatorial Africa* (1990) that traditions are not fixed: they are, indeed, continuities, but also discontinuities; they are "processes," "unique developments flowing out of static basic principles." In brief, as Vansina puts it, traditions are self-regulating processes. They consist of a changing, inherited, collective body of cognitive and physical representations shared by their members. The cognitive representations are the core. They inform the understanding of the physical world and develop innovations to give meaning to changing circumstances in the physical realm, and do so in terms of the guiding principles of the tradition. Such innovations in turn alter the substance of the cognitive world itself. (Vansina 1990: 259–60)

Thus, we cannot but be willing to note historical and intellectual discontinuities, social ruptures, and political negotiations of African traditions. Discursive formations in Africa or elsewhere do not constitute smooth genealogies of *savoirs* and *connaissances* but offer tables of intellectual and epistemological dissensions witnessing to fabulous acculturations.

An African Practice of Philosophy

In the name of philosophy, more exactly, in allegiance to rigorous practice of the discipline, my colleague and friend Kwasi Wiredu from Ghana has been, these last years, interrogating the Akans' conception of the universe. His main argument stems from three points. First, he makes a distinction between naturalists and their opponents in the Western philsophical practice, which, logically, posits antagonist interpretations about some binary oppositions such as natural versus nonnatural, material versus nonmaterial, natural versus supernatural, etc. Second, from deductions following from the preceding analysis, Wiredu can affirm that these oppositions are not intelligible in the Akan conception. Yet, contrary to Wiredu's affirmation, they are, since he is himself, as a Western-trained philosopher, commenting upon them and explaining them to his Akan fellows and to all of us and, in the name of philosophy, claiming to transcend at least two traditions, the Western and his own. Finally, focusing on Akan cosmology, Wiredu describes its main characteristics: it is an empirical ensemble based on the belief that there is an inherent order in the creation. Indeed, one could wonder if this order is not a reconstructed model of a proto-practice that Wiredu thinks he faced during his research. Throughout his project, he prudently avoids a clear distinction between *savoir* and *pensée,* although he alludes to it in the tension he creates between *okra* and *sansum,* in which, naively, I would tend to read the Kantian opposition between *Verstand* and *Vernunft.*

Wiredu's philosophical practice or that of the encyclopedia challenges the boundaries circumscribing knowledges, their migrations, and their capacities to alter and transform memories. Since I began my work on the encyclopedia project I have felt the certainty of being "colonized" by three main types of ancient knowledges. The first is a knowledge (*savoirs* and *connaissances*) depending on a political power: it expands itself "in the name of God the Father, the Son, and the Holy Ghost"; or, from the absolute revelation of the Koran: this is the Word of God to His Prophet. It is a knowledge which, in terms of Pierre Bourdieu's studies, maximizes the material and symbolic wealth of the prophets and missionaries. The second type is a genealogical one: why do I have to go back to Plato or St. Augustine in order to face the intellectual history of African cultures? This leads me to the last type of knowledge that confronts me: it is, methodologically, secular, and by definition usable because of its efficiency and the moralities of its effects on my mind. This would be, for example, the knowledge of disciplines such as anthropology and history.

All these knowledges seem to function like fiction for me. Are they real? In any case, they seem to be of the same nature as the myths magnificently analyzed by Luc de Heusch in his *The Drunken King* (1982). Yet, I cannot conceive the encyclopedia I am directing without them. Michel de Certeau, in *The Practice of Everyday Life* (1984), rightly noted that "the ancient postulate of the invisibility of the real has been replaced by the postulation of its visibility. The modern sociocultural scene refers to a 'myth'. This scene defines the social referent by its visibility (and thus by its scientific or political representativeness); it articulates on this new postulate (the belief that the real is visible) the possibility of our knowledge, observations, proofs and practices."

I have tried to show, in this book, that the epistemological and intellectual disorder represented by my reading is, indeed, also a political issue. The knowledge articulated in the encyclopedia to come will witness to a will to truth and, thus, can already be questioned.

CODA

On demandait à Socrate d'où il était. Il ne
répondait pas: d'Athènes; mais: du monde.
Lui, qui avait son imagination plus pleine et
plus étendue, embrassait l'univers comme sa
ville, jetait ses connaissances, sa société et ses
affections à tout le genre humain, non pas
comme nous qui ne regardons que sous nous.

—MONTAIGNE, *Essais*, 2, 26.

These are thus my stories to my children. They might seem difficult. They are
not really. It all depends on how they are told. One could ask: why these and
not others? And why, indeed, have I reduced the complexity of what the
diverse chapters might mean to a subjective consideration? Does this mean
that my reflection explicitly chose not to go beyond such an exercise and, in
terms of the practice of African Studies, what such would imply, particularly
when actualized by an African?

There are voids in my stories. That I have arranged themes and motives,
historical periods and discourses in order to convey to my children, and those
of their generation who might read me, what I believe to be the most important
dimension of an alienation and the exercise of its formulations is obvious.
Should I have to face an opponent who, playing on my worst nightmares,
would argue, in the voice, say, of the invisible enemy of Michel Foucault, "it
is as if you had used not the empirical, serious work [. . .], but two or three
themes that are really extrapolations rather than necessary principles," I
would say: speaking to my children, I have been speaking to myself; I have
been reflecting upon alienations, and the interpretations that made them possible in concrete and real "languages"; I worked from a reactivation of lessons
learned from those of the generation that preceded mine, and, among them,
my former professor, Willy Bal, Emeritus of the University of Louvain, to
whom this book is also dedicated. In the very practice of my storytelling I do
incarnate a silent wish: speaking as in suspense between past discourses and
the silence of a promise, I chose not to exclude connections (in terms of
possible analogies), and still least not to impose an intellectual genealogy (in
terms of interpreting traditions and ideas; analyzing, displacing, exposing, and
resisting this past; these ideas in which genealogies reflect themselves in turn).

Suspended between and foreign to the two moments, in fact my past and my after, I knew that I could rigorously make explicit the Kantian theme of permanence and, in the contradictions of my methodological commitment, identify with all the questions that, *ad vallem,* could concern themselves with what Willy Bal has been facing for years.

In his communication of June 9, 1990, to the Belgian Academy on "Confidences d'un Wallon 'wallonnant' et 'tiers-mondialiste,'" Willy Bal comments on the practice of his discipline through a meditation about his life and human milieu, and exposes an analysis that could for many function as an illustration of the fusion between the Same and the Other, thanks to a conscious will to bring together in an analogue what might seem to be different and even antagonistic memories.

> I see all of these men stripped of their humanity, then recorded and accounted for only as "pieces of ebony." I hear the Very Christian King launching his ships on a conquest "of souls and of spices." The fleshly covering of souls can be emptied by scurvy and by dysentery, for in any case, the soul is saved by the grace of baptism. The spices, however, must arrive guaranteed in flavor, safe and sound in port, ready to refloat the royal treasury. *Ile de Gorée:* sunset on a choppy sea, contemplated between the bars of captivity. Confinement facing the infinity of a free horizon. Who will ever tell the secret or screaming despair of those hearts of ebony wood?
>
> Thus I traverse the barrenness of registers, of archives, of relations, of the history so tight-lipped about the "small ones," trying to decipher the palimpsest of the peasants. But I also grope in the living matter of my own memories, of things seen, heard, and lived.
>
> I am fortunate to have two memories: one immediate, close, raw, forged of experience, incrusted like sometimes painful calcium deposits in my bones, in my joints, my muscles, my hands; the memory of a cow-herder, of a wood-cutter, of a harvester, of a captive, of a comrade.
>
> And then a memory that is deep, distant, cellular, a memory of the salmon swimming against currents and up dams until the spawning waters, a secret memory stuck to the limestone rock, deciphering the rustle of underground water irrigating my genes.
>
> In this way I go forth, reconstructing a global Third World, of North and South, of past and present, of our villages and of distant Amazonian *quilombos,* of traditional hut-villages and of modern shantytowns, *favelas, musseques,* from my birthplace, Odrimont, to the *Bahia de todos os santos (e de todos os pecados),* dear to Jorge Amado.
>
> All of these peasants, landed or landless, attached or torn from the earth, used to talk, and still do talk. Some, the rooted, have to our day (or used to have, until very recently) as sole means of daily communications their traditional languages, local, regional. These communication systems are generally non-legitimized by the powers that be, and, for this reason, are not called languages. Others, uprooted, wandering, immigrants, people in search of means to survive, have had to find ways of communicating with humans who exhibit economic, military, and technical superiority. Corresponding to the economy of coastal colonial counters, of purely commercial transactions, are the so-called Pidgin

languages. Plantation economy, built first on slavery and ethnic mixing, gave rise to so-called Creole vernacular. Colonization and neocolonialism of the modern era have introduced to each other languages and cultures of unequal power and prestige. The result is linguistic interference, as witnessed in Black Africa. A further result is the piecing together of approximating means of communications when the necessity and the urgency of communication go far beyond the possibilities of learning. Thus the birth of *français-tiraillou, petit nègre,* and *pretoguês* of Luanda. Sometimes an intermediary language is later formed, such as "popular" Ivorian French.

In short, the entire variety plays a role, that mosaic of languages of all origins, of all functions, that honest French authors of previous centuries commonly called, according to the latitudes and the continents, by formulas as synthetic as they were symmetric and without appeal: "the patois of wild men, the patois of Negroes, the patois of peasants." The good philologist J. Marouzeau defined the word "patois" (which, as an aside, is particular to French, having no exact equivalent in any other European language that I know of) in these terms: "One generally designates by this name local languages used by a population inferior to that which represents the common surrounding language."

That's what I was telling you: wild men, Negroes, and peasants. . . . (Bal 1990: 112–14)

From this magnificent formulation by Willy Bal, I may then simply say: this book is made up of a construct toward which I have tended through enunciations and descriptions of a polysemic 'idea' of Africa, convinced that its interpretations (in colonialism, for example) do not coincide with the complexity of the rules for its formation if, indeed, after Bal, we accept the rigor of conceiving difference seriously, and if, also, we submit to the demands of a regressive analysis and then to those of facing and following the constricting figures of this idea till our days. I have tried to demonstrate, and to define the formation of, this idea and its complexity and thus call attention to its aspects in cognitive apprehensions. That this book began and is ending as a subjective monologue about memories and interpretations indicates also *a way* of treating and interpreting the history of concepts. More mundanely, as Jack Goody put it, does writing down this 'story' make it also a modern event? In effect,

> Writing gives us the opportunity for [. . .] a monologue that oral intercourse so often prevents. It enables an individual to 'express' his thoughts at length, without interruption, with corrections and deletions, and according to some appropriate formula. Of course what is required for this purpose is not simply a mode of writing, but a cursive script and the kind of instruments that permit rapid recording. For the purpose of recording internal or external discourse, thoughts, or speech, pen and paper are clearly better than stylus and clay, just as shorthand is more efficient than longhand, the electric than the manual typewriter. (Goody 1977: 160)

One can state that there is still today an idea of Africa. On the continent, it is conceived from colonial disconnections and articulates itself as a rereading of the past and as contemporary searches for an identity. In its prudent expressions, this idea presents itself as a statement of a project born from the conjunction of different and often contradictory elements such as African traditions, Islam, colonization, and Christianity, which Ali Mazrui unites in his series *The Africans: A Triple Heritage.* In its operations, this idea is also a product of complex and incessant enunciative and practical negotiations between, on the one hand, the polysemic notions of race, *ethnos,* nation, individual, and humanity (and thus it can hardly be reduced to an essence), and, on the other hand, those peoples using, delimiting, or dealing with these terms. In effect, the idea is qualified by sets of composite memories, which are gratuitous systems of recollection. They bring together a number of things and experiences; and in them one might choose to emphasize certain aspects and, voluntarily or accidentally, to forget or, at least, to minimize others.

The sequence of analyses in this book has focused on two main significant issues: first, the Greco-Roman thematization of otherness and its articulation in such concepts as 'barbarism' and 'savagery'; second, the complex process that has organized in Europe the idea of Africa. It is, in any case, troubling to note that since the fifteenth century the will to truth in Europe seems to espouse perfectly a will to power. They cadence each other, justify each other, and, in three recent extraordinary moments, compromised each other in the production of three major monstrosities: the slave trade, colonialism, and nazism. With the blessing of the highest intellectual and religious authorities, the expansion of Europe overseas parallels that of slavery and its practice in the name of both civilization and Christianity. It is in the same name that Europe implements the rules of colonialism in the nineteenth century, and, in the twentieth, produces from within its own historical and cultural framework a number of troubling formations and among them nazism. These monstrosities impacted upon the idea of Africa. One might thus reflect about the similitudes and structural connections they have with both the Western will to knowledge and the will to power. The cases of the slave trade and colonialism seem obvious. As to that of nazism, which somehow sums them, let me simply quote Aimé Césaire's strong, radical, polemical stance:

> It would be useful to study clinically, in detail, the behavior of Hitler, and of Hitlerism and to reveal to the very distinguished, the very humanist, very Christian twentieth century bourgeois that he has a silent Hitler in him, that Hitler *inhabits* him, that Hitler is his *demon,* that if he vituperates, it is by lack of logic, and, in sum, what he does not forgive Hitler is not *the crime* in itself, *the crime against man,* it is not the *humiliation of the man in himself,* but the crime against the white man, the humiliation of the white man, of having applied to Europe colonialist procedures which till now were reserved to Arabs in Algeria, coolies in India, and Negroes of Africa. (Césaire 1955: 12)

To sum up the essentials of the book, two things appear clear. The first is the complexity of the idea of Africa and the multiple and contradictory discursive practices it has suscitated and which, I am afraid, are not all well and explicitly described, or even suggested, in this contribution. I would like to believe that my focus on perfectly unrepresentative texts (such as the fable on Hercules and Burton's treatise on melancholy) and on essentially theoretical issues (as in the case of cultural relativism and that of primitive art), despite its limitations, shows at least one possible way of filtering out an idea of Africa from an immense literature and complex debates.

The second thing concerns the reaction to *"this"* idea of Africa. I have, for example, emphasized a black Grecomania because it seemed exemplary to me as a revolt against the Western representation of itself and others. In effect, this revolt plays on one of the most important and most fragile areas of Western culture. In the name of philology and history, the revolt articulated its arguments as a challenge for a more correct interpretation of Greek history, for a more credible understanding of the genesis of Western civilization.

The idea of Africa presented in this book may seem, indeed, too dependent upon Western texts. Nonetheless, I think this choice makes sense. To comprehend the archaeological organization of this very idea of Africa and its resonances, it seems to me, it is impossible not to consider Western literature and, particularly, its culmination in the "colonial library." I agree that it should be possible to begin from an African context and to trace its own effects. I am afraid, however, that such a perspective would minimize the signification of its own conceptual instruments. It is true that the slave trade or the colonization of the continent could be visualized differently, but on the whole such visualizations would lose their historical and conceptual coherence. As Immanuel Wallerstein notes: "the capitalist world-economy, posing the question of whether a set of ideas, or a way of thinking, is universal [European] or African returns us only to the double bind which the system itself has created. If we are to get out of this double bind, we must take advantage of the contradictions of the system itself to go beyond it" (1988: 332).

Telling stories is a way of disarticulating an author's pretensions, as well as of reformulating the supposed logical derivations of even a mathematical demonstration. In effect, the story organizes its own basis, operations, objectives, and anticipations. The master of the storytelling performance is the listener who, when bored, can stop at any time or simply cease to listen. Moving in my imaginary library, which includes the best and the worst books about the idea of Africa, I chose my own path. It led me beyond the classically historical boundaries (in terms of references and texts) and, at the same time, maintained me firmly in what is a line of desolation. In its transparency, whatever angle one might choose, the will to truth of this history (that claims to be back to the Greeks) exemplifies a negative paradigm: any successful will to truth, converted into a dominating knowledge and actualized as an imperialist project (geographically internal or external), might transform itself into a will to "essentialist" prejudices, divisions, and destructions. I would hope that my stories about the idea of Africa have demonstrated this and, at the same time, clarified the singularity of this idea.

BIBLIOGRAPHY

A. Catalogues

AKA Circle of Exhibiting Artists
   (1988). *AKA 88: 3rd Annual Exhibition Catalogue.* Enugu, Nsukka, and Lagos.
   (1990). *AKA 90: 5th Annual Exhibition Catalogue.* Enugu.
Arte Animista. Ery Camara (AA). Mexico: Sahop. s.d.
Contemporary African Art (CAA). Published by Studio International and Africana Publishing Corporation as the Catalogue of an exhibition of Contemporary African Art held at the Camden Arts Centre. London. 10 Aug.–8 Sept. 1969.
Contemporary African Artists: Changing Tradition (CAACT). The Studio Museum in Harlem, New York 1990.
Contemporary Art from the Republic of Senegal (CARS). Wally Findlay Galleries, New York, 27 Sept.–25 Oct. 1983.
From Two Worlds (FTW). 30 July–7 Sept. 1986. The Whitechapel Art Gallery, London.
Iba Ndiaye (IN1). Musée Dynamique. Dakar 1977. Realisé et edité par l'Agence de Coopération Culturelle et Technique. Paris.
Iba Ndiaye (IN2). *Un peintre, un humaniste.* Exposition, 19 Aug.–19 Sept. 1987. Chapelle des Jésuites, Nîmes, France.
—— Munich, Staatliches Museum für Völkerkunde. (1987).
Moderne Kunst aus Afrika (MKA) Horizonte '79, Festivel der Weltkulturen. Berlin, 24 June–12 Aug. 1979.
Narrative Paintings. Senegal (SEN). University Art Museum, University of Southwestern Louisiana, Lafayette, 1986.
Neue Kunst in Afrika (NKA). Berlin: Bietrich Reimer, 1980.
Original Prints from the Third Nsukka Workshop 1987. Nsukka, University of Nigeria, Department of Fine & Applied Arts. (1987).
Ouattara (O). Edited by Vrij Baghoomian and Michael Warren, published by Kyoto Shoin International, Kyoto, 1989.
Révolution Française sous les Tropiques (RFT) Exposition d'Art Contemporain, Musée National des Arts Africains et Océaniens, 9 June–4 Sept. 1989. Réalisée par le Ministère de la Coopération et du Développement.

B. Other Works Consulted

ABDOULAY, Ly. (1956). *Les masses africaines et l'actuelle condition humaine.* Paris: Présence Africaine.
ABRAHAM, W. E. (1966). *The Mind of Africa.* Chicago: The University of Chicago Press.
ACHEBE, Ch. (1958). *Things Fall Apart.* London and Ibadan.
ACOSTA, J. de. (1588). *The Natural and Moral History of the Indies,* new edit. London: Hakluyt Society.
AGTHE, J. (1990a). *Wegzeichen. Signs: Art from East Africa 1974–89.* Frankfurt.
——. (1990b). "Signs of the Times: Art from East Africa." Unpublished manuscript.
AJAYI, J. F. A. (1969). "Colonialism: An Episode in African History." In *Colonialism in Africa 1870–1960,* L. H. Gann and P. Duignan, eds. Cambridge: Cambridge University Press.

ALPERS, E. A. (1988). "Representation and Historical Consciousness in the Art of Modern Mozambique." *Canadian Journal of African Studies* 22 (1): 73–94.

———. (1989). "Representation and Historical Consciousness in the Art of Modern Mozambique" In *Art and Politics in Black Africa,* B. Jewsiewicki, ed. Canadian Association of African Studies.

ALTHUSSER, L. (1979). *For Marx.* London: Verso.

AMMIANUS MARCELLINUS. 3 vol., with an English translation by John C. Rolfe (1935–1940). Cambridge, MA: Harvard University Press.

AMSELLE, J. L. (1990). *Logiques métisses. Anthropologie de l'identité en Afrique et ailleurs.* Paris: Payot.

AMSELLE, J. L., and M'BOKOLO, E., eds. (1985). *Au coeur de l'ethnie: Ethnie, tribalism et état en Afrique.* Paris: La Découverte.

Anon. (1900 sq.). *Thesaurus Linguae Latinae.* Lipsiae: in aed. B. G. Teubneri.

Anon. *Magnum Bullarium Romanum Seu Ejusdem Continuatio.* Luxemburg.

ARENDT, H. (1968). *Imperialism.* Part Two of *The Origins of Totalitarianism.* New York and London: Harcourt Brace Jovanovich.

ARON, R. (1964). *La lutte de classes: Nouvelles leçons sur les sociétés industrielles.* Paris: Gallimard.

ARNOLD, A. J. (1981). *Modernism and Negritude: The Poetry and Poetics of Aimé Césaire.* Cambridge, MA: Harvard University Press.

ARNOLDI, M. J. (1983). Puppet Theatre in the Segu Region in Mali. Unpublished Ph.D. dissertation, Indiana University.

———. (1987). "Rethinking Definitions of African Traditional and Popular Art." *African Studies Review* 30 (3): 79–84.

ARISTOTLE. *Problems I. 6. I–XXI,* with an English translation by W. S. Hett (1936). Cambridge, MA: Harvard University Press.

———. *The Basic Works of Aristotle.* R. McKeon, ed. (1941). New York: Random House.

———. *Historia Animalium.* I, 6. I–III, with an English translation, edited by A. L. Peck (1955). Cambridge, MA: Harvard University Press.

———. *De Generatione Animalium.* Edited by H. J. Drossaart Lulofs (1965). Oxoni: E. Typografeo Clarendoniano.

ASCH, S. (1983). *L'Eglise du prophète Kimbangu. De ses oigines à son rôle actuel au Zaïre.* Paris: Karthala.

AUBENQUE, P. (1963). *La Prudence chez Aristote.* Paris.

AXT, F., and BABACAR SY El Hadji, M. (1989). *Anthology of Contemporary Fine Arts in Senegal.* Frankfurt am Main: Museum für Völkerkunde.

BADI-BANGA, N. M. (1977). *Contribution à l'étude historique de l'art plastique zaïrois moderne,* Kinshasa.

———. (1987). *Art contemporain bantu: deuxième Biennale du CICIBA Kinshasa.* Libreville.

BAL, W. (1963). *Le Royaume du Congo aux XVᵉ et XVIᵉ Siècles.* Léopoldville: INEP.

———. (1990). "Confidences d'un Wallon 'wallonnant' et 'tiers-mondialiste.'" Séance mensuelle, 9 juin 1990. Bruxelles: *Bulletin de l'Académie Royale de langue et de littérature françaises* 68: 105–115.

BALANDIER, G. (1955). *Sociologie des Brazzavilles noires.* Paris: Armand Colin.

BAMBA, N. K., and MUSANGI, N. (1987) *Anthologie des sculpteurs et peintres zaïrois contemporains.* Paris.

BARBER, K. (1987). "Popular Arts in Africa." *African Studies Review* 30 (3): 1–78, 105–111.

BARNET, M. (1968). *Biographia de un Cimarrón.* Barcelona: Ariel.

BAUDRILLARD, J. (1987). "The Precession of Simulacra." In *Art after Modernism: Rethinking Representations,* Brian Wallis, ed. New York: Godine.

BEARDSLEY, G. H. (1929). *The Negro in Greek and Roman Civilization. A Study of the Ethiopian Type.* Baltimore: The Johns Hopkins University Press.

BEIDELMAN, T. O. (1986). *Moral Imagination in Kaguru Modes of Thought.* Bloomington: Indiana University Press.

BEIER, U. (1968). *Contemporary Art in Africa.* London: Frederick A. Praeger.

———. (1971). "Signwriters Art in Nigeria." *African Arts* 4 (3): 22–27.

———. (1976). "Middle Art: The Paintings of War." *African Arts* 9 (2): 20–23.

BEN-AMOS, P. (1977). "Pidgin Languages and Tourist Arts." *Studies in the Anthropology of Visual Communication* 4 (2): 128–139.

BENABOU, M. (1976). *La Résistance africaine à la romanisation.* Paris: Maspero.

BENJAMIN, W. (1974). *Gesammelte Schriften.* Frankfurt am Main: R. Tiedemann H. Schweppenhauser.

BENOT, Y. (1969). *Idéologies des indépendances africaines.* Paris: Maspero.

BENVENISTE, E. (1973). *Indo-European Language and Society.* Coral Gables, FL: University of Miami Press.

BERNAL, M. (1987/1991). *Black Athena. The Afroasiatic Roots of Classical Civilization.* New Brunswick, NJ: Rutgers University Press. Vol. I: *The Fabrication of Ancient Greece 1785–1985;* Vol. II: *The Archeological and Documentary Evidence.*

———. (1989). "*Black Athena* and the APA." In *Arethusa.* Special issue, Fall: 17–38.

BERTHELOT, A. (1927). *L'Afrique saharienne et soudanaise, ce qu'en ont connu les Anciens.* Paris.

BERTIEAUX, R. (1953). *Aspects de l'industrialisation en Afrique Centrale.* Bruxelles: Institut des Relations Internationales.

BHABHA, H. K. (1986). "The Other Question: Difference, Discrimination and the Discourse of Colonialism." In *Literature, Politics and Theory,* F. Barker, P. Hulme, M. Iversen, D. Loxley, eds. London: Methuen.

———, ed. (1990). *Nation and Narration.* London.

BIAYA, T. K. (1989). "L'impasse de la crise zaïroise dans la peinture populaire urbaine, 1970–1985." In Jewsiewicki 1989b: 95–120.

BIEBUYCK, D. P., ed. (1969). *Tradition and Creativity in Tribal Art.* Berkeley and Los Angeles: University of California Press.

BLOCH, R. (1963). *Les Prodiges dans l'antiquité classique.* Paris: Presses Universitaires de France.

BOEMUS, J. (1611). *The Manners, Lawes, and Customes of All Nations.* London: Eld and Burton.

BONTINCK, F. (1966). *Aux origines de l'Etat Indépendant du Congo.* Paris-Louvain: B. Nauwelaerts.

BOOTH, N. S., ed. (1977). *African Religions: A Symposium.* New York: Ndk.

BORYNACK, J. R. (1983). *Contemporary Art from the Republic of Senegal.* New York.

BOURDIER, J. P., and MINH-HA, Trinh T. (1985). *African Spaces. Designs for Living in Upper Volta.* New York: African Publishing Company, Holmes and Meier.

BOURDIEU, P. (1984). *Distinction. A Social Critique of the Judgement of Taste.* Cambridge, MA: Harvard University Press.

———. (1990a). *The Logic of Practice.* Stanford: Stanford University Press.

———. (1990b). *In Other Words.* Stanford: Stanford University Press.

———. (1991). *Language and Symbolic Power.* Cambridge, MA: Harvard University Press.

BOURDIEU, P., and PASSERON, J. (1977). *Reproduction in Education, Society and Culture.* London: Sage.

BOURGEOIS, A. (1971). *La Grèce antique devant la négritude,* Paris: Présence Africaine.

BRAIN, R. (1980). *Art and Society in Africa.* London and New York: Longman.

BRAUDEL, F. (1980). *On History*. Chicago: The University of Chicago Press.

BRAUN, L. (1973). *Histoire de l'histoire de la philosophie*. Paris: Ophrys.

BRAVMANN, R. A. (1973). *Open Frontiers: The Mobility of Art in Black Africa*. Seattle and London.

BRENNER, L. (1984). *West African Sufi: The Religious Heritage and Spiritual Search of Cerno Bokar Saalif Taal*. Berkeley and Los Angeles: University of California Press.

BRETT, G. (1986). *Through Our Own Eyes. Popular Art and Modern History*. Philadelphia: New Society Publishers.

BROWN, J. L. (1939). *The Methodus ad facilem historiarum cognitionem of Jean Bodin: A Critical Study*. Washington: Catholic University of America Press.

BRUNSCHWICG, H. (1963). *L'avènement de l'Afrique Noire*. Paris: Armand Colin.

BUCHMANN, J. (1962). *L'Afrique Noire indépendante*. Paris: R. Pichon et R. Durand-Auzias; Librairie générale de Droit et de Jurisprudence.

BURGIN, V. (1986). *The End of Art Theory: Criticism and Postmodernity*. Atlantic Highlands, NJ: Humanities Press.

BURN, M. (1948). *The Modern Everyman*. London: Rupert Hart-Davis.

BURNS, V. F. (1974). "Travel to Heaven: Fantasy Coffins." *African Arts* 7 (2): 24–25.

BURTON, R. (1932). *The Anatomy of Melancholy*. H. Jackson, ed. New York: Random House.

CAILLER, B. (1988). *Conquérants de la nuit nue: Edouard Glissant et l'H(h)istoire antillaise*. Tubingen: Gunter Narr Verlag.

CALAME-GRIAULE, G. (1965). *Ethnologie et langage: la parole chez les Dogon*. Paris.

CALVEZ, J. Y. (1956). *La pensée de Karl Marx*. Paris: Seuil.

CESAIRE, A. (1955). *Discours sur le colonialisme*. Paris: Présence Africaine.

CHAMBERS, I. (1990). *Border Dialogues: Journeys in Postmodernity*. London.

CHARLES, P. (1956). *Etudes missiologiques*. Louvain: Museum Lessianum, Desclée De Brouwer.

CHATELET, F. (1962). *La Naissance de l'histoire*. Paris: Minuit.

CHINWEIZU; JEMIE; MADUBUIKE. (1983). *Toward the Decolonization of African Literature*. Washington, D.C.: Howard University Press.

CHOME, J. (1959). *La passion de Simon Kimbangu*. Bruxelles: Les Amis de Présence Africaine.

COLUMBUS, C. *The Journal of Christopher Columbus*. Trans. by Jane Vigneras, revised by L. A. Vigneras (1960). London.

CORNET, J. A. (1975). "African Art and Authenticity." *African Arts* 9 (1): 52–55.

———. (1989). "Précurseurs de la peinture moderne au Zaïre." In Cornet et al., 1989, pp. 9–57.

CORNET, J. A.; CNODDER, R. de; TOEBOSCH, W. (1989). *60 ans de peinture au Zaïre*. Bruxelles: Les Editeurs Associés.

COTGRAVE, R. (1611). *A Dictionnaire of the French and English Tongues*. London: Adam Islip.

COURTNEY-CLARKE, M. (1986). *Ndebele. The Art of an African Tribe*. New York: Rizzoli.

COUSSEMENT, G. (1932). "L'Action Catholique dans les Missions." In *Les Actes de la Première Conférence Plénière des Ordinaires de Missions du Congo belge et du Ruanda-Urundi*. Léopoldville: Imprimerie du Courrier d'Afrique. 185–199.

CUYPERS, L. (1970). "La coopération de l'Etat Indépendant avec les missions catholiques." *Revue d'Histoire Ecclésiastique* 65 (1): 30–50.

Dakar Musée Dynamique. (1975). *Art nègre et civilisation de l'universel*. Proceedings of colloquium, "Picasso, Art Nègre et Civilisation de l'universel." 1972. Dakar and Abidjan.

DE BOSSCHÈRE, G. (1969). *Les deux versants de l'histoire*. Paris: Albin-Michel.

DE CERTEAU, M. (1975). *Politica e Mistica. Questioni di storia Religiosa.* Milan: Jaca-Book.
———. (1982). *La Fable mystique.* Paris: Gallimard.
———. (1984). *The Practice of Everyday Life.* Berkeley: University of California Press.
DE CORTE, M. (1959). "Colonisation et morale." In *Lovania* 50: 23–28. Elisabethville.
DE DEKEN, J. (n.d.). "Notre ami Pierre Romain-Desfossés." In *Hommage à Pierre Romain-Desfossés.* CEPSI, Elisabethville. pp. 5–10.
DE HEMPTINNE, J. F. (1911). "Une fondation Bénédictine au Katanga." In *Bulletin des oeuvres et Missions bénédictines au Brésil et au Congo.* Abbaye St. André, 122–132.
DE HEUSCH, L. (1982). *The Drunken King.* Bloomington: Indiana University Press.
———. (1987). *Ecrits sur la royauté sacrée.* Bruxelles: Université Libre de Bruxelles.
DE JONGHE, E. (1947). "Contre le colonialisme, pour la colonisation." In *Bulletin des Séances,* 17. Bruxelles: I.R.C.B.
DELANGE, J. (1967). *Arts et peuples de l'Afrique Noire.* Paris: Gallimard.
DELAVIGNETTE, A. (1960). *Christianisme et colonialisme.* Paris: A. Fayard.
DE MOREAU, E. (1944). *Les Missionnaires Belges de 1804 à nos jours.* Bruxelles: Editions Universitaires.
DEPELCHIN, J. (1992). *De l'Etat Indépendant du Congo au Zaïre contemporain 1885–1974.* Dakar: Codesria.
DERI, M. (1921). *Die Neue Malerei: Sex Vortrage.* Leipzig: Seeman.
DERRIDA, J. (1983). "Le Retrait de la Métaphore." In *Analecta Husserliana,* A. T. Tymiemecka ed., Vol. 14: 273–300.
DETIENNE, M. (1967). *Les Maîtres de vérité dans la Grèce archaïque.* Paris: Maspero.
DE VLEESCHAUWER, A. (1947). "Courants actuels d'idées sur les peuples non autonomes." *Bulletin des Séances,* 18:700–713. Bruxelles: I.R.C.B.
DIETERLEN, G. (1989). "Masks and Mythology among the Dogon." *African Arts* 22 (3): 34–43.
———. (1990). "Mythologie, histoire et masques." *Journal de la Société des Africanistes* 59 (1/2): 7–37.
DIETERLEN, G., and ROUCHE, J. (1971). "Les fêtes soixantenaires chez les Dogon." *Africa* 41:1–11.
DIODORUS SICULUS. 12 vol. with an English translation by C. H. Oldfather, C. L. Sherman, C. Bradford Welles, Russel M. Geer, and F. R. Walton. 1933–1967.
DIOGENES LAERTIUS. *Lives of Eminent Philosophers.* 2 vol., with an English translation by R. D. Hicks (1925). London: William Heinemann.
DIOP, C. A. (1954). *Nations nègres et culture.* Paris: Présence Africaine.
———. (1960). *L'Unité culturelle de l'Afrique Noire.* Paris: Présence Africaine.
———. (1967). *Antériorité des civilisations nègres.* Paris: Présence Africaine.
DREWAL, H. J., and DREWAL, M. (1983). *Gelede: Art and Female Power among the Yoruba.* Bloomington: Indiana University Press.
DUBOIS, J; LAGANE, R.; LEROND, A. *Dictionnaire du Français de la Langue Classique.* Paris: Larousse.
DUCHET, M. (1971). *Anthropologie et histoire au siècle des lumières.* Paris: Maspero.
DUMEZIL, G. (1980). *Camillus: A Study of Indo-European Religion as Roman History.* Berkeley: University of California Press.
ELOKO-A-N. (1976). "L'Imaginaire et l'argumentation." In V. Y. Mudimbe, *Le Vocabulaire politique Zärois. Une étude de sociolinguistique.* Lubumbashi: Centre de Linguistique Théorique et Appliquée.
ESTIENNE, R. (1740). *Thesaurus Linguae Latinae.* Basileae: Typis J. R. Turnisiorum Fr.
———. (1816–1818). *Thesaurus Graecae Linguae.* Londini: in aed. Vapianis.

FABIAN, J., and SZOMBATI-FABIAN, I. (1980). "Folk Art from an Anthropological Perspective." In *Perspectives on American Folk Art,* I. Quimby and S. Swank, eds. New York: W. W. Norton.

FAGG, W. (1963). *Nigerian Images.* New York: F. A. Praeger.

———. (1965). *Tribes and Forms in African Art.* New York.

———. (1970). *Divine Kingship in Africa.* London: The British Museum.

FANON, F. (1961). *The Wretched of the Earth.* New York: Grove Press.

———. (1967). *Black Skin White Masks.* New York: Grove Press.

———. (1968). *Toward the African Revolution.* New York: Grove Press.

FECI, D. (1972). *Vie cachée et vie publique de Simon Kimbangu selon la littérature coloniale et missionnaire belge.* Bruxelles: Cedaf.

FERNANDEZ, J. W. (1982). *Bwiti: An Ethnography of the Religious Imagination in Africa.* Princeton University Press.

FETTER, B. (1973). "L'UMHK, 1920–1940: la naissance d'une sous-culture totalitaire." *Les Cahiers du CEDAF* no. 6.

———. (1974). "African Associations in Elisabethville, 1910–1935: Their Origins and Development." In *Etudes d'Histoire Africaine,* VI, 205–223.

FINLEY, M. I. (1987). *The Use and Abuse of History.* New York: Penguin.

FOCILLON, H. (1934). *La Vie des formes.* Paris.

FORDE, D., ed. (1966). *The New Elites of Tropical Africa.* Oxford: Oxford University Press.

FORTES, M., and EVANS-PRITCHARD, E. E., eds. (1940). *African Political Systems.* Published for the International African Institute. London: Oxford University Press.

FOSU, K. (1986). *20th Century Art of Africa.* Zaria.

FOUCAULT, M. (1973). *The Order of Things: An Archaeology of the Human Sciences.* New York: Random House.

———. (1982). *The Archaeology of Knowledge.* New York: Pantheon.

———. (1982). *The Discourse on Language.* Appendix to *The Archaeology of Knowledge.* New York: Pantheon.

FREUD, S. (1927–1931). *The Complete Psychological Works of Sigmund Freud.* J. Strachey, ed. London.

FRY, J., ed. (1978). *Twenty-Five African Sculptures.* Ottawa.

FRYE, N. (1975). "Expanding Eyes." *Critical Inquiry* Winter 2 (2): 206.

GADAMER, H.-G. (1979). "The Problem of Historical Consciousness." In *Interpretive Social Science,* Paul Rabinow and William M. Sullivan, eds. Berkeley: University of California Press.

GEERTZ, C. (1973). *The Interpretation of Cultures.* New York: Basic Books.

———. (1988). *Works and Lives: The Anthropologist as Author.* Stanford University Press.

GEORIS, P. (1962). *Essai d'acculturation par l'enseignement primaire au Congo.* Bruxelles: CEMUBAC.

GILLS, C. A. (1960). *Kimbangu, fondateur d'Eglise.* Bruxelles: Librairie Encyclopédique.

GOLDWATER, R. (1986). *Primitivism in Modern Art.* Belknap: Harvard University Press.

GOODY, J. (1977). *The Domestication of the Savage Mind.* Cambridge: Cambridge University Press.

GORDON, R. L., ed. (1982). *Myth, Religion and Society.* Cambridge: Cambridge University Press.

GOUARD, C. (1989). *Fodé Camara ou L'oeuvre ouverte: Essai d'approche anthropologique d'une jeune peinture Sénégalaise.* Unpublished Mémoire de Maîtrise d'esthétique, Université Paris I—Panthéon Sorbonne.

GREVISSE, F. (1950). *Le Centre Extra-Coutumier d'Elisabethville—Quelques aspects de la politique indigène du Haut-Katanga industriel.* Gembloux: J. Duculot.

GRIAULE, M. (1938). "Masques Dogons." *Travaux et Mémoires de l'Institut d'Ethnologie* 33. Paris.

GROETHUYSEN, B. (1953). *Anthropologie philosophique.* Paris: Gallimard.

GUERNIER, E. (1952). *L'Apport de l'Afrique à la pensée humaine.* Paris: Payot.

GUGELBERGER, G. M., ed. (1985). *Marxism and African Literature.* Trenton, NJ: African World Press.

GUILBERT, D. (1956). "Le Droit de la colonisation." In *Lovania* 38: 15–43; 40: 67–87. Elisabethville.

HAMMOND, D., and JABLOW, A. (1977). *The Myth of Africa.* New York: The Library of Social Science.

HANNON's *Periplus.* In Muller, C. (1882). *Geographici Graeci Minores.* Paris: Firmin Didot.

HARDING, S. (1991). *Whose Science? Whose Knowledge? Thinking from Women's Lives.* Ithaca: Cornell University Press.

HAUSER, M. (1982). *Essai sur la poétique de la négritude.* Lille.

HERDECK, D. (1973). *African Authors.* Washington: Black Orpheus Press.

HERODOTUS. 4 vol., with an English translation by A. D. Godley (1920–1925). Cambridge, MA: Harvard University Press.

HERSKOVITS, M. (1929). "The Civilizations of Prehistory." In *Man and His World,* B. Brownell, ed. New York: Van Nostrand Company.

———. (1940). *The Economic Life of Primitive Peoples.* New York: Knopf.

———. (1941). *The Myth of the Negro Past.* New York and London: Harper.

———. (1967). *The Human Factor in Changing Africa.* New York: Knopf.

———. (1972). *Cultural Relativism.* Edited by Frances Herskovits. New York: Random House.

HERSKOVITS, M., and BASCOM, W. R. (1959). *Continuity and Change in African Cultures.* Chicago: Chicago University Press.

HERSKOVITS, M., and HERSKOVITS, F. *Dahomean Narratives.*

HIRSCHMAN, A. (1979). "The Search for Paradigms as a Hindrance to Understanding." In *Interpretive Social Science. A Reader,* Paul Rabinow and William M. Sullivan, eds. Berkeley: University of California Press.

HOBSBAWM, E., and RANGER, T., eds. (1983). *The Invention of Tradition.* Cambridge: Cambridge University Press.

HODGEN, M. T. (1971). *Early Anthropology in the Sixteenth and Seventeenth Centuries.* Philadelphia: University of Pennsylvania Press.

HOMER. *The Odyssey.* 2 vol., with an English translation by A. T. Murray (1919). Cambridge, MA: Harvard University Press.

———. *The Iliad.* 2 vol., with an English translation by A. T. Murray (1924 and 1925). Cambridge, MA: Harvard University Press.

HORTON, R. (1981). "African Traditional Thought and Western Science." In *Rationality,* B. R. Wilson, ed. Oxford: Basil Blackwell.

HOUSTON, D. D. (1985). *Wonderful Ethiopians of the Ancient Cushite Empire.* Baltimore: Black Classic Press.

HULME, P., ed. (1986). *Colonial Encounters. European and the Native Caribbean 1492–1797.* London and New York: Methuen.

HULSTAERT, G. (1980). "Le Dieu des Mongo." In *Religions africaines et christianisme* 2: 33–84. Kinshasa: Faculté de Théologe Catholique.

HUNTINGFORD, G. W. B., ed. and trans. (1980). *The Periplus of The Erythraean Sea.* London: The Hakluyt Society.

HUSSERL, E. (1959). *Erste Philosophie. Husserliana,* vol. 8. The Hague: Martinus Nijhoff.

———. (1970). *The Crisis of European Sciences and Transcendental Phenomenology.* Evanston: Northwestern University Press.

ILUNGA, K. (1984). "Déroutante Afrique ou la syncope d'un discours." In *Etat Indépendant du Congo, Congo Belge, République Démocratique du Congo, République du Zaïre,* B. Jewsiewicki, ed. Quebec: Editions Safi.

IMPERATO, P. J. (1971). "Contemporary Adapted Dances of the Dogon." *African Arts* 5 (1): 28–33, 68–72, 84.

IRELE, A. (1965). "Negritude—Literature and Ideology." *The Journal of Modern African Studies* 3 (4): 499–526.

———. (1981). *The African Experience in Literature and Ideology.* London.

———. (1986). "Contemporary Thought in French Speaking Africa." In *Africa and the West: The Legacies of Empire,* Isaac James Mowoe and Richard Bjornson, eds. New York: Greenwood.

ISIDORE of SEVILLE. (1911) *Isidori Hispalensis episcopi, Etymologiarum sive originum libri XX.* W. M. Lindsay, ed. Oxford: Clarendon Press.

JACKSON, H., ed. (1932). *The Anatomy of Melancholy* by Robert Burton (1621). New York: Random House.

JACQUEMIN, J. P. (1990). "Saint Chéri Samba, vie et oeuvres (im)pies." In Ostend, Provinciaal Museum voor Moderne Kunst, 9–33.

JAHN, J. (1961). *Muntu. An Outline of the New African Culture.* New York: Grove Press.

———. (1968). *A History of Neo-African Literature.* London: Faber and Faber.

JANSON, H. W. (1986). *History of Art.* New York: Abrams.

JEWSIEWICKI, B. (1984) *Etat Indépendant du Congo, Congo Belge, République Démocratique du Congo, République du Zaire.* Québec: Editions Safi.

———. (1985). *Marx, Afrique et Occident.* Montreal. McGill University: Centre for Developing Area Studies.

———. (1986a). "Collective Memory and the Stakes of Power. A Reading of Popular Zairean Historical Discourse." *History in Africa* 13.

———. (1986b). "Collective Memory and Its Images: Popular Urban Painting in Zaire—A Source of 'Present Past.'" *History and Anthropology* 2.

———. (1989a). "Présentation: Le Language politique et les arts plastiques en Afrique." In Jewsiewicki 1989b: 1–10.

———, ed. (1989b). *Art and Politics in Black Africa.* Ottawa. Canadian Association of African Studies.

JEWSIEWICKI, B., and Newbury, D., eds. (1986). *African Historiographies: What History for Which Africa?* Beverly Hills: Sage.

JEWSIEWICKI, B., et al., eds. (1990). *Moi, l'autre, nous autres: Vies zaïroises ordinaires, 1930–1980. Dix récits.* Quebec and Paris.

JULES-ROSETTE, B. (1977). "The Potters and the Painters: Art By and About Women in Urban Africa." *Studies in the Anthropology of Visual Communication* 4 (2): 112–127.

———. (1984). *The Messages of Tourist Art: An African Semiotic System in Comparative Perspective.* New York.

———. (1987). "Rethinking the Popular Arts in Africa: Problems of Interpretation." *African Studies Review* 30 (3): 91–98.

JUNG, C. J. (1980). *The Archetypes and the Collective Unconscious.* Translated by R. F. C. Hull. Princeton: Bollingen Foundation and Princeton University Press.

KAGAME, A. (1956). *La philosophie bantu-rwandaise de lêtre.* Bruxelles: Académie Royale des Sciences Coloniales.

———. (1976). *La philosophie bantu comparée.* Paris: Présence Africaine.

KANDINSKY, W. (1914). *The Art of Spiritual Harmony.* London: Constable.

KANE, C. H. (1961). *L'aventure ambiguë.* Paris: Julliard.

KARP, I. (1988). "Laughter at Marriage: Subversion in Performance." *Journal of Folklore Research* 15 (1–2): 35–52.

KEITA, F. B., and ALBARET, L. (1990). *Bogolan et arts graphiques du Mali.* Paris.

KELLER, A. S.; LISSITZYN, O. J.; and MANN, J. F. (1938). *Creation of Rights of Sovereignty through Symbolic Acts 1400–1800.* New York: Columbia University Press.

KESTELOOT, L. (1965). *Les écrivains noirs de langue francaise: Naissance d'une littérature.* Bruxelles: Institut de Sociologie.

KILSON, M. (1975). *New States in the Modern World.* Cambridge, MA (U.S.) and London (U.K.): Harvard University Press.

KIRWEN, M. (1987). *The Missionary and the Diviner.* New York: Orbis Books.

KI-ZERBO, J. (1972). *Histoire de l'Afrique d'hier à demain.* Paris: Hatier.

———, ed. (1980). *General History of Africa.* Vol. 1, *Methodology and African Prehistory.* London.

KLUCKHON, C. (1955). "Ethical Relativity and Value Conflict." In *Philosophy of Science* 12: 54–57.

KLUCKHON, C., and MURRAY, H. A. (1940). *Personality in Nature, Society and Culture.* New York: Knopf.

KOLOSS, H. J. (1990). *Art of Central Africa: Masterpieces from the Berlin Museum für Völkerkunde.* New York.

KRISTEVA, J. (1980). *Desire in Language. A Semiotic Approach to Literature and Art.* New York: Columbia University Press.

LACAN, J. (1975). *Le Séminaire. Livre XX. Encore.* Paris: Seuil.

LAROUI, A. (1967). *L'idéologie arabe contemporaine.* Paris: Maspéro.

LAS CASAS, B. de. (1951). *Historia de las Indias.* 3 vols. Mexico City: Ed. A. Millares Carlo.

LEACH, E. R. (1980). "Genesis as Myth." In *Myth and Cosmos,* J. Middleton, ed. Austin: University of Texas Press.

LEACH, E., and AYCOCK, A. D. (1983). *Structuralist Interpretations of Biblical Myth.* Cambridge, MA: Cambridge University Press.

LECLAIRE, S. (1968). *Psychanalyser.* Paris: Seuil.

———. (1971). *Démasquer le Réel.* Paris: Seuil.

LE FEBVE DE VIVY, L. (1955). *Documents d'histoire précoloniale belge (1861–1865). Les idées coloniales de Léopold, duc de Brabant.* Bruxelles: A.R.S.C.

LEIRIS, M. (1948). "La Langue secrète des Dogons de Sanga (Soudan Français)." *Travaux et Mémoires de l'Institut d'Ethnologie* 50. Paris.

LENIN, V. I. (1967). *On Literature and Art.* Moscow: Progress Publishers.

LÉVI-STRAUSS, Claude. (1952). *Race et Histoire.* Paris: Unesco.

———. (1963). *Structural Anthropology.* New York: Basic Books.

———. (1966). *The Savage Mind.* Chicago: University of Chicago Press.

———. (1976). *Structural Anthropology.* Vol. II. Chicago: University of Chicago Press.

———. (1978). *The Origin of Table Manners.* New York: Harper and Row.

LITT, J. L. (1970). *Analyse d'un processus d'acculturation. Les débuts de l'enseignement supérieur au Congo et la constitution d'une élite orientée vers le statut.* Mémoire de Licence, Sciences Politiques et Sociales, Université Catholique de Louvain.

LOHISSE, J. (1974). *La Communication tribale.* Paris: Editions Universitaires.

LONIS, R. (1981). "Les Trois approches de l'Ethiopien par l'opinion gréco-Romaine." In *Ktema,* 6.

LOTAR, L. (1923). "Le statut des immatriculés." In *Congo* 1 (4): 451–466.

———. (1937). "L'immatriculation des indigènes à l'Etat-civil." In *Bulletin des Séances,* ARSOM, 6 (1): 54–58.

LOUGHRAN, K. S.; LOUGHRAN, J. L.; JOHNSON, J. W.; and SAMATAR, S. S., eds. (1986). *Somalia in Word and Image*. Washington, D.C.: Foundation for Cross-Cultural Understanding.

MABANZA, K. (1979). *Politique coloniale et stratification sociale*. Lubumbashi, mémoire de licence, Unaza.

MACCLINTOCK, D. (1984). *African Images*. Pictures by Ugo Mochi. New York: Charles Scribner's Sons.

MACGAFFEY, W. (1983) *Modern Kongo Prophets. Religion in a Plural Society*. Bloomington: Indiana University Press.

MAQUET, J. (1967). *Africanité traditionnelle et moderne*. Paris: Présence Africaine.

MARCUS, G., and FISCHER, M. M. J. (1986). *Anthropology as Cultural Critique: An Experimental Moment in the Human Sciences*. Chicago: University of Chicago Press.

MASSON, J. (1936). *Le Roi Albert et les missions*. Louvain: Aucam.

MATUMELE, M. 1976. "Mouvement général du vocabulaire de 1959 à 1963." In V. Y. Mudimbe, *Le Vocabulaire politique Zaïrois. Une étude de sociolinguistique*. Lubumbashi: Centre de Linguistique Théorique et Appliquée.

MAURIER, H. (1974). *Philosophie de l'Afrique noire*. St. Augustin bei Bonn: Verlag des Anthropes–Instituts.

MAZRUI, Ali. (1972). *Cultural Engineering and Nation-Building in East Africa*. Evanston: Northwestern University Press.

MBITI, J. (1971). *New Testament Eschatology in an African Background*. Oxford: Oxford University Press.

MCEWEN, F. (1970). "The Workshop School." In *Camden Arts Centre*, London.

MELS, B. (1946). *Instructions*. Luluabourg: Pro Manuscripto.

MERCIER, P. (1966). *Histoire de l'anthropologie*. Paris: Presses Universitaires de France.

MERLE, M. (1969). *L'Anticolonialisme européen de Las Casas à Marx*. Paris: Armand Colin.

MERLEAU-PONTY, M. (1973). *The Prose of the World*. Evanston: Northwestern University Press.

MERLIER, M. (1962). *Le Congo de la colonisation belge à l'indépendance*. Paris: Maspero.

MILLER, C. (1990). *Theories of Africans. Francophone Literature and Anthropology in Africa*. Chicago: University of Chicago Press.

MILLER, J. (1975). *Art in East Africa: A Guide to Contemporary Art*. London and Nairobi.

MINON, P. (1957). "Quelques aspects de l'évolution récente du CEC d'Elisabethville." In *Bulletin du CEPSI*, 36.

MOMMSEN, T. (1921). *Römische Geschichte* II. Berlin.

MOMMSEN, T., and MARQUARDT, J. (1892). *Manuel des Antiquités Romaines*, XI, II.

MONHEIM, C. (n.d.). *Le Congo et les livres*. Bruxelles: Dewit, Anthologie coloniale.

MOORE, S. F. (1986). *Social Facts and Fabrications: 'Customary' Law on Kilimanjaro, 1880–1980*. Cambridge: Cambridge University Press.

MOORE, W. (1971). *Les changements sociaux*. Gembloux: Duculot.

MOUNT, M. W. (1973) (1989). *African Art: The Years Since 1920*. Bloomington and London: Indiana University Press (reprint, with a new introduction, New York: Da Copo).

MOURALIS, B. (1975). *Les Contre-Littératures*. Paris: Presses Universitaires de France.

———. (1988). "L'Afrique comme figure de la folie." In *L'Exotisme*. Paris: Didier.

MUDIMBE, V. Y. (1979). "Le chant d'un africain sous les Antonins." In *Africa et Roma*. Roma: L'Erma di Bretschneider.

———. (1986). "African Art as a Question Mark." In *African Studies Review* 29, 1.

————. (1988). *The Invention of Africa*. Bloomington: Indiana University Press.

————. (1991). *Parables and Fables*. Madison: The University of Wisconsin Press.

————, ed. (1992). *The Surreptitious Speech*. Chicago: The University of Chicago Press.

MULLER, C. (1882). *Geographi Graeci Minores*, Paris: Firmin Didot.

MVENG, E. (1965). *L'Art d'Afrique Noire*. Paris: Mame.

————. (1972). *Les Sources grecques de l'histoire négro-africaine depuis Homère jusqu'à Strabon*. Paris: Présence Africaine.

————. (1980). *L'Art et l'artisanat africains*. Yaoundé: Editions CLE.

NIMAL, N. (1935). "Le Droit de colonisation." In *Revue de l'Aucam* 10 (2) (February): 253–256.

NKRUMAH, K. (1970). *Consciencism*. London: Panaf Books.

NORA, P. (1989). "Between Memory and History: Les Lieux de Mémoire." In *Representations* Spring, 26.

NORTHERN, T. (1973). *Royal Art of Cameroon*. Hanover, NH: Dartmouth College.

NZONGOLA, G. N. (1970). "Les classes sociales et la révolution anti-coloniale au Congo-Kinshasa: le rôle de la bourgeoisie." In *Cahiers Economiques et Sociaux*, Vol. 8, no. 3, IRES-Kinshasa.

OLBRECHTS, F. M. (1959). *Les Arts Plastiques du Congo Belge*. Brussels and Anvers-Amsterdam.

OLEMA, D. (1984). "Société zaïroise dans le miroir de la chanson populaire." *Canadian Journal of African Studies* 18 (1): 122–130.

PAGDEN, A. (1982). *The Fall of Natural Man*. Cambridge: Cambridge University Press.

PEEK, P. M. (1981). "The Power of Words in African Verbal Arts." *Journal of American Folklore* 94 (371): 19–45.

————. (1985). "Ovia Idah and Eture Egbede: Traditional Nigerian Artists." *African Arts* 18 (2): 54–59, 102.

PÉRIER, G.-D. (1948). *Les Arts Populaires du Congo Belge*. Brussels.

PERROIS, L. (1989). "Through the Eyes of the White Man. From 'Negro Art' to 'African Art'." In *Third Text 6* (Spring).

PETILLON, A. M. (1967). *Témoignage et réflexions*. Bruxelles: La Renaissance du Livre.

PHILOSTRATUS, F. [1614]. *Les Images*. Translated by Blaise de Vigenère, New York and London: Garland. Reprint, 1976.

————. *Imagines*. With an English translation by A. Fairbanks (1931). Cambridge, MA: Harvard University Press.

————. *Life of Apollonius*. Translated by C. P. Jones; Edited, abridged and introduced by G. W. Bowersock (1970). Harmondsworth: Penguin Books.

PIGAFETTA, F., and LOPEZ, D. (1591). *Description du Royaume de Congo et des contrée environnantes*. Edited and translated by W. Bal. Louvain and Paris: B. Nauwelearts.

PINDAR. With an English translation by Sir J. Sandys (1915). Cambridge, MA: Harvard University Press.

PIROTTE, J. (1973). *Périodiques missionaires belges d'expression française. Reflets de cinquante années d'évolution d'une mentalité (1889–1940)*. Louvain.

PLINY. *Natural History*. 10 vols., with an English translation by H. Rackham, W. H. S. Jones (books XX–XXIII), and D. E. Eichholz (books XXXVI–XXXVII) (1938–1952). Cambridge, MA: Harvard University Press.

POGGIOLI, R. (1968). *The Theory of the Avant-Garde*. Cambridge, MA: Harvard University Press.

POIRIER, J. (1966). "Dépendance et aliénation: de la situation coloniale à la situation condominiale." In *Cahiers Internationaux de Sociologie* 40: 73–88.

POLYBIUS, *The Histories,* 6 vols., with an English translation by W. R. Paton (1922–1927). Cambridge, MA: Harvard University Press.

POULANTZAS, N. (1968). *Pouvoir politique et classes sociales,* Paris: Maspero.

PRICE, S. (1989a). *Primitive Art in Civilized Places.* Chicago: The University of Chicago Press.

———. (1989b). "Our Art—Their Art." In *Third Text* 6 (Spring).

PRUSSIN, L. (1986). *Hatumere, Islamic Design in West Africa.* Berkeley, Los Angeles, and London: University of California Press.

RAD, G. von. (1962). *Theology of the Old Testament.* Vol. I: *Theology of the Historical Tradition of Israel.* Edinburgh: Oliver and Boyd.

RALEGH, W. (1848). *The Discovery of the Large (. . .) empire of Guiana (. . .) performed in the year 1595.* London: Hakluyt Society.

RAY, B. C. (1991). *Myth, Ritual and Kingship in Buganda.* New York: Oxford University Press.

REY, P. P. (1973). *Les alliances de classes.* Paris: Maspéro.

RICOEUR, P. (1965). *History and Truth.* Evanston: Northwestern University Press.

———. (1974). *The Conflict of Interpretations. Essays on Hermeneutics.* Evanston: Northwestern University Press.

ROBERTS, A., and MAURER, E. (1985). *Tabwa. The Rising of a New Moon: A Century of Tabwa Art.* Ann Arbor: The University of Michigan Museum of Art.

———. (1987). "'Insidious Conquests': Wartime Politics Along the South-western Shore of Lake Tanganyika." In *Africa and the First World War,* M. Page, ed. London: MacMillan Press.

———. (1989). "History, Ethnicity and Change in the 'Christian Kingdom' of Southeastern Zaïre." In *The Creation of Tribalism in Southern Africa,* Leroy Vail, ed. London: James Curry.

ROELENS (mgr.). (n.d.). *Esquisse psychologique de nos Noirs.* Namur.

———. (n.d.). [1913] *Situation des Missions Catholiques du Congo Belge. Historique de la Campagne 1913.* Anvers: Imprimerie "De Vlijt."

———. (1932). "La formation du Clergé Indigène." In *Actes de la Première Conférence Plénière des Ordinaires de Missions du Congo-Belge et du Rwanda-Urundi,* Léopoldville: Imprimerie du Courrier d'Afrique.

———. (1938). *Instructions aux Missionnaires Pères Blancs du Haut-Congo.* Baudouinville: Vicariat Apostolique du Haut-Congo.

ROEYKENS, P. A. (1957). *La période initiale de l'oeuvre africaine de Léopold II (1875–1883).* Vol. 10. Bruxelles: Académie Royale de Sciences Coloniales.

———. (1958). *Léopold II et l'Afrique (1855–1880).* Vol. 14. Bruxelles: Académie Royale de Sciences Coloniales.

RORTY, R. (1979). *Philosophy and the Mirror of Nature.* Princeton University Press.

RUBBENS, A., ed. (1945). *Dettes de guerre.* Elisabethville: L'Essor du Congo.

———. (1949). "Le colour-bar au Congo belge." In *Zaïre* 3 (5): 503–513.

———. (1958). "La politique congolaise." In *La Revue Nouvelle* 27, 1 (January): 59–65.

———. (1970). *Le Droit Judiciaire Congolais.* Ferdinand Larcier, T.I. Le pouvoir, l'organisation et la compétence judiciaires, Université Lovanium-Kinshasa.

RYCKBOST, J. (1945). "Liberté d'association au Congo." In *Lovania* 53 (1959): 1–28.

RYCKMANS, P. (1945). *Messages de Guerre.* Bruxelles: Ferdinand Larcier.

———. (1946). *Etapes et jalons.* Bruxelles: Ferdinand Larcier.

SALLUST. With an English translation by J. C. Rolfe (1921). Cambridge, MA: Harvard University Press.

SAMB, I. (1989a). "Criticism of Representation." In Axt and Babacar Sy, 129–130.

———. (1989b). "The Social and Economic Situation of the Artists of the 'École de Dakar.'" In Axt and Babacar Sy, 117–120.

SANGARI, K. (1989). "Representations in History." *Journal of Arts and Ideas* 17–18: 3–7.

SARTRE, J.-P. (1956). *Being and Nothingness*. New York: Washington Square Press.

———. (1974). *Between Existentialism and Marxism*. New York: Pantheon.

SCHILDKROUT, E, and KEIM, C. A. (1990). *African Reflections: Art from Northeastern Zaire*. Seattle, London, and New York: University of Washington Press.

SCHNEIDER, B. (1972). "Malangatana of Mozambique." *African Arts* 5 (2): 40–45.

SENGHOR, L. S. (1977). *Liberté III: Négritude et civilisation de l'universel*. Paris: Seuil.

———. (1988). *Ce que je Crois*. Paris: Grasset.

———. (1989). "Introduction." In Axt and Babacar Sy, 19–20.

SERRES, M. (1979). "The Algebra of Literature: The Wolf's Game." In J. V. Harari, *Textual Strategies*. Ithaca, NY: Cornell University Press.

SIEBOLD, P. F. de. (1843). *Lettre sur l'utilité des Musées Ethnographiques et sur l'importance de leur création dans les états européens qui possèdent des colonies*. Paris: Librairie de l'Institut.

SIEBER, R., and WALKER, R. A. (1987). *African Art in the Cycle of Life*. Washington, D.C.: National Museum of African Art, Smithsonian Institution Press.

SINDA, M. (1972). *Le messianisme congolais*. Paris: Payor.

SLADE, R. (1959). *English Speaking Missions in the Congo Independent State*. Bruxelles: Académie Royale de Sciences Coloniales.

SNOWDEN, JR., F. M. (1970). *Blacks in Antiquity*. Cambridge, MA: Harvard University Press.

SOHIER, A. (1949). "Le problème des indigènes évolués et la Commission du Statut des Congolais civilisés." In *Zaïre* 3 (8): 843–880.

———. (1951). "La politique d'intégration." In *Zaïre* 5 (9): 899–928.

STENGERS, J. (1965). "L'anticolonialisme libéral au XIXᵉ siècle et son influence en Belgique." In *Bulletin des Séances*, A.R.S.O.M., 481–521.

STRABO, *The Geography of Strabo*, 8 vols., with an English translation by H. L. Jones (1917–1932). Cambridge, MA: Harvard University Press.

SURET-CANALE, J. (1958). *Afrique noire occidentale et centrale*. Paris: Editions Sociales.

SZOMBATI-FABIAN, I., and FABIAN, J. (1976). "Art, History and Society." In *Studies in the Anthropology of Visual Communication* 3, 1.

TEMPELS, P. (1949). *La Philosophie bantoue*. Paris: Présence Africaine.

———. (1959). *Bantu Philosophie*, trans. C. King, 1969. Paris: Présence Africaine.

———. (1962). *Notre Rencontre I*. Léopoldville: Centre d'Etudes Pastorales.

———. (1979). *Philosophie bantu*. A new version adapted from the English translation by A. J. Smet. Kinshasa: Faculté de Théologie Catholique.

THOMPSON, J. O. (1948). *History of Ancient Geography*. Cambridge: Cambridge University Press.

THOMPSON, R. F., and CORNET, J. A. (1981). *The Four Moments of the Sun: Kongo Art in Two Worlds*. Washington, D.C.

TODOROV, T. (1984). *The Conquest of America*. New York: Harper and Row.

TSHIAMALENGA, N. (1974). "La Philosophie de la faute dans la tradition luba." In *Cahiers des religions africaines* 8: 167–186.

———. (1977a). "Que'est—ce que la 'philosophie africaine.'" In *La Philosophie africaine* 33–46. Kinshasa: Faculté de Théologie Catholique.

———. (1977b). "Langues bantu et philosophie. Le cas du ciluba." In *La Philosophie africaine* 147–158. Kinshasa: Faculté de Théologie Catholique.

———. (1980). *Denken und Sprechen: Ein Beitrag zum linguistischen Relativitäts Prinzip am Beispiel einer Bantusprache (Ciluba)*. Dissertation, Johann Wolfgang Goethe Universität.

TYLOR, E. (1871). *Primitive Culture*. London: Murray.

VAN BILSEN, A. A. J. (1977). *Vers l'indépendance du Congo et du Ruanda-Urundi.* 2nd ed. Kinshasa: Presses Universitaires du Zaïre.

VAN CAENEGHEM, P. R. (1956). *La notion de Dieu chez les baluba du Kasai.* Bruxelles: Académie Royale de Sciences Coloniales.

VAN LIERDE, J. 1963, *La Pensée politique de Lumumba.* Paris: Présence Africaine.

VANSINA, J. (1961). *De la tradition orale. Essai de méthode historique.* Tervuren: Musée Royal de l'Afrique Centrale.

———. (1978). *The Children of Woot: A History of the Kuba Peoples.* Madison: The University of Wisconsin Press.

———. (1984). *Art History in Africa.* London: Longman.

———. (1990). *Paths in the Rainforests. Towards a History of Political Tradition in Equatorial Africa.* Madison: The University of Wisconsin Press.

VANSINA, J.; MAUNY, R.; and THOMAS, L. V., eds. (1964). *The Historian in Tropical Africa.* London: Oxford University Press.

VAN ZUYLEN, P. (1959). *L'échiquier congolais ou le secret du Roi.* Bruxelles: Charles Dessart.

VERHAEGEN, B. (1974). *Introduction à l'Histoire Immédiate.* Gembloux: Duculot.

VEYNE, P. (1984). *Writing History.* Middletown, CT: Wesleyan University Press.

———. (1988). *Did the Greeks Believe in Their Myths?* Chicago: University of Chicago Press.

VIDAL-NAQUET, P. (1986). *The Black Hunter.* Baltimore: The Johns Hopkins University Press.

VIGENÈRE, B. de. (1614). *Les Images ou Tableaux de Platte Peinture des Deux Philostrates Sophistes Grecs,* mis en François par Blaise de Vigenère. Paris: Chez la Veuve Abel L'Angellier.

VIRET, P. (1551). *De la Source et la Difference.* Genève: Jean Gerard.

VOGEL, S., and N'DIAYE, F. (1985). *African Masterpieces from the Musée de l'Homme.* New York: The Center for African Art.

VOGEL, S., and EBOND, I., eds. (1991). *Africa Explores.* New York: The Center for African Art.

WAGNER, C. (1967). *L'enseignement dans l'Etat Indépendant du Congo et le Congo Belge. Objectifs et Réalisations (1890–1918).* Mémoire de Licence, Histoire, Université Catholique de Louvain.

WAGNER, J. (1962). *Les poètes noirs des Etats-Unis.* Paris: Istra.

WALLERSTEIN, I. (1983). "The Evolving Role of the African Scholar in African Studies." In *Canadian Journal of African Studies.* 14: 9–16.

WRIGHT, R. (1975). "The Art of Independence." New York: The Alicia Patterson Foundation.

YOUNG, C. (1978). "Zaïre: The Unending Crisis," In *Foreign Affairs* (Fall): 167–185.

———. (1984). "Zaïre: Is There a State?" In B. Jewsiewicki, *Etat Indépendant du Congo, Congo Belge, République Démocratique du Congo, République du Zaïre.* Québec: Editions Safi.

INDEX

Abraham, Willy, 172
Abu Dulama Ibn al-Djaun, 176
Académie des Beaux Arts (Zaire), 159
Aethiopia, use of term, 26–27
Africa: in Burton's *Anatomy of Melancholy,* 9, 10; European "discovery" of, 16–19; idea of, xi–xvi, 211–13; ideological climate of since 1960s and traditional artworks, 172–74; image of and nature in contemporary African art, 169; naming and metaphorizing of by Europeans, 26–30; and reactivation of ancient texts, 19–26. *See also* Belgian Congo; Zaire
Africa et Roma (Mudimbe), 176
African Images (MacClintock), 167–69
Africanism, in anthropology, 38–40
African Mission Society, 159
Agbasiere, Joseph T., 205
Akan philosophy, 197–201, 207
Akoto, Anthony, 165
Albertus Magnus, 4
Alexander VI, Pope, 30–37
Althusser, Louis, 202
Amazons, in Greek ethnographic narratives, 80–92
America, image of in Burton's *Anatomy of Melancholy,* 9, 10
Amselle, Jean-Loup, 52, 187, 206
Anatomy of Melancholy (Burton), 5–14
Anaximander, 80
Antar, 176
anthropology: and Africanism, 38–40; Amselle's critique of "ethnological reason," 52–55; and colonialism in eighteenth and nineteenth centuries, 29–30; concept of "proper interpretation," 198–99; and contemporary African literature, 184; cultural relativism and, 47–52; historicizing of cultures in eighteenth-century, 28–29. *See also* cultural anthropology
antisemitism, Bernal's critique of Aryan Model, 99, 103
apprentice, concept of in West African societies, 69
architecture, vernacular and Gurunsi culture in Burkina Faso, 169–70, 172
Arendt, Hannah, 100
Aristotle, 21, 86, 90, 92, 96, 185
art: concept of primitivism in, 55–70; enunciations and strategies in contemporary African, 154–75
Asch, Susan, 150–52

Asia, image of in Burton's *Anatomy of Melancholy,* 9–10
Association Internationale Africaine (AIA), 105–106
Augustine of Hippo, 26, 176

Baba, Ahmad, 176
Bal, Willy, 29, 209, 210–11
Balandier, Georges, 43
Barnet, Miguel, 193–94
Beardsley, Grace Hadley, 25
Beidelman, T. O., 206
Beier, Ulli, 160, 163–64, 169
Belgian Congo: Bernard Mels and Catholic program of conversion in, 123–29; colonialism, geography, and African memories, 129–44; colonization of by Belgium, 105–10; Victor Roelens as paradigm for conversion in, 110–23. *See also* Zaire
Belgium: colonization of the Congo, 105–10. *See also* Belgian Congo
Benjamin, Walter, 55
Bergson, Henri, 195
Bernal, Martin, 24, 26, 93–104
Berthelot, A., 20
Between Existentialism and Marxism (Sartre), 185
Black Athena (Bernal), 93–104
Black Orpheus (Sartre), 44–45, 179
Blacks in Antiquity (Snowden), 25
Blomfield, Tome, 159
Boniface VIII, Pope, 32, 37
Borynack, James R., 162
Bourdier, Jean-Paul, 169–70
Bourdieu, Pierre, xiii, 207
Bourgeois, Alain, xii, 19–21, 103
Brain, Robert, 67
Brancusi, Constantin, 60
Braun, Lucien, xiv
Brenner, Louis, 206
Brerewood, Edward, 11
bricolage, concept of, 50–51
Budge, E. A. Wallis, 103
Burkina Faso, Gurunsi culture and vernacular architecture, 169–70, 172
Burn, Michael, 30
Burton, Robert, 5–15

Cabral, Amilcar, 184–85
Cailler, Bernadette, 181, 191–97
Camara, Ery, 164
Camara, Fodé, 164
Camara, Sory, 191
Camp, Sokari Douglas, 164

V. Y. MUDIMBE is the Ruth F. DeVernay Professor of Romance Studies, Professor of Comparative Literature, and Professor of Anthropology at Duke University. His books include *The Invention of Africa: Gnosis, Philosophy and the Order of Knowledge, Fables and Parables,* and *The Surreptitious Speech.*